Home Sweat Home

Home Sweat Home

*Perspectives on Housework and
Modern Relationships*

Edited by
Elizabeth Patton
Mimi Choi

ROWMAN & LITTLEFIELD
Lanham • Boulder • New York • Toronto • Plymouth, UK

Published by Rowman & Littlefield
4501 Forbes Boulevard, Suite 200, Lanham, Maryland 20706
www.rowman.com

10 Thornbury Road, Plymouth PL6 7PP, United Kingdom

British Library Cataloguing in Publication Information Available

Library of Congress Cataloging-in-Publication Data

Home sweat home : perspectives on housework and modern relationships / edited by: Elizabeth Patton, Mimi Choi.
pages cm
Includes bibliographical references and index.
ISBN 978-1-4422-2969-3 (cloth : alk. paper) — ISBN 978-1-4422-2970-9 (ebook) 1. Homemakers.
2. Housekeeping. 3. Second-wave feminism. I. Patton, Elizabeth, 1975– II. Choi, Mimi, 1963–
TX147.H747 2014
640.92—dc23
2013037131

61.20

∞™ The paper used in this publication meets the minimum requirements of American National Standard for Information Sciences Permanence of Paper for Printed Library Materials, ANSI/NISO Z39.48-1992.

640.92
Hom

Printed in the United States of America

To John,
who always believed that I can do anything I put my mind to,
and Cian,
for letting mommy work quietly on her laptop!
—Elizabeth Patton

To Larry and Oliver,
whose love and support have sustained me through all my endeavors.
—Mimi Choi

Contents

List of Figures

Acknowledgments

This journey began at the 2012 PCA/ACA Conference in Boston. Although we were previously unacquainted, we almost immediately recognized each other's common interest in the images of housework in popular culture. Since then, we've deepened that shared interest through discussing related scholarship, and not coincidentally, establishing a valued friendship and professional connection through this project.

Mimi would like to thank her many mentors who have advised her on *Home Sweat Home* and throughout her academic and professional careers, including Dr. Ruth Panofsky, Elizabeth Podnieks, Linda Hutcheon, Julia Reibetanz, Rahul Sapra, and Alan Shepard. Each has provided priceless and wise thoughts that continue to influence and provoke questions and ideas. She would also like to thank her family for their encouragement and sometimes challenging commentary that keeps everything interesting. Mimi would especially like to thank Elizabeth Patton, her excellent fellow traveler on this engaging project, and the wonderful contributors—Nicole Barnes, Kristi Branham, Nancy Bressler, Nicola Goc, Christopher Holliday, Kristi Humphreys, Rita Jones, Andrea Krafft, Ryan Lescure, Hannah Swamidoss, Gust Yep—who astounded us with their unexpected insights and depth of scholarship.

Elizabeth would like to express her appreciation to Marita Sturken, her dissertation chair, whose support of her research and scholarship was outstanding. She would also like to thank the staff at the archives she visited to conduct her research for this project, specifically, the staff at the Paley Center for Media in New York. Elizabeth owes her deepest thanks to her family. She would like to thank her son Cian and husband John for all their love and support while she worked on the book for the last year. Finally, she would like to thank the excellent contributors and her coeditor, Mimi Choi, for making the writing and editorial process so enjoyable.

Mimi and Elizabeth would also like to thank Chris Nasso, who initially approached us with the idea of turning our conference papers into the book you are now reading, and Bennett Graff, whose clear-eyed advice and buoyant sense of humor kept us on course.

Introduction

Mimi Choi and Elizabeth Patton

Just over fifty years ago, Betty Friedan wrote about the discontented housewife living in a suburban trap. Recognizing themselves in that image helped many women break free, mentally and physically, as well as individually and across society. By any standard, half a century is a long time, time enough for sweeping changes to take hold and transform a culture. Or so we would like to think. While Friedan's assessment of a housewife's lot still has much relevance, more astounding may be to consider that the upheaval she triggered and influenced—the women's movement and second-wave feminism—is all too frequently disavowed by many who are direct beneficiaries.

Although Friedan's text helped ignite second-wave feminism, age-old images of housework hold firm. In many ways, *The Feminine Mystique*, first published in January 1963, complicated the idea of who is responsible for domestic issues both fundamentally and on a daily basis as more women began to enter the workforce and no longer reflexively filled their entire days with housework and child care. If the 1950s TV mother, exemplified by *Leave It to Beaver*'s June Cleaver and Donna Stone of *The Donna Reed Show*, propagated the image of an immaculate house effortlessly achieved, this idea was starting to be challenged in the 1960s even as it was further perpetuated by advertisers and others who wanted to protect patriarchal institutions. But while the image of the housewife was becoming a conflicted identity with this bifurcation, the issue of housework has received less attention and, in our view, not enough debate.

Many, of course, have written about housework or some aspects of domesticity. From *The American Woman's Home* (1869) by Catharine Beecher and Harriet Beecher Stowe to numerous how-to manuals and popular women's magazines over the last 150 years to design periodicals and publications devoted to beautiful houses and interiors as spotless as their 1950s TV counterparts, idealized domesticity has been very visible. But, all too frequently, these texts have focused on showcasing domestic spaces as gleaming tableaux, seemingly unoccupied, unrealistic in their unlived-in appearance and never the site of conflict regarding sharing domestic responsibilities.

The issue of sharing domestic responsibilities seems to exist in a completely different sphere of thought. Such commentary, in addition to Friedan's perspectives, do include such notable works as Pat Mainardi's "The Politics of Housework" (1970), Barbara Ehrenreich and Deirdre English's "The Manufacture of Housework" (1975), Angela Davis's "The Approaching Obsolescence of Housework: A Working-Class Perspective" in *Women, Race and Class* (1981), and Arlie Hochschild's *The Second Shift* (1989, 2012). Recently, bloggers and some mainstream journalists have given some attention to domestic tension under the catchy label of "chore wars." But we would argue that the paucity of discourse, particularly in the deep gap between the popular and the serious, hampers the reception whenever a new perspective seeking to examine the issues emerges. Too often, the new perspective suggests a negligence or unawareness of the spectrum of earlier voices, as well as the implications of images from media and advertising that constantly swirl around all of us. The territory is not necessarily uncharted, but it is too thinly explored; we want to delve deeper, as well as broader.

Consequently, we believe the time for a more involved examination of media images of housework from the mid-nineteenth century to the early twenty-first century is due, perhaps even overdue. As we started developing this project, we wondered how many others had a scholarly interest in not just the "work" aspect of housework but also the implications of the pervasively aspirational images in advertising, photography, magazines, TV, movies, and literature. After soliciting for submissions, we were impressed by the spectrum of interest and ideas by other scholars. We received far more proposals than we anticipated, and selecting those for our collection here was not an easy decision—this text could easily be twice the length. Moreover, we were struck by the widespread consciousness of the still-vivid standard-bearers of the "perfect" housewives and how that specter continues to largely inform our culture on the assumptions and expectations of housework.

How did we get there and why do these images still persist? Although Friedan looked critically at the postwar era, an extended scope reveals much more, much earlier. Although we conceptualize (house)work as an economic system that has produced domestic commodities and interior spaces that have transformed our socioeconomic system, an important recurring theme among many of our authors is the perspective of housework as invisible, marginalized, and devalued. As Ehrenreich and English acutely observe, "No one notices it until it isn't done—we notice the unmade bed, not the scrubbed and polished floor" (26). In other words the work, specifically, the labor, is most palpable as an absence, particularly when it confounds expectations. This sensibility underlies the image of domestic perfection from the 1950s sitcom and becomes increasingly problematic as the pattern toward dual-income households prevails, when dirty dishes are a more likely greeting at the end of a long, hard day. The home-cooked meal and an attractive maternal figure in pearls and an apron exist only in fiction or fantasy, possibly always having been in that realm, as much as we look to that image in reality.

This still-enduring image not only prolongs our expectations of idealized domestic standards and has been problematic as the pattern—and necessity—of dual-income households has been perceived as the norm for the last several decades. But, as these essays seek to demonstrate, this complication has tended not to engender substantive discourse, perhaps to some extent because the invisibility and devaluation of housework has been too effective. With these essays, lively with fresh ideas and meticulously incisive in their scholarship, our objective is to wrest and make visible the awkward issues from the margins, to validate and make prominent the range of perspectives, and ultimately contribute to and enlarge the discourse.

The Industrial Revolution that brought technological advances and the beginning of modern conveniences to the flourishing middle class also helped to entrench the conventions we regard as fixtures of middle-class life—a comfortable home, indoor plumbing, heat and electricity. These features defined what we now reflexively regard as the basic standard of living, as well as other infrequently examined aspects. Therefore, we start our examination of housework in the second half of the nineteenth century. The "cult of domesticity" or "cult of true womanhood" established the Victorian middle-class home as the separate, proper sphere for the family, a refuge from the hostility, violence, contamination, and strangeness that was associated with the city and modern life. This new ideology could be traced to advice books and women's magazines such as *Godey's Lady's Book* (1830–1878), a popular monthly that influenced the trend of wearing a white wedding dress as Queen Victoria had done. After *Godey's* copied and "Americanized" a woodcut of the British Royal Family in front of a Christmas tree in 1850, the practice of Christmas trees in American households was firmly established. This tendency to idealize the domestic sphere depended on a specific image of middle-class women, an erasure of labor in relation to housework, and a reorganization of the relationship between family members, work, and home. Jeanne Boydston argues that as "romantic narrative played against lived experience, the labor and economic value of housework ceased to exist [. . .] It became work's opposite: a new form of leisure" (146). The essays in *Home Sweat Home* demonstrate that the construction of women as homemakers and the erasure of "labor" (what Boydston called the "pastoralization" of housework) in the middle-class home are evident in representations of housework in popular culture.

Kristi Branham's "Hung Out to Dry: Laundry Advertising and the American Woman, 1890–1920" dissects laundry advertising as early home washing machines appeared and the commercial laundry industry declined. Critiquing the rhetoric of marketing laundry soap and the new machines, Branham examines the marketers' appeal for nationalism directed toward their target demographic, the white, middle-class housewife. By focusing on the jingoistic language, which played upon fears of "racial contamination," Branham effectively argues that these forces isolated and burdened women. "Due in large part to marketing strategies that espoused the reality of the machine over the servant coupled with the democratic ideal of independence," she notes, "the circle of responsibility for the work required within the home narrowed to include only the woman, the wife and mother, in the home." As would be the case over much of the twentieth century, many machines that were meant to ease labor also brought unforeseen difficulties.

Another example of a consumer product in this era that created extra responsibilities for women was the simplified camera. In "Snapshot Photography, Women's Domestic Work and the 'Kodak Moment,' 1910s–1960s," Nicola Goc analyzes early amateur photography and the pivotal role of the Eastman Kodak Company in situating the mother as the family historian. Through an examination of Kodak's advertising and how-to texts, Goc places the humble and much-maligned family snapshot at the center of her inquiry. Arguing for its value as a text, Goc articulates how snapshots from this period helped to construct the meaning of women's lives for much of the twentieth century. By focusing on six family snapshots, Goc further aligns Kodak's persistent message that it was the *duty* of mothers to record happy family moments with a Foucauldian perspective. Through conscious and self-conscious presentation the maternal family photographer came into being, even though she was frequently not visible in the image. As instant and now digital photography have been overtaking the practice of composed family portraits, Goc's examination sheds important light on the residual effects of a once-familiar ritual.

Hannah Swamidoss looks at several key texts of children's fantasy literature in "From Chimney Sweeps to House Elves: Housework, Subject Formation, Agency, and British Fantasy Children's Literature." Focusing on Charles Kingsley's *The Water-Babies*, Lewis Carroll's *Alice's Adventures in Wonderland*, Beatrix Potter's *The Tale of Two Bad Mice* and *The Tale of Mrs. Tittlemouse*, Kenneth Grahame's *The Wind in the Willows*, and J. K. Rowling's *Harry Potter* series, Swamidoss constructs a compelling and insightful relationship between housework, morality, and class. As she argues, the act of housekeeping in these texts "becomes a thin Victorian veneer which barely covers up the class anger displayed by the working class and the disorder, tedium, and purposelessness of daily living experienced by all classes." By adding Rowling to "the canonical authors of the Golden Age of children's literature," Swamidoss updates the moral values of the Victorian and Edwardian period into the context of the new millennium. The continued focus on housework in children's literature "offers a means to explore profound ethical questions of how one should live." The enduring theme of the "need to maintain home" is not just visited but given renewed relevance.

Completely different perspectives are taken up by Andrea Krafft and Nicole Williams Barnes, who both explore subversive and political aspects through postwar speculative fiction and Cold War rhetoric. In "Appliance Reliance: Domestic Technologies and the Depersonalization of Housework in Postwar American Speculative Fiction," Krafft focuses on short stories by Shirley Jackson, Ray Bradbury, and Ira Levin's 1972 novel *The Stepford Wives*, along with General Electric's "Live Better Electrically" marketing campaign. Although as she notes, advances in domestic technologies "dramatically altered the nature of housework for American women," Jackson, Bradbury, and Levin "embraced speculative fiction as a means of critiquing the dislocating effects these technologies had for American housewives." Krafft notes that postwar economic prosperity in the United States made home ownership more accessible for more Americans, thus propelling the growth of the appliance industry. After women gave up their wartime factory jobs for soldiers back from the war, their return to the domestic sphere accommodated "the desire of a postwar patriarchal culture to reclaim the public sphere as a male domain." The implications, as Krafft argues, make for haunting literature.

Postwar advertising for domestic appliances and gadgets conveyed the message that new technological advancements meant less grunt work for the average housewife who did not have servants like her nineteenth-century counterparts. From the Proctor iron that "does all the work" and "banishes ironing fatigue forever!" to the vacuum cleaners that "lighten labor" and "walk on air," enabling the housewife, if she wished, to clean her house in high heels even on the stairs, the advertising emphasizes how women were targeted as the apparent key decision maker over household products. Despite the fact that the more expensive items, such as cars and houses, were still largely chosen by husbands, the advertising industry concentrated on communicating the idea of women as the primary consumer. Friedan excoriated "the men who make the images to see women only as thing-buyers" (119) because, as she cogently detailed, despite labor-saving technology, middle-class housewives in the 1950s were spending *more* time doing housework. Stephanie Coontz estimates that since the 1920s, the amount of time women spent taking care of children had more than doubled (27). Guilt, Friedan observed, was an effective tactic wielded by the advertising industry as products such as cake mixes that *required* extra ingredients and work to simulate the from-scratch process of previous generations were developed and introduced (306).

Until Friedan articulated such strategies, suburban housewives were inclined to believe that their guilt and sense of inadequacy were manifestations of their ambivalence regarding their domestic responsibilities and specific only to them. As Friedan memorably stated, "I [. . .] thought there was something wrong with *me* because I didn't have an orgasm waxing the kitchen floor" (43). But, as Nicole Williams Barnes argues, there was actually a larger agenda that promoted the ideal of the happy housewife. In "Making Easier the Lives of Our Housewives: Visions of Domestic Technology in the Kitchen Debate," Barnes examines the 1959 summit between then U.S. vice president Richard Nixon and Nikita Khrushchev, premier of the Soviet Union, providing fascinating glimpses into how domestic images were conscripted by the two superpowers. We might expect a high-level political discussion in that era to focus on satellites and missiles, but Barnes argues that Nixon pivoted the discussion to vacuum cleaners, dishwashers, and color TVs. Like Krafft, Barnes focuses on appliances as the locus of new technology, implicitly the core of power and influence, and therefore of crisis and anxiety. Characterizing domestic appliances as the "metric of evaluation," Barnes argues that Nixon "redefined the ideological battlefield of the Cold War through a manipulation of gender roles and expectations to measure the strength of a nation through its housewives and their work." But although women and their domestic work was central to Nixon's agenda, Barnes asserts that he effectively expanded masculine control over the feminine space of the home by "asserting the essential nature of gendered characteristics" in both the debate with Khrushchev and in the reinforcement of established American social conventions.

On postwar television, housewives' household labor is frequently glossed over—the appliances and gadgets seem to fulfill their promise—and so are usually, at most, incidental to the storyline, if not barely acknowledged or entirely ignored. The television mothers are depicted preparing meals and cleaning up after dinner, sometimes with the help of the father, yet avoiding any real grunt work—did television housewives have housekeepers we didn't see? Donna Stone occasionally folds clothes, cooks, and serves meals (all with seemingly little effort) and is shown only a few times cleaning or doing any grueling work in appropriate attire—like June Cleaver, she wears pearls and nice dresses throughout the day, and grabs an apron when necessary, as if it is an accessory that nominally identifies her as a housewife. These representations of middle-class housewives diminish the concept of labor or the awareness of the cost of being a homemaker. Consequently, as feminist scholars such as Eileen Boris have noted, mothering is not valued as an authentic form of work equal to the jobs done by men in the public sphere. Depictions of fathers helping to wash the dishes (now a vanished rite since dishwashers became a standard household appliance) was right in line with postwar notions of marriage and family experts calling upon men to participate more in parenting and household duties. However, the act of fathering within the domestic sphere is all too frequently depicted as a form of leisure activity and less productive (and meaningful) than their work in the public sphere. Even though fathers were encouraged to be more involved in domestic life, men were still expected to remain the sole breadwinner as their primary contribution to fatherhood.

This sensibility, as well as aspects of speculative fiction and 1950s sitcoms, underlies Kristi Rowan Humphreys's "Supernatural Housework: Magic and Domesticity in 1960s Television" as she examines 1960s TV shows *Bewitched, I Dream of Jeannie*, and *The Addams Family*. With these popular programs, Humphreys analyzes the predicament of the gifted housewives repressing or circumscribing their inherent powers to accommodate their domestic challenges defined by mortal husbands or external social conventions. The ensuing tensions, expressed within an overt comedic framework, can be regarded as essentially critiquing mainstream middle-class sensibilities of that era and, to some extent, providing an implied and somewhat ambivalent response to Friedan's text. As Humphreys observes, "'Supernatural housework' became the mechanism by which television portrayed women who possessed the hidden powers to change men into dogs or to make storm clouds appear, but who often were unwilling to use these powers for much more than vacuuming the drapes." It is hard to imagine audiences today—and perhaps in the 1960s as well—limiting magical powers they might possess just to clean drapes on the sly. If Samantha, Jeannie, and Morticia, as well as their rapt fans, were encouraged to use their secret powers to their full potential, what could they accomplish?

To some extent, *The Feminine Mystique* encouraged women to believe that they did possess an inherent strength that they weren't utilizing fully when it was dedicated only to housework. Friedan's influence on second-wave feminists is perhaps most visible in the founding of groups like the National Organization for Women (NOW) and *Ms.* magazine. This empowered sensibility also inspired actor and activist Marlo Thomas to conceive and develop *Free to Be . . . You and Me*, a multimedia project in the early 1970s that encouraged parents and children to explore non-sexist images and ideas. With the involvement of prominent feminists such as Gloria Steinem and many *Ms.* contributors, part of this agenda included a nod to sharing housework. But, as Mimi Choi argues in "Every Day Should Be Like Sunny Weather," "Housework," a three-minute skit written by Sheldon Harnick and voiced by Carol Channing, was fairly cursory rather than fully embraced by the project's creators. Although *Free to Be* was popular and critically acclaimed as a record, book, and TV special, "Housework" (which was not included in the TV special) generated an uneasy response and was marginalized while other segments were more enthusiastically promoted. Choi conjectures that this exclusion inadvertently created a vacuum not just in the discourse of sharing housework but also in encouraging children to regard domestic responsibilities as a fundamental aspect of growing up.

Although the 1970s marked a revolutionary period for women as record numbers entered the paid workforce, perspectives on housework have shifted far more slowly. In 1981, Angela Davis observed, "Housework, after all, is virtually invisible [. . .] Invisible, repetitive, exhausting, unproductive, un-creative—these are the adjectives which most perfectly capture the nature of housework" (222). As many women pursued advanced degrees, white-collar careers, and economic autonomy, the housework they frequently left behind (or took care of in the term coined by Arlie Hochschild, during their "second shift") was sometimes picked up or supplemented by men, but not always with the same sense of obligation women had routinely practiced. Hochs-child captures and examines much of the tension in households as these roles were changing, sometimes dramatically, to the point where *The Second Shift* is familiar to many who have not read her landmark text, similar to Friedan's *The Feminine Mystique*. Arguably, gendered domestic roles have always been in flux, but Hochschild's vital study guided many, including several essays in *Home Sweat Home*, perspectives on media images of masculinity that were shifting very visibly.

As Elizabeth Patton discusses in "Spaces of Masculinity and Work: Bringing Men Back into the Domestic Sphere," domestic masculinity has become significantly more visible on TV sitcoms. From the sporadic appear-ances in earlier programs, such as Bub and Uncle Charlie in *My Three Sons*, to the more recent portrayals of the professional father at home, particularly in *The Cosby Show* and *Growing Pains*, we see the rise of the New Father as a defined media representation. This figure, eager to demonstrate his domes-tic abilities as his wife pursues a career outside the home, is for the first time part of the ongoing narrative, regularly reinforcing such circumstances in the television landscape and possibly beyond. These shows depict professional lifestyles as flexible, rewarding, and desirable; transitions between work and home life appeared seamless. More importantly, representations of masculin-ity do not preclude the practice of domesticity and make masculine domestic-ity specifically consistently visible. Still, these representations of new father-hood are problematic, as Patton argues that men "still appear as heads of households, albeit domesticated and progressive," and consequently may have undermined "the expanding professionalism" of working mothers.

Also exploring domestic masculinity and sexuality is "Kuaering 'Home' in Ang Lee's *The Wedding Banquet*" by Gust Yep and Ryan Lescure. This essay complicates commonly held notions of home as a non-politicized space. Yep and Lescure argue that the home is a social construction and represents "multiple dimensions and meanings," including notions of sexual-ity and domesticity. Although *The Wedding Banquet* was first released in 1993, Yep and Lescure contend that its images of non-heteronormative and multicultural domesticity are still rare in our culture despite increasing representations of transcultural and same-sex households. In fact, they assert, nonnormative performances of masculinity and sexuality remain acceptable only when they support existing power structures. Their hybrid reading of *The Wedding Banquet* recognizes that the meaning of home is not limited to heteropatriarchal or queer representations but incorporates elements of both. Yep and Lescure's conception of the home that "demonstrates the elasticity of power structures in adapting to re-exert social control even in the face of changing conditions and tensions" is very much applicable today.

In "Good Luck Raising the Modern Family: Analyzing Portrayals of Sexual Division of Labor and Socioeconomic Class on Family Sitcoms," Nancy Bressler examines several recent TV shows and considers how class stratifications still tend to reinforce a sexual division of labor in the home. In contemporary domestic sitcoms, such as *Modern Family*, *Good Luck Charlie*, *The Middle*, and *Raising Hope*, Bressler notes that "working-class families talk about domestic labor, while middle-class and upper middle-class/ wealthy characters readily ignore it." For the more affluent, negotiating housework is a non-issue largely due to domestic workers, present but consistently invisible and upon whom the characters are routinely dependent. Bressler argues that despite increasing gender equality in the workforce and in the domestic sphere, television appears to represent the sexual division of labor in the home as equal while simultaneously bolstering the division. Bressler concludes that gender roles on family sitcoms are just as prevalent as they were in the postwar period, "but are even more deeply concealed in these media images in the early twenty-first century."

The new millennium prompts us to look forward, backward, and possibly back to the future. In "No Longer Whistling While You Work? Reanimating the Cult of Domesticity in *The Incredibles*," Christopher Holliday outlines a particularly mid-century aesthetic and elaborates upon the narrative significance of its period setting, reading the suburban struggles of superhero Helen Parr/Elastigirl as retroactively steeped in the feminine malaise documented in Friedan's seminal research. Departing from previous animated depictions of housework, such as *Snow White and the Seven Dwarfs* and *Cinderella* as "performative spectacle," *The Incredibles* depicts housework as a "more socially determined and altogether less enchanting enterprise." Holliday deftly notes that Elastigirl's physical adjustment (her ability to reshape her body to meet household demands) and quiet retreat to civilian life as homemaker "betrays a degree of ambivalence towards the historical legacy of second-wave feminism." Like Humphreys's discussion in "Supernatural Housework," Holliday raises questions of the implications of women who must (temporarily) reduce their fundamental powers to satisfy official definitions of where authority should reside in service to the family.

Also examining a kind of millennial bifurcation, Rita Jones explores the construction of domesticity on television representations of polygamous households in "I Couldn't Do It Without Her: *Big Love, Sister Wives,* and Housework." Through the multiplicity of work and plural marriage, Jones argues that housework is made visible, in contrast to non-plural marriage representations. Images of plural marriage on TV and the sharing of housework reference early feminists' demand for shared housework, particularly in Charlotte Perkins Gilman's advocacy for co-operative kitchens in city apartment buildings in *Women and Economics—A Study of the Economic Relation Between Men and Women as a Factor in Social Evolution* (1898). However, Jones observes, the highlighting of housework within patriarchal spaces consequently devalues household labor and makes women who choose these roles appear regressive and outside the sanitized versions of domesticity. As Jones contends, *Big Love* and *Sister Wives* "demonstrate how difficult it is to provide a space to reassess housework, particularly to reassess it as something positive and worthwhile." Can these perspectives be reconciled?

Have we made progress, or just come full circle to a moment at which Betty Friedan would not just recognize but shudder? With the recent discussion of chore wars, (not) having it all, and sharing domestic responsibilities by "leaning in," prompted by Anne-Marie Slaughter, Marissa Mayer, and Sheryl Sandberg whose high-profile careers in government, academia, and business inspire, intimidate, and infuriate many serious and casual observers of gender relationships, we may feel not very far from Friedan in 1963. We are also often inclined to feel we are in a brave new world constructed by advertisers who have succeeded in stoking our desires for consumer products which, soon after occupying our domestic spaces, require organization and negotiation with partners and families to share domestic responsibilities. Popular culture represents an apparently new middle class and the aspirations and privileges that go with it. In such images, professional middle-class family lives are represented as ideal. But all too often in reality, the participation of fathers and mothers conflicts with institutions and conventions that lag along with the slow pace of the discourse on housework. School still ends before the workday does; lack of child care programs, low wages for service (and domestic) workers, and dismantling of unions reduce opportunities to monitor children, manage educational options, and participate in extracurricular activities that reproduce class privilege. Will it take another fifty years to really resolve the issue of housework?

WORKS CITED

Beecher, Catharine, and Harriet Beecher Stowe. *The American Woman's Home.* New York: J. B. Ford & Co., 1869. Google Books.

Boydston, Jeanne. *Home and Work: Housework, Waves, and the Ideology of Labor in the Early Republic*. New York: Oxford University Press, 1990. Print.

Coontz, Stephanie. *The Way We Never Were: American Families and the Nostalgia Trap*. New York: Basic, 2000. Print.

Davis, Angela. "The Approaching Obsolescence of Housework: A Working-Class Perspective." *Women, Race and Class*. New York: Vintage, 1981. 222–44. Print.

Ehrenreich, Barbara, and Deirdre English. "The Manufacture of Housework." *Socialist Revolution* 5.4 (1975): 5–40. Print.

Friedan, Betty. *The Feminine Mystique*. 1963. New York: Norton, 2001. Print.

Gilman, Charlotte Perkins. *Women and Economics—A Study of the Economic Relation Between Men and Women as a Factor in Social Evolution*. 1898. New York: Cosimo, 2007. Print.

Hochschild, Arlie. *The Second Shift: Working Families and the Revolution at Home*. Rev. ed. New York: Penguin, 2012. Print.

Mainardi, Pat. "The Politics of Housework." 1970. CWLU Herstory Archive.Web.

Chapter One

Hung Out to Dry

Laundry Advertising and the American Woman,
1890–1920

Kristi Branham

In this chapter, I trace the history of laundry in the United States in order to map the ways in which popular ideology regarding women's work and responsibilities resulted in the failure of a nascent commercial laundry industry, and the location of this responsibility in the home and with women. Advertising campaigns for laundry products and services employed nationalist ideals about the *true* American woman set against popular fears regarding racial contamination. These advertisements have the simultaneous effect of elevating the arduous task of cleaning clothes and fabrics as the representation of a mother's love and declaiming commercial laundries, laundresses, and hand laundries as unhygienic and ultimately un-American, due to racist and classist notions. Through an examination of advertisements for laundry services and products found in two women's popular magazines (*The Ladies' Home Journal* and *Woman's Home Companion*), as well as pamphlets and trade cards between 1890 to 1920, I argue that laundry becomes a metonymic expression of women's love for family in order to serve corporate and nationalist interests.

That housework and the responsibility of maintaining domestic life, for which laundry is but one of many chores, has fallen to women over the centuries is not groundbreaking news. Scholars have documented well the history, evolutions, and technologies affecting and influencing the gendered division of labor within the home.[1] Even today in the postfeminist twenty-first century, women still dominate popular culture's representations of domestic chores. Such representations prevail in all forms of women's popular

media, including household handbooks, film, television, women's magazines, and advertising. Indeed, advertising plays a significant role in situating
and reinforcing domestic work as the responsibility of women, a fact not
unknown to businesses. For example, in a 1975 speech to the Newcomen
Society, a nonprofit, educationally focused business organization, then chair-
man and president of the Colgate-Palmolive Company, David R. Foster,
stated that "a good description for the history of the company would be '170
years overcoming housewife resistance through advertising'" (64). The "resistance" Foster references figures in two ways. First, as mass production
increased manufacturers' capabilities to create and produce new products for
the home, they quickly realized the need to convince consumers that the
products were better than traditional methods of completing household work.
Marketing strategies included instructional information to demonstrate how
to use the new products, as well as promises of efficiency and economic
benefits. The new products would save time and money. Second, advertising
campaigns countered "housewife resistance" in order to shift the work of the
homemaker from one of production within the home to one of consumption
for the home.

This insistence on women's responsibility for maintaining the home,
whether through production or consumption, began to take hold during the
tumultuous social, political, and economic changes of the nineteenth century.
As the United States moved from a mercantile economy to laissez-faire capitalism, home production, too, shifted to the public sphere through the increased ability of mass production. "In the colonial period," Ruth Schwartz
Cowan explains, "when most households were rural and rooted in European
traditions, the labor of both men and women was required to bring any
substantial meal to the table" (*Social History* 193). However, as such activities as cloth-making, candle-making, and food preservation moved from the
home, men and children relocated their labor to the factories and wage work.
The private sphere became the responsibility and realm solely of the woman
in the home, discursively constructed to buttress against the corruption of the
public sphere as both a place of refuge and of renewal for its inhabitants.

The transformation from an agrarian to an industrial society was a long
and difficult process characterized by anxiety and exuberance, great wealth
and great poverty, and social, cultural, and political unrest, not just in the
United States but globally. The political unrest around the globe sent waves
of populations to the United States in search of financial means to support
families in their home country, or to begin life anew in a country that from its
beginnings promised individual autonomy and freedom. During the mid-
nineteenth century, Chinese migration to the United States increased significantly. In his book *Chinese Laundries: Tickets to Survival on Gold Mountain*, John Jung explains that unrest in China during the early nineteenth
century, along with the discovery of gold in California, led to waves of

Chinese male migration. The Opium Wars between 1839 and 1860 left many Chinese villages, especially in the southern region, impoverished, and many of the men in these villages migrated to California, Canada, Alaska, and Australia to find gold or work.

In addition to the Chinese migration to the West, waves of immigrants came from Europe. According to John Chambers, "Until the 1890s most of these immigrants came from the countries that had sent immigrants before the Civil War [. . .] Beginning in the mid-1880s, however, increasing numbers began to arrive from southern and eastern Europe" (11). Reasons for the migration are generally universal—political and religious oppression, economic depression, and poverty. Chambers notes that during the Progressive Era (1890–1920), immigrants "accounted for nearly a third of the nation's population growth" (81). Much like the mixed consequences of the Industrial Revolution (great wealth and great misery), the mass migration to the United States was simultaneously welcomed and feared, encouraged by industrialists in search of cheap labor and discouraged by nativist movements fearful of racial contamination. The result included legislation limiting the movement of distinct peoples as well as an ideological war over what constituted a *true* American citizen.

Immigration and other post–Civil War changes exacerbated the discursive ideal of "True Womanhood" that historian Barbara Welter famously detailed as emerging in the early nineteenth century. As Welter explains, the discursive ideal of "True Womanhood" resided in the white race and was characterized by "piety, purity, submissiveness, and domesticity" (152). Situated firmly within the home, white womanhood provided the bulwark necessary to justify the rapidly emerging free-market economy. Welter notes that "[i]n a society where values changed frequently, where fortunes rose and fell with frightening rapidity, where social and economic mobility provided instability as well as hope, one thing at least remained the same—a true woman was a true woman" (151–52). The source of this message, as Welter explains, was the "women's magazines, gift annuals, and religious literature of the nineteenth century" (151). Clearly, this representation of womanhood was idealistic, and most American women at the turn of the twentieth century, no matter what their ethnicity, did not enjoy the luxury of achieving the four tenets of "True Womanhood."

Although Welter's groundbreaking study focuses on women's popular culture from the early nineteenth century, the ideal of the private sphere as the realm of the wife and mother persists well into the twentieth century. During the height of the First World War, the 1917 marketing campaign for Fels-Naptha soap reflected this expectation with its creation of the Fels-Naptha Home Maker, a white middle-class wife and mother who appears in most of the ads from that year. Early ads for this campaign introduced the Fels-Naptha Home Maker and describe her as "sympathetic, kindly, she understands woman and her problems" (figure 1.1). This campaign offered sage advice for the homemaker such as the following: "A house is just four walls. A home is four walls built 'round a mother. And the less time a mother needs to devote to house cleaning, the more time she has for home making."

The distinction between "house cleaning" and "home making" reflects society's bifurcated relationship to the roles and responsibilities associated with women and with women's work. Of course, American society reveres motherhood along with the other familial roles of women, but the countless responsibilities necessary for a family's growth and well-being are not in-cluded in the dominant ideal of "mother" or "wife." Instead, society elevates women's familial roles to iconic status while simultaneously devaluing "women's work" as menial and degrading.

Efforts to professionalize and value the work required within the home began as the Industrial Revolution brought about immense changes in all aspects of American life. In the early to mid-nineteenth century, proponents of the domestic sphere such as Sarah Josepha Hale, editor of *Godey's Lady's Book*, Catharine Beecher, and Harriet Beecher Stowe offered household manuals and advice in all aspects of domestic production, advising women on both the housekeeping and *healthkeeping* (menial and nurturing) of the home.[2] The term "healthkeeping" comes from the Beecher sisters' household manual *The American Woman's Home*, first published in 1869, where they articulate women's "profession as both housekeepers and health-keepers" (14). By the Progressive Era, home economists and home scientists such as Ellen Swallow Richards and Christine Frederick replaced the emphasis on household production with household manuals focused on the housewife as business manager and purchasing agent for the home.[3] This change in focus for household work both signals and reflects the dramatic shift in economic purpose of the home from one of production to one of consumption.

LAUNDRY *IS* WOMEN'S WORK: "THE BURDENS OF THE AMERICAN HOUSEKEEPER"

Laundry is but one component of a larger sphere of responsibility that the patriarchal social contract assigns to women and refers to (often derogatorily) as "women's work." This term includes the gamut of work required to keep domestic life going and is tied up with women's intimate roles of wife, mother, daughter, and sister. The idealization of these roles belies the actual work and caring labor these roles require, the kind of work that American poet Adrienne Rich so aptly describes as "work that others constantly undo" (43). In other words, as soon as dishes are washed, there are more dishes to wash. Obviously, the idealized social roles for women—wife, mother, daughter, sister—significantly conflict with the actual degraded work re-

Figure 1.1. Fels-Naptha Home Maker. Source: Periodical Collection in the Sophia Smith Collection at Smith College, Northampton, MA

quired to fulfill these socially mandated roles. This work exacts a high emotional cost from the worker because it (1) is always *for* others, (2) demands sacrifice of autonomous self, (3) is repetitive, (4) is thankless because it is expected, (5) is "work others constantly undo," and thus (6) never ending. There are many responsibilities tied up with these idealized roles, each with a limitless supply of tasks. Laundry is but one; however, it can stand as representative of all these responsibilities. Laundry work exemplifies the drudgery and repetitiveness of household labor even while media and advertising representations increasingly present it as a labor of love. As we continuously redefine gendered divisions of labor within the home and by extension the private sphere, laundry in our representational field remains predominantly women's responsibility.

There is no doubt about it, doing laundry before the technological advances of the industrial age was arduous and labor-intensive work. In her comprehensive history of women's work and domestic labor, *Never Done*, Susan Strasser details the tasks and labor necessary to maintain the average U.S. household. She notes that although today we celebrate the nineteenth century as the industrial age full of time- and work-saving technological advances, most of these life-changing advances did not reach the average American home until well into the twentieth century. For instance, electricity did not reach the majority of U.S. homes until the 1930s, and even then only 85 percent of urban area nonfarm dwelling units had electricity (Strasser, *Never Done* 81). The lack of access to modern fuel or water systems meant washing clothes required not only scrubbing, rinsing, drying, and ironing but also hauling water and stoking wood or coal fires. Every bit of water used in household work had to be carried in from streams, wells, or urban hydrants, and hauled back out. As Strasser so powerfully notes, "One wash, one boiling, and one rinse used about fifty gallons of water—or four hundred pounds" (*Never Done* 105).

The labor was so intensive, it compelled the Beecher sisters, two of the nineteenth century's most vocal proponents for the American woman's presence in the domestic sphere, to exclaim in their influential how-to book *The American Woman's Home*: "How would it simplify the burdens of the American housekeeper to have washing and ironing day expunged from her calendar! [. . .] Whoever sets neighborhood-laundries on foot will do much to solve the American housekeeper's hardest problem" (334). Indeed, the Beecher sisters' prescription for a healthy and happy domestic space included networks of families and neighborhoods as a central component. Within these networks, families and specifically women would share resources necessary to maintain the household, and well into the early decades of the twentieth century, women relied on these networks and communities of other women to complete laundry tasks, among other domestic responsibilities.

Clearly, maintaining the clothes and fabrics of the average nineteenth-century household was not work women could do alone. Indeed, women sought help with laundry from a variety of avenues. Girl children were kept from school on laundry days. Families hired out their daughters to other families to assist with laundry. Any money women were able to save or earn often went to laundry assistance, either through hired help or sending out certain pieces to individual laundresses or to commercial laundries, a budding and welcome business in the late nineteenth and early twentieth century. Further, neighborhood laundries (an early form of the Laundromat) emerged to provide access to the resources women needed to complete laundry tasks such as tubs, water, and soap. Indeed, the burden of this labor led to several time-saving inventions including separate shirt collars and cuffs that could be washed much more easily than an entire shirt without the damaging wear of heavy scrubbing.

FROM PRODUCING TO CARING: "THE AMERICAN WOMAN'S GREATEST JOB"

Commercial laundries sprouted in urban areas and for a short while benefited from technological advances of the industrial age. Some of the early automatic washing machines powered manually or by steam were manufactured for commercial laundries. Strasser notes in *Satisfaction Guaranteed*, her study of the growth of consumer culture in the United States, that mechanized systems for production such as conveyer belts and gravity slides had been in use since colonial times (6). However, as the nineteenth century came to a close, advances in fuel and water systems brought about giant leaps in production capabilities. Even as industrialization was changing the way manufacturers produced products, it was also changing the landscape of the American home. Ruth Schwartz Cowan remarks in "Coal Stoves and Clean Sinks" that "in the forty years between 1890 and 1930, the equipment with which housework was done underwent a veritable industrial revolution" (211).

As the technology for mass production improved, the variety and amount of goods available increased exponentially. The slow hand of industrialization brought with it the transition from mercantile to laissez-faire capitalism. During the thirty years of the Progressive Era, small independent merchants and craftsmen gave way to the larger industrial factories. Large manufacturers became the dominant force in the production of goods. Initially, manufacturers sold their products to local wholesalers that distributed the product to retailers and individuals. Strasser describes how "modern organizational systems and advanced technologies for production and distribution transformed industry itself. Countless new products—some of them packaged versions of goods people had used for centuries, others completely new—may be understood as material representations of that transition and its effects on American daily life" (*Satisfaction Guaranteed* 5). Advances in fuel and water systems spurred this transition, and small, locally based manufacturers gave way to the emerging corporate system of nationally based manufacturers and distribution.

The evolution of the washing machine itself is an example of the development Strasser describes. Washing machine technology evolved from the washboard to manual crank-turned agitators, manglers, and wringers, to the automatic gas or electric-powered washing machine. Manufacturers also introduced other items required for completing laundry. The gas iron replaced the "sad iron," which required heating on a stove and presented the danger of burning oneself at every turn. Industrialization brought technological advances to laundry work, yet these advances surprisingly resulted in more time spent on housework in the twentieth century than at the end of the nineteenth. According to Cowan, the cause of this increase between 1890 and 1920 "has three components. First, the number of domestic servants had declined. Second, the number of commercial services provided to households also had declined. Third, standards for housework had risen" (214). The reasons for these changes include a myriad of economic and social factors.

In the span of approximately forty years, the American home changed drastically. These changes were in large part due to the national increase in manufacturing and the emphasis during the Progressive Era on technology and efficiency. Nancy A. Walker explains that "[t]he application of scientific principles to the duties of the homemaker paralleled the 'efficiency' movement in the nation's industrial production, assuring women that they too could benefit in their jobs from developments in science and technology. By the early twentieth century, the rhetoric of advertising reflected this correspondence" (34–35). Manufacturers created products and marketed them as revolutionary technological advances. The increased production and marketing of these new products changed the way women interacted with and interpreted everyday objects and tasks. According to Strasser,

> [d]uring the decades around the turn of the twentieth century, branded, standardized products came to represent and embody the new networks and systems of production and distribution, the social relationships that brought people the things they used. Household routines involved making fewer things and purchasing more; consumption became a major part of the work of the household. (*Satisfaction Guaranteed* 15)

Due in large part to marketing strategies that espoused the reliability of the machine over the servant, coupled with the democratic ideal of independence, the circle of responsibility for the work required within the home narrowed to include only the woman, wife and mother, in the home.

Although most middle-class families employed servants into the first decades of the twentieth century, American disdain for relying on servants evidences in the mid-nineteenth century and figures as a rejection of aristocratic European and Old World ways in contrast to the idealized democratic egalitarianism of the New World. As early as 1841, Sarah Josepha Hale, the influential editor of *Godey's Lady's Book*, argues in her household manual *The Good Housekeeper* that

> [i]n our republican land, thanks to its rational institutions which preserve in a high degree of purity the moral relations of domestic life . . . The most delicate lady, unless her ill health were the pretext, would scarcely boast of retaining a hired housekeeper to perform her duties; and no lady would gain credit or consequence in society by so doing. (127)

Not only was this labor presented as the definition of an American lady, it was also constructed as work to be done not for pay but as an expression of love and patriotism.[4] Access to and acceptability of servants diminished along with an increased expectation for cleanliness. Many ads for laundry products in the Progressive Era promised better service than a servant could provide. For example, a 1920 advertisement for the Simplex Ironer from the American Ironing Machine Company claimed the product to be "a faithful servant." Similarly, in an advertisement for the manufacturing company Universal Home Needs, the copy promised "Housewives need not worry over the servant problem."

Manufacturers quickly realized they would do better bypassing the wholesaler by taking over the marketing and distribution of goods. For manufacturers of laundry products and services, this meant selling many smaller machines and other laundry products to individual families rather than selling a few products to commercial laundries, and the marketing campaign in support of this goal began. In addition to washing machines, other products required for laundry employed similar advertising messages. As Strasser notes, these marketing campaigns were so successful that laundry is the only home production that did not follow the progression of other industries (such as textiles and food preservation) from home production to craft stage to mass production. Instead, laundry went from home production to craft stage (with laundresses and then commercial laundries) and finally back to the home (*Never Done* 120).

In the world of industry and commerce, the odds were stacked against individual laundresses, hand laundries, and family-owned steam and commercial laundries. In contrast to the local unions and trade organizations, manufacturers formed larger, more powerful conglomerates than individual or family-owned businesses. Chambers explains that "[b]efore the turn of the century there were only a few supercorporations. Yet in only a half dozen years, from 1897 to 1903, a sudden wave of reorganization and consolidation created vast new empires" (55). In addition, they could sell a tangible product as opposed to less measurable services. Further, manufacturers could take advantage of the many venues on a national scale for advertising their products, including trade cards and advertising space in women's periodicals, newspapers, and other ephemera. The sheer number of available ads for laundry products in contrast to the very limited availability of advertising for commercial laundries attests to this difference. Further, these ads relied on marketing strategies that played into nationalist concerns regarding the "American Woman" and reflected anxieties regarding the identity of a still nascent nation reeling from the failure of Reconstruction in the South and the great influx of immigrants in the West and North that characterized the second half of the nineteenth century.

These ideals converged with significant shifts in magazine sales and publication. The last two decades of the nineteenth century mark a sea change in the relationship between advertising and American periodicals. First, as Daniel Hill explains, "[a]s manufacturers developed more efficient, lower cost methods of production, the need to sell higher volumes of products rapidly expanded. Marketing strategies evolved that were specifically designed to convert a population accustomed to homemade products and generic bulk merchandise into consumers of branded products" (2). Second, in the early 1890s, several popular magazines lowered their per-issue price from thirty-five cents to ten cents. The lower price resulted in significant increases in circulation. As a result of this change, advertising took a more prominent place in the monthlies, moving from the back pages to integration throughout the magazine and in concert with the magazine's content. Significantly, the cost of publication shifted from subscriptions to advertising revenue.

In *The Adman in the Parlor*, Ellen Garvey argues that the resulting interconnection of magazine advertising and magazine content functioned as a tool by which American women were transformed into consumers. She explains that "magazines addressed to middle-class women [. . .] discouraged autonomous work for married women and encouraged them to seek fulfillment in shopping and the emotional caretaking of their families" (8). In the last decade of the nineteenth century, "shopping" for women meant purchasing products for the home and the comfort of its inhabitants, encouraging the connecting pleasures of *shopping-for* and *emotional caretaking-of* the home's inhabitants. As the actual labor involved to maintain a household decreased with the addition of such technological advancements as the washing machine and the gas iron, the emphasis for women moved from the *work produced* within the domestic space to the *care given* in that space. According to Cowan, by 1940 the middle-class housewife "was expected to spend much more time with her children than her mother had spent—playing with them on the living room floor, taking them to playgrounds, providing nurturance and education at all hours of the day and night" (218). As a result, this *care work* became hyperidealized in the sociocultural field, giving way to the enshrinement of the nuclear family, the fetishization of the child, and the worship of *Mother*.

This move to *care giving* is clearly represented in the instructional piece "The American Woman's Greatest Job," published in *The Ladies' Home Journal* in 1917. Here the anonymous author admonishes the readers that "a woman at the head of her house can do her 'bit' in no more direct or efficient manner than to get on her job as a homekeeper" (9). The rationing required during the war demanded "homekeepers" to adhere to a "wise economy and elimination of waste that is asked of her." The Progressive Era's emphasis on efficiency found fertile ground during the First World War. This brief instructional piece does empathize with the housewife, acknowledging that "suddenly has housekeeping been transformed from a daily round to a science and a business. . . . Nine-tenths of the success or the failure of the war depends upon the way that every American woman meets the situation in her own home" (9).

Clearly, there existed intense pressure from the discursive messages addressed to women for their patriotic participation by way of housekeeping. Walker notes that "the family was rhetorically posited as equivalent to the nation, so that a woman's domestic duty was also her patriotic duty" (33). The marketing for laundry products and services reflected this idealization, erasing the actual work required while elevating the care demanded as impetus for such labor. The ads for such products and services are consistent in the marketing campaigns' imagined audience and the rhetorical strategies employed to overcome "housewife resistance" and entice this audience to become consumers rather than producers of goods and services.

GETTING THE DIRT OUT: "FREE FROM IMPURITIES"

The advertisements and marketing strategies I discuss in this section represent a sample from a set of over 200 images from *The Ladies'Home Journal* and *Woman's Home Companion*, two popular women's magazines, as well as advertising trade cards and pamphlets published in the period between 1890 and 1920. Mary Zuckerman explains the role of women's popular magazines at the close of the nineteenth century. After the Civil War, women's magazines increased in popularity due to new, more reliable printing and distribution methods. Billed as "trade papers," these early periodicals contained "service departments designed to help middle-class women in their jobs as housewives, a change from the ante-bellum publications targeted primarily at the elite. Now columns advised readers about cleaning, cooking, making clothes, buying goods, supervising servants, child care, and the home needs of husbands" (xiii). *The Ladies'Home Journal* and *Woman's Home Companion* were leaders in the field and part of the "Big Six," six women's magazines that set the standards for mass publication at the end of the nineteenth century.[5] Zuckerman notes that "these magazines led in circulation, attracted large advertising dollars, and were treasured in the homes of thousands of loyal readers" (3).

It shouldn't come as a surprise that advertising for laundry products and services addresses a female audience. Women are traditionally primarily responsible for doing laundry, therefore, the assumed and expected consumers of laundry products and services. Most advertising for laundry products and services referenced the responsibility of maintaining the clothes of a family, reinforcing the expectation that the wife and mother of the home completed this household chore. Further, this woman and her family are always represented as white and middle class. The repeated rhetorical strategies employed in advertising for laundry products and services focuses on three central messages for its intended audience: (1) the product or service will save time and labor, (2) it is economical, (3) and/or the product or service will be hygienic. Advertisements for laundry products and services between 1890 and 1920 cover three categories of product: washing compounds or soap; irons, ironing boards, and starch; and washers and wringers. Advertisements for soaps, irons, and manual washers dominate during the 1890s, while ads for the quickly evolving washer begin to increase by the turn of the century. Ads for each of these products clearly address a female audience. An 1894 print advertisement for the Western Washer exemplifies this imagined audience (figure 1.2).

In bold letters the ad proclaims, "Women Welcome the Western Washer." Rather suggestively, this ad states the Western Washer "is guaranteed to satisfy you," connecting the labor necessary to clean clothes to the pleasure of caring for family. In addition, this ad exemplifies the theme of labor and time saving. The copy reads, "It is simple, attractive, durable, saves much time and labor." The Western Washer, along with several other early versions of an "automatic" washer, consisted of an enclosed tub for clothes and water and a crank handle with which to rock or agitate the tub. At the end of the nineteenth century, many of these early prototypes were produced by small manufacturers and sold by individual agents. Advertising for these products had to convince women, who were suspicious of their quality, that these automatic agitators were as good if not better than the accustomed method of scrubbing clothes on a washboard.

Marketing strategists promised that the new products would reduce the drudgery and burden of laundry duties for women. The ads argued that there were more elevated tasks that women could perform instead of laboring over the laundry. Advertising for products such as the Western Washer and the Rocker Washer (1894) promised the time-saving qualities of its product,

WOMEN WELCOME THE WESTERN WASHER.

They cannot afford to be without one. It is simple, attractive, durable, saves much time and labor, and is guaranteed to satisfy you. Over 200,000 in use. We want energetic Agents, and offer excellent inducements. Address for prices, etc.,

HORTON MFG. CO.,
Fort Wayne, Ind.

Mention this Paper.

Figure 1.2.   Western Washer. Source: Periodical Collection in the Sophia Smith Collection at Smith College, Northampton, MA

which, as the ad for the Rocker Washer explains, "is warranted to wash 100 pieces in one hour as clean as can be washed on the washboard" (figure 1.3).

The 1920 advertising campaign for the Crystal Electric Washer and Wringer exemplifies the popular attitudes toward laundry as drudge work relegated to women. This full-page ad includes a large medallion image of ancient Greek-like figures of a man and a woman (figure 1.4). The male figure lifts a large bundle of clothes from the back of the bent figure of the woman. The copy on the medallion reads, "To lighten the load of womankind." The image reflects the faith of the Progressive Era in technological and scientific advancements. In addition, the advertisement explains, "The solid faith of the American woman in her Crystal is the result of her own satisfying experience." The connection of satisfaction, and by extension, pleasure, with the work of maintaining a home indicates the move from production to consumption. This connection is evident not only in the copy for the Western Washer and the Crystal Electric Washer, but also in the names of the products themselves. Between 1890 and 1920, a plethora of manufacturers experimented with different designs for automatic washers; the Bluebird Washer and the Eden Washer are two examples. Clearly referencing the biblical Garden of Eden, a 1920 advertisement for the Eden Wash-

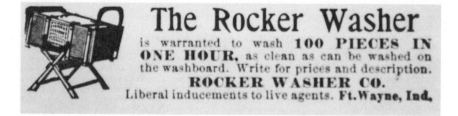

Figure 1.3.   Rocker Washer. Source: Periodical Collection in the Sophia Smith Collection at Smith College, Northampton, MA

er asked readers, "Does your home know the joy of an abundance of clean things?"

Advertising for Pearline Soap, one of the most widely advertised laundry products during the 1890s, especially emphasized the message of labor, time, and money savings for the new American housewife. In one popular print ad, the copy exclaims, "Let the *men* wash, if they won't get you Pearline" (figure 1.5). The use of the second person pronoun in this sentence implies a female audience. In acknowledging the amount of labor required "for any woman" to wash clothes, the ad also makes recourse to the claim of saving money—"it saves money, too"—because clothes will not be needlessly worn out through excessive rubbing on a washboard.

These same rhetorical strategies are exemplified in a second ad for Pearline Soap, which claims to save time and labor for the homemaker: "What a difference in the evening—when a woman has cleaned house all day with Pearline" (figure 1.6). The image included with the copy shows the contrast between a woman who cleaned with Pearline Soap and a woman who did not. From the copy, it is clear that the woman on the left did not use Pearline and is therefore exhausted and unable to interact positively with her family. The woman on the right demonstrates how much better a woman will feel in the evening if she uses Pearline. The advertisement emphasizes the benefits Pearline offers the whole family in the form of a more cheerful and rested wife and mother: "And what a difference to everyone in the house when the cleaning is done quickly and easily without any fuming or fretting!" The ad suggests that the woman of the house has fumed and fretted under the labor of cleaning. However, it is also implied that the woman of the house has fumed and fretted due to the amount of labor required to clean and maintain a nineteenth-century home, causing "everyone in the house" much *discomfort.* However, by using Pearline Soap, the woman of the house can now complete her cleaning responsibilities much faster and have more time to give *care and comfort* to the household inhabitants.

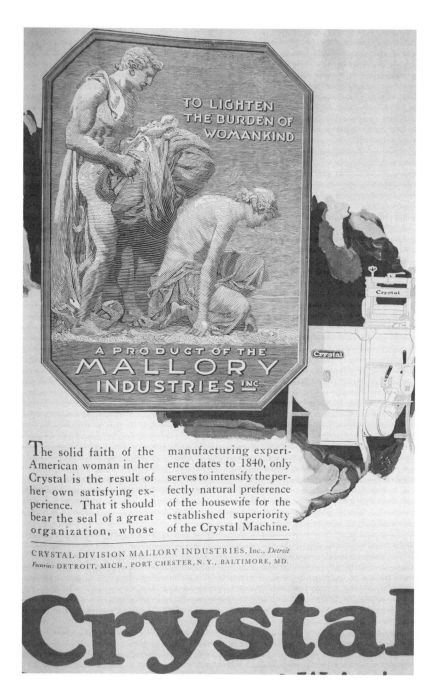

TO LIGHTEN
THE BURDEN OF
WOMANKIND

A PRODUCT OF THE
MALLORY
INDUSTRIES INC.

The solid faith of the American woman in her Crystal is the result of her own satisfying experience. That it should bear the seal of a great organization, whose manufacturing experience dates to 1840, only serves to intensify the perfectly natural preference of the housewife for the established superiority of the Crystal Machine.

CRYSTAL DIVISION MALLORY INDUSTRIES, Inc., *Detroit*
Factories: DETROIT, MICH., PORT CHESTER, N.Y., BALTIMORE, MD.

Crystal

Figure 1.4.   Crystal Washer medallion. Source: Periodical Collection in the Sophia Smith Collection at Smith College, Northampton, MA

Figure 1.5.   Pearline Washing Compound. Source: Periodical Collection in the
Sophia Smith Collection at Smith College, Northampton, MA

Even though popular domestic scientists were criticizing as un-American the practice of hiring servants to assist with maintaining the domestic space, the reality was that the labor and resources required to meet these new middle-class standards necessitated hiring help or sending work out of the home. Middle-class families made up only a small portion of the population during the Progressive Era. Cowan notes that "before World War II roughly two-thirds of the population lived below what was then considered the standard of 'health and decency'" (213). Despite this disparity, as Tera Hunter explains, "low wages made domestic workers accessible to virtually the entire white population" (108). At the same time, employment opportunities for blacks and immigrants were severely constrained, leaving very few options for work other than domestic labor. The sheer amount of work required to maintain a home to the new standards brought on by the industrial age made it virtually impossible for one woman to complete this work alone. "But good servants were hard to find," explains Cowan. "Indeed, good servants had always been hard to find in North America [. . .] In the land of the free, no one was eager to become a servant, and few people, even if forced into service, were willing to be subservient" (196). Yet the use of servants raised fears of contamination at a time when science, nationalism, and xenophobia

Oh! What a difference

in the evening — when a woman has cleaned house all day with **Pearline,** instead of the old fashioned way. It's so much easier. There isn't a thing anywhere about the house (that you'd take water to) but **Pearline** can save you time and work on it.' Saves that wearing rubbing on your paint and wood work, too. And what a difference to every one in the house when the cleaning is done quickly and easily and without any fuming and fretting! **You men ought to get together and insist on Pearline.**

Beware Peddlers and some unscrupulous grocers will tell you, "this is as good as" or "the same as Pearline." IT'S FALSE—Pearline is never peddled; if your grocer sends you an imitation, be honest—*send it back.* 443 JAMES PYLE, New York.

Figure 1.6.   Pearline Washing Compound. Source: Periodical Collection in the Sophia Smith Collection at Smith College, Northampton, MA

combined to demonize those groups relegated to perform such services. Further, the responsibility for the maintenance of the domestic space landed squarely in the lap of the American woman, who was not only to fight the battle on a literal level but also symbolically.

The new germ theory that influenced reform in hygiene and standards of cleanliness at the end of the nineteenth century also influenced the population's understanding of nationalism. By the beginning of the twentieth century, germ theory, the understanding that disease was transmitted through microscopic particles, had replaced the miasma theory, a belief that disease and plagues were the result of a noxious or putrescent environment, or "bad air." Thus, a new understanding of the spread of disease meant the responsibility for germ transmission moved from a specific place to individuals. This symbolic war against dirt and contamination played out most prominently against those who did not meet the American white ideal. In the South, this battle attacked the newly freed blacks, and at this time in the West and North, the contamination was marked as coming from Chinese immigrants. Industrialized commercial and steam laundries attacked black washerwomen and Chinese hand laundries from several fronts. They combined marketing strategies with lobbying pressure for local and federal legislation designed to restrict or discourage independent laundresses and family-owned Chinese hand laundries.

Advertising emphasized the sterilizing function of the new laundry products. An 1892 advertisement for Ivory Soap in *The Ladies' Home Journal* expounds the value of "clean air, clean linen, clean, pure food, and personal cleanliness." The copy promises Ivory Soap "has been examined for animalcular or vegetable germ life by microscopists and chemists, and found to be free from impurities." The marketing campaign for the 1920 Percolo Washer, an agitator that functioned inside a boiling tub, promised that "the steaming suds continually circulate . . . cleaning and boiling and STERILIZING the biggest wash" (original emphasis). In the New South, fear of disease, specifically tuberculosis, influenced many municipalities to enact efforts to regulate black washerwomen. For instance, "in 1904 the city of Macon, Georgia, passed a law to require washerwomen to buy badges. . . . The badges were designed to keep tabs on washerwomen and to prevent stealing. Sanitary inspections of the homes of washerwomen were also included in the provision" (Hunter 204).

The large number of black women and Chinese men in the laundry business resulted from several factors. Tera Hunter details the conditions for black women in *To 'Joy My Freedom*, explaining that "[m]odernization and Jim Crow grew to maturity together in the New South. African American women's lives and labor were severely circumscribed by the harsh consequences of this pairing" (99). Similarly, as John Jung notes, Chinese immigrants, initially encouraged to migrate to the United States by industrialists in need of cheap labor, found their opportunities for work sorely limited. Jung notes that "once the transcontinental railroad was completed . . . in 1869, more than 10,000 Chinese who had worked on its construction for over four years became unemployed overnight" (ch. 1). As these displaced laborers followed available work on smaller railroads, they moved to other regions of the United States.

The low status of laundry work coupled with an increasing emphasis on cleanliness created a stronger need for laundry services. At the turn into the twentieth century, this was not work that could be completed at home by an individual woman. As Jung explains, "In large cities, crowded housing conditions did not allow laundry to be done easily in city residences." In the West, there were few women to perform this job. Jung notes that "[s]hips transported laundry to Hawaii for washing, an expensive and slow solution requiring several weeks." The new germ theory increased the emphasis on cleaning clothes and on bathing. Further, there was a class and moral element attached to the increase in the need for laundry services. Jung notes that "being able to afford clean clothes became a marker of higher social standing [and] . . . from a moral view, cleanliness became a virtue 'next to Godliness'" (ch. 1).

A 1918 advertisement for Lux laundry soap illustrates common attitudes toward the laundress or washerwoman (figure 1.7). The copy reads, "If only you knew the heartless laundress would not rub the life and the newness out of your dainty things! You cannot afford to have your nicest things go so fast. You, yourself, with a fraction of the energy you spent hating the laundress can now gently rinse the dirt out of your filmiest things."

Similarly, an advertising pamphlet for Miami Laundry Company (figure 1.8), a large commercial laundry, offers a clear choice: either a clean, industrial, modernized laundry or the unsanitary and untrustworthy backyard of a black laundress. The copy states that families may feel stuck with the "old fashioned, unsanitary household methods" and warns against the "unknown sanitary conditions . . . where disease germs may start their journey to your home and children." The implication is clear: laundry done by black laundresses results in contamination.

One of the most iconic advertisements from the end of the nineteenth century is the trade card for Magic Washer soap (figure 1.9). This advertisement made recourse to nationalist concerns and fears against contamination. In it, Uncle Sam figures prominently, holding a "proclamation" demanding that American women use Magic Washer soap not only to clean clothes but also as a way to rid the nation of what was referred to as the "yellow peril": the influx of Chinese immigrants during the nineteenth century. The Chinese in the advertisement are shown in traditional national garb with washtubs, literally being kicked out of the country. Anti-Chinese sentiment was so strong that in 1882 President Chester Arthur signed into law the Chinese

Figure 1.7.   Lux Laundry Soap. Source: Periodical Collection in the Sophia Smith Collection at Smith College, Northampton, MA

WHAT DOES "WASH DAY" MEAN TO YOU?

Figure 1.8.   Miami Laundry Co. Source: *Emergence of Advertising in America,* *1850–1920.* **Digital Collections. Duke Libraries.**

Exclusion Act, which banned Chinese immigration to the United States. Explicit in the copy on the left side of the ad is the association of dirt with racial contamination, which reads, "don't use this if you want to be dirty." Certainly, however, there is no subtlety in the copy at the bottom of the ad: "the Chinese must go."

CONCLUSION

In her 1963 analysis of American women's social and cultural role, *The Feminine Mystique*, Betty Friedan devotes an entire chapter to "the sexual sell" that advertisers and manufacturers employed in postwar America to

Figure 1.9. Magic Washer. Source: The History Project, University of California–Davis. Online.

enshrine woman's home- and health-keeping as the ultimate expression of a wife and mother's love. Making extensive references to "a thousand-odd studies for business and industry, 300,000 individual 'depth interviews,' mostly with American housewives" conducted by the Institute for Motivational Research, Friedan argues that marketing strategists advised manufacturers that "(p)roperly manipulated [. . .], American housewives can be given the sense of identity, purpose, creativity, the self-realization, even the sexual joy they lack—by the buying of things" (108). Although feminists have widely criticized Friedan's book for universalizing women's experience, the postwar consumer system she describes results from Progressive Era social, political, and economic changes.

Several factors converged in the last decades of the nineteenth century to influence the advertising campaigns for laundry products and services. Industrialization during the latter half of the nineteenth century led to innumerable technological advances in the equipment, products, and ways laundry duties were performed. The consolidation of smaller manufacturers into larger national firms changed the economy. The evolving relationship between advertising and popular magazines resulted in a greater incorporation of advertising within the monthlies and an increase in advertising numbers. The nationally perceived threat of racial contamination from now-freed blacks and waves of immigration permeated the rhetorical messages of the advertising. The American woman's place within the home as a bulwark against such contamination figures prominently not only within advertising, but also in other women's popular ephemera. Sending laundry back to the home enshrined an ideal of American womanhood that isolated women and solidified the ideal of the nuclear family for the twentieth century.

NOTES

1. See, for example, Teresa Amott and Julie Matthaei, *Race, Gender, and Work: A Multicultural Economic History of Women in the United States*; Jeanne Boydston, *Home and Work: Housework, Wages, and the Ideology of Labor in the Early Republic*; and Arlie Russell Hochschild, *The Commercialization of Intimate Life: Notes from Home and Work*.

2. One of the earliest mass-published periodicals in the United States, *Godey's Lady's Book* ran from 1830 to 1878. Under the editorship of Sarah Josepha Hale, it focused on enhancements for the American home and woman. Hale along with Catharine Beecher and Harriet Beecher Stowe advocated for women's education in order to enhance their performance within the home.

3. For a comprehensive analysis of the home economist movement, see Carolyn M. Goldstein, *Creating Consumers: Home Economists in Twentieth-Century America*.

4. Many household manuals and handbooks published at the same time also presented the work of maintaining a home as a unique expression of American independence and egalitarianism. See, for example, Lydia Marie Child, *The American Frugal Housewife*, and Catharine Beecher, *A Treatise on Domestic Economy*.

5. In addition to *The Ladies' Home Journal* (1863–present) and *Woman's Home Companion* (1873–1957), the "Big Six" included one more magazine focused on homekeeping, *Good Housekeeping* (1885–present), and three women's magazines directed toward fashion and dress patterns: *McCall's* (1897–2000), *The Delineator* (1873–1937), and *Pictorial Review* (1889–1939).

WORKS CITED

"The American Woman's Greatest Job." *The Ladies' Home Journal* 34.9 (Sept. 1917): 9. Periodicals Collection. Sophia Smith Collection. Smith College, MA. Print.

Amott, Teresa, and Julie Matthaei. *Race, Gender, and Work: A Multicultural Economic History of Women in the United States*. Boston: South End Press, 1991. Print.

Beecher, Catharine. *A Treatise on Domestic Economy*. Boston: T. H. Webb & Co., 1841, 1842. Print.

Beecher, Catharine E., and Harriet Beecher Stowe. *The American Woman's Home, or, Principles of Domestic Science*. New York: Fords, Howard & Hulbert, 1881. Print.

Boydston, Jeanne. *Home and Work: Housework, Wages, and the Ideology of Labor in the Early Republic*. New York: Oxford University Press, 1990. Print.

Chambers, John Whiteclay II. *The Tyranny of Change: America in the Progressive Era, 1890–1920*. New Brunswick, NJ: Rutgers University Press, 1992. Print.

Child, Lydia Marie. *The American Frugal Housewife*. Boston: American Stationer's Co., 1830, 1836. Print.

Cowan, Ruth Schwartz. "Coal Stoves and Clean Sinks: Housework between 1890 and 1930." *American Home Life, 1880–1930: A Social History of Spaces and Services*. Ed. Jessica H. Foy and Thomas J. Schlereth. Knoxville: University of Tennessee Press, 1997. 211–24. Print.

———. *A Social History of American Technology*. New York and Oxford: Oxford University Press, 1997. Print.

Foster, David R. "170 Years Quelling Housewife Resistance via Ads." Rpt. in *How It Was in Advertising: 1776¬1976*. Compiled by the editors of *Advertising Age*. Chicago: Crain Books, 1976. 64–67. Print.

Friedan, Betty. *The Feminine Mystique*. 1963. Twentieth Anniversary Ed. New York: Dell, 1983. Print.

Garvey, Ellen Gruber. *The Adman in the Parlor: Magazines and the Gendering of Consumer Culture, 1880s to 1910s*. New York and Oxford: Oxford University Press, 1996. Print.

Goldstein, Carolyn M. *Creating Consumers: Home Economists in Twentieth-Century America*. Chapel Hill: University of North Carolina Press, 2012. Print.

Hale, Sarah Josepha. *The Good Housekeeper*. 1841. Early American Cookery. Ed. Anice Blustein Longone. New York: Dover, 1996. Print.

Hill, Daniel Delis. *Advertising to the American Woman, 1900–1999*. Columbus: Ohio State University Press, 2002. Print.

Hochschild, Arlie Russell. *The Commercialization of Intimate Life: Notes from Home and Work*. Berkeley and Los Angeles: University of California Press, 2003. Print.

How It Was in Advertising: 1776–1976. Compiled by the editors of *Advertising Age*. Chicago: Crain Books, 1976. Print.

Hunter, Tera W. *To 'Joy My Freedom: Southern Black Women's Lives and Labors after the Civil War*. Cambridge: Harvard University Press, 1997. Print.

Ivory Soap. *The Ladies' Home Journal* 11.2 (Jan 1894): 29. Periodicals Collection, Sophia Smith Collection. Smith College, MA. Print.

Jung, John. *Chinese Laundries: Tickets to Survival on Gold Mountain*. California: Yin & Yang P, 2007. Kindle file.

"Let the Men Wash." Pearline. *The Ladies' Home Journal* 11.9 (Aug 1894): 25. Periodicals Collection, Sophia Smith Collection. Smith College, MA. Print.

Lux. *The Ladies' Home Journal* 35.4 (April 1918): 107. Periodicals Collection, Sophia Smith Collection. Smith College, MA. Print.

Magic Washer Soap. The History Project. University of California–Davis. Web. April 20, 2011.

Miami Laundry. *Emergence of Advertising in America, 1850–1920*. Digital Collection. Duke Libraries. Web. June 18, 2010.

"Oh What a Difference." Pearline Soap. *The Ladies' Home Journal* 11.1 (Dec. 1895): 39. Periodicals Collection, Sophia Smith Collection. Smith College, MA. Print.

Percolo Washer. *Woman's Home Companion* 47.6 (June 1920): 128. Periodicals Collection, Sophia Smith Collection. Smith College, MA. Print.

Rich, Adrienne. "When We Dead Awaken: Writing as Re-Vision." *On Lies, Secrets, and Silence: Selected Prose 1966–1978*. New York: Norton, 1979. 33–49. Print.

Rocker Washer. *The Ladies' Home Journal* 11.5 (Apr 1894): 39. Periodicals Collection, Sophia Smith Collection. Smith College, MA. Print.

Simplex Ironer. *The Ladies' Home Journal* 37.1 (June 1920): 177. Periodicals Collection, Sophia Smith Collection. Smith College, MA. Print.

Strasser, Susan. *Never Done: A History of American Housework*. New York: Henry Holt, 2000. Print.

————. *Satisfaction Guaranteed: The Making of the American Mass Market*. Washington, D.C.: Smithsonian Books, 1989. Print.

Universal Home Needs. *The Ladies' Home Journal* 37.1 (June 1920): 152. Periodicals Collection, Sophia Smith Collection. Smith College, MA. Print.

Walker, Nancy A. *Shaping Our Mothers' World: American Women's Magazines*. Jackson: University Press of Mississippi, 2000. Print.

Welter, Barbara. "The Cult of True Womanhood: 1820–1860." *American Quarterly* 18.2 (Summer 1966): 151–74. Print.

Western Washer. *The Ladies' Home Journal* 11.3 (Feb 1894): 37. Periodicals Collection. Sophia Smith Collection. Smith College, MA. Print.

Zuckerman, Mary Ellen. *A History of Popular Women's Magazines in the United States, 1792–1995*. Contributions in Women's Studies. No. 65. Westport, CT, and London: Greenwood Press, 1998. Print.

Chapter Two

Snapshot Photography, Women's Domestic Work, and the "Kodak Moment," 1910s–1960s

Nicola Goc

I hold in my hand a small rectangular sepia 1920s snapshot photograph; it shows a young girl of about four sitting on the back doorstep of a sun-drenched American house (figure 2.1).

Behind the child, beyond the fly-wire screen door, a cane basket sits on a table, signifying recent domestic activity. The girl's hair is neatly bobbed and she is wearing a freshly laundered cotton dress and bright white socks that have been neatly rolled down her legs to rest just above her polished shoes, indicating dedicated care. Three small dogs surround the little girl—one sits on her lap, the others stand beside her—providing the perfect composition for a "Kodak moment." The girl is smiling as she looks away from the female photographer, presumably her mother, whose shadow is interjected in the scene.[1]

This chapter looks at family snapshot photography from two perspectives: as part of women's domestic work and as documentary evidence of woman's work. In the period 1910s–1960s, mothers and housewives regularly used the snapshot camera as a tool to record family life and to map the development of their children by photographing milestones, special occasions, and every-day family moments, thus according to Kodak, fulfilling the role of "family historian" ("All Out-doors"). For most of the twentieth century the product of women's maternal labor—healthy, happy, and often beautifully presented children—was the dominant subject matter of family snapshots. In 1960, for example, it is estimated that 55 percent of the 2.2 billion photographs taken in America were of babies ("SIC 3861 Photographic"). Female domestic photographic practice not only produced a tangible product for family con-

27

Figure 2.1. Anonymous American snapshot, circa 1920s, 9 cm x 6.5 cm, sepia Kodak Velox gloss print; brown paper album residue on verso. *Author's collection*

sumption, but the snapshot photographs could also be duplicated and sent outside the family as evidence of family life. The snapshot camera was also at times employed by women and others to document women undertaking household work, although, as will be argued later in this chapter, women's labor in the home was generally not the subject of family photographs.

The ubiquitous family snapshot is on one level a banal, technically poor amateur photograph of little aesthetic merit, but it is also a visual text saturated with meaning. It is both clichéd—the same poses and settings for example are replicated in all of our family snapshots—and a one-off, capturing as it does a unique moment in time. It also reflects the photographer's and the subject's acceptance, whether knowingly or unknowingly, of Kodak's photographic ideology.

Through a textual analysis of Kodak's global publishing phenomenon, *How to Make Good Pictures* (1951), a selection of Kodak advertisements, and an analysis of six anonymous family snapshot photographs from the period 1910s–1960s, this chapter explores the ways in which the Eastman Kodak Company constructed the universally accepted rules for family photography and how it placed the woman within the home as the family photographer.

With the introduction in 1900 of Kodak's first affordable easy-to-use Box Brownie,[2] for the first time the private lives of ordinary people could be visually recorded. By simplifying the photographic process to "You press the button and we do the rest," and reducing photography's motive from an aesthetic artistic pursuit to one of simply recording and memorializing specific lived experiences, Kodak transformed photography.

This transformation would not have eventuated, however, without Kodak founder George Eastman's personal vision to universalize family photography. Eastman regarded amateur photographers as two specific gendered groups—enthusiastic male amateurs willing to devote time and expense "to acquire skills in developing, printing, toning, etc." who "valued photography as something between a challenging craft and an art form," and the "snap-happy group who wanted to produce a kind of personal record of their everyday life" (Brayer 30). Through instructional texts, literature, and a global advertising campaign, Eastman placed women photographers in this second category and set about making them the largest consumers of Kodak's snapshot cameras, film, and products (Muir, "Demise of Kodak").

KODAK'S MARKETING AND INSTRUCTIONAL DISCOURSES

Kodak Advertisements

Kodak's marketing and instructional discourses were highly influential in establishing snapshot photography as a family practice. So intent was the company to link all amateur photography to Kodak that they introduced a new verb, "Kodaking," into the literature in the early twentieth century. The 1914 edition of the Webster dictionary defined "Kodaking" as a verb meaning "to photograph with a Kodak" (Lester 383) and while this term did not become universal, the phrase "Kodak moment," introduced in the early 1900s to signify a snapshot photo opportunity, did become part of the global photographic lexicon and remains with us today in the post-Kodak era.

A 1908 Kodak advertisement for "The Kodak Baby Book," an instruction booklet for parents on how to photograph babies published by Eastman Kodak Company, features a young mother photographing her baby, reinforcing the role of the mother as the family photographer ("The Baby's Picture"). Tapping into the early twentieth-century doctrine of "mother love" and the notion of the adored child being at the heart of family life, Kodak's advertising campaigns placed the mother as the family photographer and the child at the center of family photography. The woman whose shadow cuts across the frame in figure 2.1 was fulfilling the maternal role in recording the milestones of childhood—in this instance the arrival of a litter of cute puppies, a subject Kodak encouraged family photographers to capture.

To create a growth market for the consumption of Kodak film, the company created the notion that the everyday family events were also snapshot opportunities: "It's the small things—the daily, intimate events—that yield the best pictures" (*How to Make* 68). The marketing rhetoric encouraged mothers to see snapshot photography as an everyday family activity: "And if such moments are overlooked, you're wasting pure gold. Capture them, no matter how trivial they may seem at the moment—and you'll treasure them forever" (*How to Make* 68). A 1915 Kodak advertisement reaffirmed the value of capturing such images of children: "You love them as much in their soiled pinafores as in their party best. And, too, you will love the Kodak pictures that hold the charm of homeyness" ("Keep a KODAK Baby Book").

Consider figure 2.2, which reflects this notion of photography as everyday practice and an acceptance of the Kodak rhetoric that ceaselessly reminded women that "the record of his infant days is incomplete unless there are home pictures to supplement the more formal studio photographs" ("The Baby's Picture"). The grubby, barefoot children pictured in this snapshot appear to have been captured in an "everyday" Kodak moment, the picture representing the "homeyness" Kodak talks about, with the washtub and wringer behind the boys butting onto the side of the house speaking to woman's laundry work. But perhaps it is not such an everyday moment for this working-class family. Perhaps the female photographer, whose shadow is cast across the photographic plane (reflecting her adherence to Kodak's prescribed photographic convention to shoot with the sun at her back), is a grandmother or aunt whose visit is a celebratory moment, who was fulfilling her duty to record a special family moment? Without identity this photograph can only provide possible readings. Nonetheless it is evidence that women photographers adhered to Kodak's advice and snapped pictures of children in the backyard dressed in everyday clothes, in soiled pinafores and overalls, as well as in their Sunday best.

Kodakery

The company's own photography magazine, *Kodakery: A Magazine for Amateur Photographers*, launched in September 1913, focused on simplicity and provided what it regarded as useful information written "by men who not only know about photography" but who "know how to write in a simple way that the amateur can understand" (West 52). According to Nancy Martha West in her study of the Kodak Company it was "women, not their husbands, brothers, or fathers," who Kodak writers were speaking to and it was women who "constituted the principal readership of *Kodakery*" (52). For the duration of its life (1913–1932) the magazine almost exclusively depicted a female photographer on the front cover, often a maternal figure taking a photograph

Figure 2.2. Anonymous snapshot, Australia, circa 1920s, Kodak sepia gloss
Velox paper, 5.5 cm x 3.5 cm, no album residue on verso. *Author's collection*

of children, reflecting the understanding that it was women who were primarily the family snapshot photographers.

The central message of Kodak's marketing campaigns in the mass magazines was that Kodak products were important to American family life (Johnston 101), but perhaps the most enduring Kodak message for photographers was the directive to record only the happy, *pleasurable* moments in life. From the early 1900s the message in Kodak advertisements was explicit:

"Kodak knows no dark days" ("Kodak knows"). Kodak's creation of a vast canon of marketing and instructive literature, published globally in numerous languages, privileged the pleasurable moments of family life as the *only* moments worthy of photographic documentation. Pleasure was fundamental to the Kodak snapshot experience: "There's a new pleasure in every phase of photography—pleasure in the taking, pleasure in the finishing, but most of all, pleasure in possessing pictures of the places and people that *you* are interested in" ("All Out-doors"). Kodak's advertising, as Nancy Martha West writes, "purged domestic photography of all traces of sorrow and death and in the process taught amateur photographers that in a consumer society, to make the real consumable is to affirm it" (1). The "real," affirmed through snapshot photography, was a heavily censored version of life's experiences.

Kodak also potently meshed feelings of longing and nostalgia into their discourse, as in this advertisement:

> Time works quick changes in the growing girl. Pig-tails and short skirts are soon forgotten in the maturer charm of the debutante. Sometimes though you will ache for a picture of her just as she romped in the school or play. Think how she would like one too, in the after years—to show her friends and possibly her children. ("There's a Photographer")

The discourse weaves a potent emotional mix designed to resonate with a mother—her children will grow up quickly and at times she will ache for the toddler her child once was. Without a photograph she has denied herself the solace of owning tangible visual evidence of the infant child she once cradled in her arms. And by not capturing the childhood moment she is selfishly denying her daughter the pleasure of owning and sharing the visual evidence of her childhood. The implication is clear—the mother owes it to herself and to her children to capture their childhood moments.

The universal effectiveness of Kodak's discourses in influencing consumer practice speaks directly to Michel Foucault's position that it is through discourse that human subjectivity is created. Foucault understands discourse as the conjunction of power and knowledge. For Foucault, discourses are "practices that systematically form the objects of which they speak [. . .] Discourses are not about objects; they do not identify objects, they constitute them and in the practice of doing so conceal their own intervention" (*Archaeology* 54; "What Is an Author" 113–38). For those of us born in the pre-digital age, our mothers (and others) in capturing our childhood selves in fact captured our Kodak selves, a distorted, clichéd view of our early life experiences and imbued the snapshot images of our early years with a sentimentality and nostalgia that has played an influential role in our adult constructions of our childhood selves.

There was, as the Kodak Company realized, an ongoing value in a product that promised to perpetually memorialize the happy pleasurable moments in consumers' lives. Unlike other consumer products that are disposable, such as newspapers, magazines, and fashion items, the snapshot photograph, capturing a transitory moment in time, is itself a lasting product whose value continues to grow over time as it becomes imbued with nostalgia when viewers long for the "happier, simpler times" depicted in their snapshots.

How to Make Good Pictures

The standard twentieth-century text for snapshot photography was the Kodak book, *How to Make Good Pictures*. George Eastman published his first guidebook for amateur photographers, *Picture Taking and Picture Making*, in 1898 and followed this with the booklets *Home Portraiture* and *Amateur Portraiture by Flash Light* in 1904. In 1905 a more comprehensive book, *The Modern Way in Picture Making*, was published, and then in 1912 the company published *How to Make Good Pictures* which quickly became a global phenomenon and over the century was translated into multiple languages. Despite a name change in 1981 to *How to Take Good Pictures,* the book remained in print until almost the end of the twentieth century, creating a universal photographic practice—what some argue led to the production of a global corpus of banal, pictorial clichés.[3] *How to Make Good Pictures* was a brilliant marketing text because it remained within families, like my own, for generations of family photographers to be indoctrinated into how and what to photograph, reflecting Foucault's thesis on the power of discourse: the family photographer came into being through Kodak discourse. The image of the female family photographer was also reinforced through the front cover of *How to Make Good Pictures*, which from the 1930s through the 1950s featured a mother figure with camera in hand. Kodak's instruction manuals and books, with their didactic discourse, brought into being the female family photographer. The Kodak ideology was hidden by rhetoric that drew on the "common-sense" notion of photography as a truthful, authentic record of life: "A picture remembers what words might easily forget" ("Kodak TV Commercial 1961") was the sustained message. Kodak positioned itself, and by extension photography, as the arbiter of reality with the slogan, "Prove It with a Kodak" (Updike, "Visual Trophies"). In 1910 John Lee Mahin, an American advertising executive, summarized much of the conventional wisdom of marketing when he wrote, "[T]he consumer nearly always purchases in unconscious obedience to what he or she believes to be the dictates of an authority which is anxiously consulted and respected" (Lears 209). In *How to Make Good Pictures* Kodak tapped into this new psychological approach and created a universally accepted photographic practice as it also created the desire for Kodak products.

The first pages of the book begin by explaining the basic principles of picture taking with a series of thirty-two photographs depicting a father with his young daughter in various poses, the inference being that mother is taking the photographs. "Pictures right around home" directs the focus of snapshot photography on the home, suggesting:

> Why roam far afield in search of picture material—when the best hunting-ground of all is at home, right under your nose? Every day, every hour, there's a new fund of picture possibilities. Such occasions as Christmas, Thanksgiving, birthdays—these are crests on the tide of events, and we'll examine them in detail later on. But in between—How many snapshots do you have of Johnny, biting into that big after-school slab of bread and jam? (*How to Make* 67)

Kodak first provided the rationale for consumption, and then, through the rhetoric of guilt, transformed the consumer's mindset into desire to purchase Kodak products:

> You didn't take them? Well, never mind. Some of the opportunities will come again. They won't be quite the same. Each member of the family will be a little older. There will be gaps in the family story that can't be patched up now. But you can begin, today, to write the rest of the story as it should be written—clear, comprehensive, and complete. (*How to Make* 68)

The language in this text was designed to persuade readers through its potent mix of emotions—guilt, regret, and desire. Advertisers from the early years of mass marketing used emotive language to create feelings of guilt and a sense of failing in the consumer, leading to a desire to consume. Female consumers, in general already predisposed toward prosocial behavior (that is, voluntary behavior intended to benefit other people and society as a whole), were regularly addressed in Kodak advertising through the use of pathos, rhetoric expected to elicit emotional responses.

Kodak's highly crafted marketing discourse begins here with a series of short hard accusatory sentences, followed by a longer but no less accusatory sentence, and ends with positive and forward-looking rhetoric, creating the imperative for the reader to begin taking pictures immediately. The collocation of the words "begin" and "today" compel the reader to immediately take up family photography while the phrase "rest of the story" is a final reminder of what has been lost and what should be done to ensure the opportunity will never be lost again. The persuasive purpose of Kodak's moralistic discourse, both in overt marketing and in their editorial texts, was to arouse interest in Kodak products and to attract and to capture lifelong consumers.

In the 1951 edition of *How to Make Good Pictures* readers were taken on a "tour around a reasonably typical household" and instructed on what activities to capture. The narrative reinforces the transitory nature of childhood and the fleeting moments that are lost forever if not photographed. A rhetoric of loss and longing is embedded into the discourse: "We come up to the front gate, and find Jenny is using it for a swing. Small girls know what gates are for—and wise parents know that an album isn't complete without pictures of that operation" (*How to Make* 69–70). The inference is clear—an unwise parent is the one who fails to visually record seemingly trivial childhood moments. The text does not specifically frame the mother as the family photographer but the rhetoric speaks to child-caring practices commonly understood as a mother's role. In this narrative Jenny is finally transformed into the classic "Kodak Girl" who no longer wants or needs her mother to record her childhood moments; she can do that herself:

> Eight or ten years from now, in another springtime, Jenny will be leaning on that same gate, swapping sweet words with the boy next door. She won't want anybody to take a picture of that, naturally; but she'll be using her own camera to picture this boy, and other boys in her high school class. (*How to Make* 69–70)

And, if Kodak's script played out, Jenny would one day become the photographer in her own family.

PUNCTUM

Let us return to figure 2.1 for a moment to consider the snapshot photograph as something other than a clichéd artifact reflecting Kodak's family photography ideology. In the corpus of boring snapshot images, relics of the predigital age, there are certain snapshot photographs that arrest the attention of the viewer—you will no doubt recall images in your own family album that elicit an unexpected emotional response and make you stop, and pause, and carefully scan the photograph. In figure 2.1 there is a slight gap between the woman's shadow and the child's feet, a sliver that attracts and holds my gaze, evoking a potent tension, the indescribable feeling Roland Barthes in *Camera Lucida* called *punctum*.

For Barthes *punctum* denotes the wounding, the personally touching detail within a photograph that establishes a direct relationship between the person viewing the photograph and the object or person within it. Barthes wrote eloquently about this inexpressible ability of the humble little snapshot, however technically imperfect, however banal and trite in form and content, to ignite in our breast a quality that shoots out of the photograph and, like an arrow, pierces our heart. And despite the fact that I know nothing of the woman who captured this photo of a golden-haired girl, a litter of puppies, and herself in a domestic backyard in 1923, the slender void between the apparition of the woman and the mortal body of the child in this snapshot captures my attention and amplifies my awareness of that fundamental truth: we are all of women born. For me this small (9 cm x 6.5 cm) snapshot photograph of an intimate sunny moment in an unknown family's life potently speaks to family snapshot photography as women's work. While this dog-eared little snapshot was commodified in the twenty-first century when it was cut away from a page in a photo album and sold at a San Francisco flea market for three dollars, it remains an artifact of 1920s domesticity; it is the material object of a woman's work, visual evidence in the shadow cast across the photographic plane, of a woman working, photographically recording a child's growing years and fulfilling her Kodak duty as the "family historian" ("All Out-doors"). And it also provides us, in the image of a healthy, well-groomed, and seemingly happy child, visual evidence of a mother's devoted labor. It is this ability of the humble snapshot image to surprise and at times to captivate the viewer, along with its documentary evidence of life, that give this vernacular text its value as a cultural document.

FAMILY SNAPSHOT PHOTOGRAPHY AND SURVEILLANCE

While Michel Foucault did not write about photography in any detail, nor about the surveillance aspect of photography, his theories on surveillance and self-surveillance in *Discipline and Punish* (1975, 2012) speak directly to the powerful surveillance role of the snapshot camera as a tool of modernity that invades the private space. In the first half of the twentieth century, at the same time Kodak exalted family life, its consumers were unconsciously using the snapshot camera as a surveillance device, performing behind and before the camera's lens in ways prescribed by the Kodak Company. On cue before the camera family members adopted normative standards of "good" family behavior—gathering as a happy group and at the command of the photographer they all, in perfect unison, cried "cheese!" as the shutter clicked—ensuring a lasting record of happy family life.

The snapshot camera is a perfect surveillance device because its hegemonic familial gaze is disguised by the accepted notion of photography, and particularly amateur snapshot photography, as simply recording authentic moments. Women were naturalized into accepting certain prescriptions about how they should behave as mothers. In their day-to-day practices they were aware of the all-pervasive patriarchal eye; they were Foucault's "docile bodies" (*Discipline and Punish*), unconsciously constrained in the way they lived their lives through a passive acceptance of society's rules. Betty Friedan, in her investigation of American women in the 1950s, argued that popular culture in the form of women's magazines and advertising in particular produced a housewife who "turns away from individual identity to become an anonymous biological robot in a docile mass. She becomes less than human, preyed upon by outside pressures, and herself preying on her husband and children" (296–97).

In its invasion of the private world of the family at the beginning of the twentieth century, the snapshot camera created a highly effective tool for the surveillance of the housewife in her private work domain, and through snapshot photographic practice we can see the ways in which women internalized the patriarchal gaze, which according to Naomi Scheman influences the way women create family snapshot photographs:

> Mothers are the objects of the social-scientific gaze, which judges the adequacy of their mothering from behind the one-way mirror in the psychologist's playroom. The maternal gaze is not unobserved and, although it can certainly be felt as powerful by those who are its objects, it is itself closely watched to ensure that actual empowerment flows from and not to it. (Hirsch 154)

Mothers as photographers are observed by society and self-censor their photographic practice to conform to societal expectations as they themselves do the watching of their offspring, inculcating their children with expectations about what it is to be a "good" child. According to Friedan, the 1950s woman lived a "vicarious life through mass daydreams and through her husband and children" (296–97). Is it any wonder, then, that she so easily slipped into Kodak's prescribed role both as the family photographer and as the subject of family photographs, willingly conforming to Kodak's family snapshot principles?

In figure 2.3 we see a young unknown American mother presenting herself before the camera as the personification of the ideal 1950s wife and mother. She stands, willingly compliant to the photographer's gaze, beautifully dressed, poised and confident in front of a family car with her beautifully groomed children. An active participant in the creation of the visual documentary evidence of her success as a wife and mother, she smiles in a moment of pride and pleasure. This photograph, we might assume, was taken by her husband, whose intention is to capture his perfect Kodak family, although again its anonymity makes definitive judgments impossible. The image reflects both the woman's and the photographer's sense of pride and achievement in the creation of the ideal 1950s family. Behind the mother we can see the modern family car and signs of a new suburbia emerging from agricultural land. From this vista we can assume that a new family home, belonging to this perfectly groomed family, sits on the land behind the photographer. This American family has clearly benefited from the Federal Aid Highway Act of 1956 which led to the suburban sprawl and "contributed to the development of gender-specific space for the suburban family: commuter husbands and homemaker mothers" (Haralovich 75). There is no evidence that this image ever occupied a family album, no residue on the back or corners, so it may have been a copy sent to family or friends distanced by the urban sprawl, reflecting the snapshot as an important social device, as a way of informing family and friends of the family's current status. The mother's demeanor appears to be saying, "Look at how well I have done." Her poise before the camera, however, belies the enormous effort she must have undertaken to have the children so well presented for this Kodak moment. In this way the snapshot photograph is a document with value that increases over time, and decades later it provides visual documentary evidence of 1950s American family life.

The Kitchen

Snapshots of happy family gatherings in the kitchen are plentiful in my own collection and in other collections I have viewed, but rarer are images of women at work in an ordinary workday kitchen environment, reflecting how

Figure 2.3. Anonymous American snapshot, April 1958, Kodak black and white Velox gloss paper, 9 cm x 9 cm, scalloped edge, no album residue. *Author's collection*

effectively Kodak created the concept of snapshot photography as a tool to memorialize special, happy, and pleasurable family moments. However, the reasons may be more complex. Perhaps they did not want to memorialize what they considered to be unpleasant drudgery, especially when advertisements in women's magazines claimed, "housewives— [. . .] You should *know* your sink, since you spend altogether about six years of your life over it! Yet do you? There's so much hidden from the human eye. Mere inches from where you wash your food, germs breed—in the waste pipe, in the overflow" ("6 Years of Your Life"). It is reasonable to assume that women in the period of this study did not approach the kitchen sink on a regular working day as a "Kodak moment" photo opportunity. Kodak and photography may have provided the tools to allow us to examine everyday aspects of our domestic lives more closely; however, the quotidian coding of a kitchen sink discourages us from looking too closely or with fresh eyes at our own kitchen snapshots. During the period of this study, when woman's primary role in society was seen as wife, mother, and domestic caregiver, society's moral judgments about housework and tidiness and cleanliness may have made women even more reluctant to capture in snapshots their kitchen in a state of culinary or domestic activity, or to have themselves captured washing the dishes or scrubbing the sink. Yet the new TV sitcoms of the 1950s almost invariably situated the action in domestic settings and more often than not in the kitchen—although the kitchen sink was rarely shown and the most favored setting was the kitchen table.

Most TV wives and mothers of the 1950s were, as Elisabeth Edwards writes, of "the old-fashioned variety. Harriet Nelson (*Ozzie and Harriet*), Margaret Anderson (*Father Knows Best*), June Cleaver (*Leave It to Beaver*) and Donna Stone (*The Donna Reed Show*) were all white, middle class and suburban," as of course was the most popular 1950s housewife of all, Lucy Ricardo (*I Love Lucy*) (141). And in the commercial breaks, advertisements for cleaning products reinforced to viewers that the pinnacle of success for a wife and mother was, as Kristin Tillotson writes, "to stay at home and keep a tidy home, raise polite children, and tend to her husband's comfort" (6). The normative expectation was that a "good" wife was to keep her husband's home tidy, orderly, and clean, an ideal that since the advent of mass-manufactured household cleaning products has been central to the advertising media's construct of the ideal housewife. This indoctrination perhaps made women reluctant to allow their workplace to be photographed while they were in the messy process of cooking and cleaning.

The 1950s young wife pictured in figure 2.4 posing in her small but beautifully presented apartment kitchen shows no such reluctance as she poses in a manner that suggests the pride and proprietorship that comes with the early years of marriage. The verso message simply reads: "my first kitchen." She wears a glamorous party dress and is the epitome of a modern, fashionable, and therefore desirable wife. Behind her on the gleaming stove-top sit the lustrous coffee pot and kettle, signifying her housewifely prowess. Likewise the two carefully positioned, fashionably patterned potholders hanging neatly from the wall and complementing the floral patterned rubbish bin signify her excellent attention to decorative detail. Her right hand rests lightly on the edge of the kitchen sink while her direct and confident gaze speaks to a relaxed familiarity; perhaps the photographer is her husband. This young wife is clearly signifying pleased satisfaction with her status as a wife and pride in her small but beautifully presented apartment kitchen, reflecting the idealized young wife captured in a perfect Kodak moment.

The Laundry and the Poultry

The two areas of domestic work in which women are, not commonly but more frequently, represented in snapshots are set in the backyard where women are captured tending to poultry or hanging out the laundry. Both

Figure 2.4. Anonymous American snapshot, circa 1950s, Kodak black and white Velox gloss paper, 9 cm x 9 cm, scalloped edge, 045L processor's stamp on verso, no album residue. *Author's collection*

these activities are, however, invariably captured in snapshots on bright sunny days in pleasant surroundings—I have yet to come across photographs of women mucking out the chicken coop on gelid winter mornings. The snapshots of women hanging out the washing usually capture the woman pausing, turning to the camera, and smiling like the woman in figure 2.5, creating a representation of laundry work as a pleasant activity and belying the reality of monotonous and backbreaking work. This young mother has paused from hanging out nappies and infant clothes to pose for the camera on a sunny California summer's day. Her relaxed smile signifies an intimate family moment, but also speaks to her compliance with Kodak's imperative to "smile" before the camera. This image provides evidence of a young mother's relentless laundry work. In the pre-disposable nappy era, washing nappies and baby clothes was a tedious daily chore. It is reasonable to assume that this mother's relaxed and happy demeanor hides a deadening exhaustion that comes with nightly broken sleep, caring for a newborn and a toddler.

THE FAMILY ALBUM

In the early twentieth century the husband, as the "head of the family," was still widely regarded as the custodian of the family's external reputation (Brown 113). However, under the influence of Kodak discourse, it was the woman within the home who was seen as the producer and custodian of the visual evidence of a family's reputation—the family album—which Kodak branded the "Kodak Album." The Kodak Album was framed as the portal for telling "family stories" which remained within the home and it was also often referred to in Kodak discourse as the "family book" which had many "chapters," reinforcing the story-telling features of snapshot photography.

From 1910 the "At Home with KODAK" advertising series, which featured images of mothers as family photographers, promoted the woman's role as the taker, keeper, and importantly, the creator of the family album: "Make Kodak your family historian. Start the history on Christmas day, the day of home gathering, and let it keep for you an intimate pictorial history of the home and all who are in it." The text accompanying a picture of a grandmother, mother, and young daughter looking at a photograph album in a 1914 advertisement both reinforces Kodak as the memory maker, and reinforces the mother's role in servicing the emotional needs of her family. According to Kodak, "The story of the Kodak Album—it's a continued and never concluded story that grips you stronger with every chapter—a story that fascinates every member of the family from grandmother to the kiddies because it's a personal story full of human interest. Let Kodak keep that story for you" ("The Kodak Story").

Figure 2.5.   Anonymous American snapshot, July 1959, Kodak black and white Velox gloss paper, 9 cm x 9 cm, scalloped edge, no album residue. *Author's collection*

In an advertisement from the 1910s, a mother is pictured showing the family album to her young daughter while the Kodak Album is positioned as "the most cherished book in all the house," a remarkably brash position for Kodak to take at a time when in their major Western market the family Bible was perhaps still considered the preeminent "family book." Another advertisement in the "Keep a KODAK Baby Book" series from the 1920s has a picture of a mother photographing her child and reinforces the rationale for the lifelong practice of family snapshot photography: "The first journey downstairs for exhibition to that secondary consideration—father. The toddling nursery days! That all-important epoch when *the baby* first trudges off to school! [. . .] In all these great events are limitless opportunities for the Kodak" ("Keep a KODAK Baby Book").

Family albums have a consistency in content and form across spatial and geographic locations that speak to this deep social inscription of what was considered appropriate content for the "family book."

SNAPSHOT PHOTOGRAPHS AS SOCIAL DEVICES

The snapshot was as much a social device in the twentieth century as Facebook is in the twenty-first-century electronic age. Facebook is the largest photography site on the Internet, with more than 200 million photos uploaded per day, or around 6 billion per month (Mitchell, "How Many Photos"). While the number of analogue snapshots taken each day, month, or indeed throughout the whole of the twentieth century is hard to quantify, we do know that the snapshot was as much a social device in the twentieth century as is the digital image in the twenty-first century.

From early in the century Kodak's rhetoric specifically framed snapshot practice as a sharing experience through the Kodak Album and also by encouraging the reproduction of prints to be sent to distant relatives and friends. Kodak capitalized on the market for photographic postcards by introducing stock specifically for postcards in 1902, and by producing from 1903 to 1941 various models of the 3A camera that used postcard-sized film (Vaule, *As We Were*).

The period of this study—1910s–1960s—was a time when, due to increasing mobility, there was a breakdown of the consanguine family unit, with young married couples in Western societies moving far away from their birth families to seek work opportunities and independence in different towns, cities, or even countries. With this displacement of the extended family, ties were maintained primarily by housewives through letters and through snapshots, which were evidence of a family's continuation of familial customs and traditions. Pierre Bourdieu's 1960s study on family photography in rural and urban France, while focusing on male photographers, found "[T]he sexual division of labour gives the wife responsibility of maintaining relations with the members of the family group who live a long way away, and first and foremost with her own family. Like letters, and better than letters, the photograph has its role to play in the continual updating of the exchange of family information" (Bourdieu 22).

As early as 1912 a Kodak advertisement depicts a mother maintaining the family ties through photography: "Nothing preserves the home atmosphere and home memories like a group picture—with father and mother in the center. And, when the family is scattered how glad you will be that you had it done in time. Photography almost puts this obligation on us" ("There's a

Photographer"). One faded photograph in my collection (not included in this chapter) depicts an unknown young Australian mother and her infant daughter, Nancy, standing on the front path of a suburban home. The mother's verso message speaks to her anxiety to be seen by her family and friends as a "good" mother and also to her utterly subjective mother love: "Nancy looks older than 1 1/2 years in this picture I think the sun was in her eyes so she is squinting. Her eyes are blue as stars and her hair still continues yellow."

The young American mother of the bonny baby pictured in figure 2.6 sent this snapshot with pride to an unknown friend or relative. The verso note simply states: "Baby 6 months—with love." Whether the mother, father, or someone else took this image, it is the mother's domestic work that is represented and it was the mother who utilized the snapshot camera to communicate her work ethic. This mother in the 1920s practiced her mothering amidst a barren built-up environment in Boston. The stark backyard setting creates an uneasy tension between the vulnerable, dependent infant and the site of industrial work. The yard, devoid of a garden and any of the appurtenances of domesticity—there is no clothesline or safe place for a child to play—is nevertheless home to both the bonny baby and the laundry van. The chubby baby and the beautiful knitted garments signify robust health and committed care—she or he is the essence and product of maternal love. The fashionable cane carriage and the carved wooden high chair (of the kind that converts to a low rocking chair) have been moved outside into the sunlight specifically for this "Kodak moment" and, along with the scallop-edged baby blanket, strategically placed across the baby carriage for display, suggest a mother's pride in her maternal labor which she was keen to communicate to distant family or friends.

CONCLUSION

The humble and much maligned family snapshot is a valuable text for both making meaning of women's lives in the domestic environment in the period 1910s–1960s and in understanding photographic practice as women's work. Through an analysis of Kodak's advertising and how-to texts, and six family snapshots, this study shows how the Eastman Kodak Company framed the maternal figure as the family photographer and how the company through multiple discourses inculcated the creation of culturally specific images that reinforced the dominant Western patriarchal view of the ideal family. Kodak's persistent message throughout the twentieth century was that it was the *duty* of mothers to record happy family moments through snapshot photography. As a result, as Pierre Bourdieu writes, women were the historiographers of their offspring's childhood; they prepared "as an heirloom for them the image of what they used to be" (Bourdieu 30). But, as I have argued, the

Figure 2.6.   Anonymous snapshot, Boston, USA, c1910s, sepia, matt paper of unknown brand, 14.5 cm x 9.5 cm, "93" pencil mark on verso. *Author's collection*

happy snapshot heirloom, imbued with sentimentality and nostalgia, reflects a distorted Kodak view of family life. Women, both as photographers and posing for the camera, fulfilled their social duties by creating culturally specific family Kodak moments. Their photographs may be technically flawed, banal, and clichéd, but as the material of women's lived experiences family snapshots are important cultural artifacts and also among a family's most prized possessions because they provide a tangible visual link to the past.

NOTES

1. In the manual of directions accompanying each Kodak camera from 1900, which I have viewed, the beginner is cautioned to stand so that the sun is behind "him" or "shining over his shoulder" and "the subject should be in the broad, open sunlight." According to Robert R. Miller, writing in *Kodakery* magazine in October 1928: "This is good advice for the new camera owner as he might otherwise ruin many pictures by permitting the sun to shine into the camera lens."
2. The first of the famous Brownie cameras was introduced in 1900 and sold for one dollar and used film that sold for 15 cents a roll. The easy use and affordability made the hobby of photography available to virtually everyone.
3. See Geoffrey Batchen's *Forget Me Not* and Marianne Hirsch's *Family Frames*.

WORKS CITED

Barthes, Roland. *Camera Lucida: Reflections on Photography*. London: Vintage, 2000. Print.

Batchen, Geoffrey. *Forget Me Not: Photography and Remembrance*. New York: Princeton Architectural Press, 2004. Print.

———. "Snapshots." *Photographies* 1:2 (2008): 121–42. Print.

Bourdieu, Pierre. *Photography: A Middle-Brow Art*. Cambridge: Polity Press, 1990. Print.

Brayer, Elizabeth. *George Eastman: A Biography*. Rochester: University of Rochester Press, 2006. Print.

Brown, Morven S. "Changing Functions of the Australian Family." *Marriage and the Family in Australia*. Ed. A. P. Elkin. Sydney and London: Angus and Robertson, 1957, 82–114. Print.

Edwards, Elisabeth. *"I Love Lucy": A Celebration of All Things Lucy: Inside the World of Television's First Great Sitcom*. Philadelphia: Running Press, 2011. Print.

Foucault, Michel. *Archaeology of Knowledge*. Sussex: Tavistock, 1972. Print.

———. "What Is an Author?" *Language, Counter-Memory, Practice: Selected Essays and Interviews*. Ed. D. F. Bouchard. Ithaca: Cornell University Press, 1977, 113–38. Print.

———. *Discipline and Punish: The Birth of the Prison*. 1975. New York: Knopf Doubleday, 2012. Print.

Friedan, Betty. *The Feminine Mystique*. New York: Dell, 1963. Print.

Haralovich, Mary Beth. "Sitcoms and Suburbs: Positioning the 1950s Homemaker." *Critiquing the Sitcom: A Reader*. Ed. Joanne Morreal. New York: Syracuse University Press, 2003, 69–86. Print.

Hirsch, Marianne. *Family Frames: Photography, Narrative, and Postmemory*. Cambridge and London: Harvard University Press, 1997. Print.

How to Make Good Pictures. Rochester: George Eastman House, 1951. Print.

Johnston, Patricia A. *Real Fantasies: Edward Steichens: Advertising Photography*. Berkeley: University of California Press, 1997. Print.

Lears, Jackson. *Fables of Abundance: A Cultural History of Advertising in America*. New York: Basic, 1994. Print.

Lester, Martin Paul. *Visual Communication: Images with Messages*. Belmont, CA: Thomson Wadsworth, 2006. Print.

Miller, Robert R. "Back Lighting and the Amateur," in *Kodakery*. October 1928. Rochester: George Eastman House, 1928. Print.

Mitchell, Justin. "How Many Photos Are Loaded to Facebook Each Day?" Quora.com. 25 Jan. 2011. Web. 8 April 2013.

Muir, Kamal. "The Demise of Kodak: Five Reasons." *Wall Street Journal* 26 Feb. 2012. Web.

"SIC 3861 Photographic Equipment and Supplies." *Reference for Business, Encyclopedia of Small Business*, 2nd edition. Advameg Inc. 2013. Web. 21 April 2013.

"6 Years of Your Life over the Sink!" SANPIC Disinfectant, Reckitt & Colman Advertisement, *Home Chat*, No. 3094, July 10, 1954. London: Amalgamated Press. Print.

Tillotson, Kristin. *Retro Housewife: A Salute to the Suburban Superwoman*. Portland, OR: Collector's Press, 2004. Print.

Updike, John. "Visual Trophies: The Art of Snapshots." *New Yorker* 24 Dec. 2007. Web.

Vaule, R. B. *As We Were: American Photographic Postcards, 1905–1930*. Jaffrey, NH: David R. Godine, 2004. Print.

West, Nancy Martha. *Kodak and the Lens of Nostalgia*. Charlottesville: University Press of Virginia, 2000. Print.

KODAK ADVERTISEMENTS

"All Out-doors Invites Your Kodak," Item No. 2006-0144-000. Rochester: George Eastman House, 1911. Web. 2 Jan. 2012.

"At Home with KODAK," Rochester: George Eastman House, 1910. Print.

"The Baby's Picture," in *Harper's Magazine*, February 1908. Kodak Advertising Collection. Rochester: George Eastman House, 1908. Web. 2 Jan. 2012.

"Keep a KODAK Baby Book." Rochester: George Eastman House, 1915. Web. 2 Jan. 2012.

"Kodak Knows No Dark Days," in *The Ladies' Home Journal*, July 1917. *Kodak Antique Camera Ad Collection 1886–1923*. Ontario: Vintage Literature Reproductions, 2012. CD.

"The Kodak Story." Rochester: George Eastman House, 1914. Web. 2 Feb. 2012.

"Kodak TV commercial." 1961. Web. 21 Feb. 2012.

"There's a Photographer in Your Town." *The Ladies' Home Journal*, July 1913. *Kodak Antique Camera Ad Collection 1886–1923*. Ontario: Vintage Literature Reproductions, 2012. CD.

Chapter Three

From Chimney Sweeps to House-Elves

Housework, Subject Formation, Agency, and British Children's Fantasy Literature, 1863–2007

Hannah Swamidoss

In J. K. Rowling's *Harry Potter* series (1997–2007), one of the lead characters, Hermione, expresses outrage when she finds out that house-elves cook and clean at Hogwarts, the boarding school for young wizards and witches that Hermione attends. Although magical, house-elves form the domestic workforce for wizards and witches and belong to families for generations unless freed, frequently facing abuse from their owners. The appalled Hermione asks, "But they get paid? [. . .] They get *holidays*, don't they? And—and sick leave, and pensions and everything?" (Rowling, *Goblet of Fire* 182). The resounding "no" to her questions makes Hermione begin the Society for Protection of Elfish Welfare. However, when Hermione begins her campaign to free elves, she receives derision both from her peers and from the elves themselves: the elves enjoy their work and position. Later, Rowling complicates the idea that this domestic labor force does not mind this subjugation: Harry's parental figure, Sirius Black, meets his death partly due to his ill-treatment of his house-elf.

Both at its earliest beginnings and in its latest developments, representations of housework in British children's fantasy literature have linked the labor involved in maintaining domestic space to moral value. Caroline Davidson points out that when John Wesley famously stated "cleanliness is indeed next to godliness," this maxim became "the favourite cliché of the nineteenth-century sanitary reformers" (117).[1] From the late 1700s onwards, Davidson notes that, for women, "a large proportion found [cleaning their homes] a creative, satisfying and thoroughly moral activity, in which they took considerable pride" (134).[2] In light of these cultural attitudes, British children's fantasy literature surprisingly portrays domestic labor as undesirable, a form of punishment, or the image of societal abuse, and does not equate the accomplishment of domestic labor with virtue. Charles Kingsley's *The Water-Babies* (1863), for instance, represents the problematic nature of its protagonist's domestic service: Tom, a chimney sweep, has undeserved misfortunes. Lewis Carroll's *Alice's Adventures in Wonderland* (1865) subverts the idea that housework creates order and focuses on its drudgery and tedium. Beatrix Potter's infamous mice, Hunca Munca and Tom Thumb, seemingly perform housework as punishment and recompense, while Potter's more compulsive Mrs. Tittlemouse demonstrates that exacting standards in cleanliness create an exclusive community. Kenneth Grahame's *The Wind in the Willows* (1908) portrays housework as limiting and cumbersome, yet necessary to maintain the pleasures of a home. Rowling, decades later, would once again explore the need to maintain a home while echoing Kingsley's concern over societal abuse.

British children's fantasy literature offers an appropriate venue for these subversive portrayals of housework. Rosemary Jackson observes that "fantasy characteristically attempts to compensate for a lack resulting from cultural constraints: it is a literature of desire, which seeks that which is experienced as absence and loss" (3). Jackson categorizes fantasy as either manifesting desire or expelling desire and consequently opening up subversive, sociopolitical spaces (3–5). In the specific context of children's fantasy literature, Maria Nikolajeva notes, "[t]he issue of power thus becomes almost from start [*sic*] the engine for children's fantasy, as well as its tangible double address" (51). The subversive treatment of housework displayed in Kingsley, Carroll, Potter, and Grahame (canonical authors of the Golden Age of children's literature) and the issues of power that go alongside domestic labor, consequently, demonstrate a new attention to domestic work and thinking about it in moral terms. Children's literature has always had representations of housework, but with the advent of Kingsley, Carroll, Potter, and Grahame, the *character* of these representations changes: housework becomes attached to moral values that run counter to contemporary norms. Initially, Rowling may seem anomalous to this grouping of Victorian and Edwardian authors, but her work finds its place in two key ways. First, Rowling inherits these texts, and her treatment of domestic work echoes many of the ethical concerns of these earlier authors. Second, Rowling anachronistically situates the series' domestic workforce in the Victorian/Edwardian era; her portrayal of a large number of servants loyal to their families and who work invisibly behind the scenes smacks of the TV series *Downton Abbey* (2010–) and not Britain of the 1990s.

The primary audience for children's fantasy literature, the child, also plays a role in Jackson's subversive sociopolitical spaces. Children's literature has a long-standing role of inculcating cultural and political values that adults frequently promote or shun; these authors' portrayal of domestic work to this particular audience consequently proves of interest. By making the abuses of domestic labor *visible* through chimney sweeps, for instance, Kingsley strategically introduces social reform to a young audience (and the adults who buy the books and perhaps read them to their children). Yet the very visibility of housework seen in these narratives—whether it be a crying sweep, an obsessively clean mouse, or an angry house-elf—points also to its intended *invisibility*. The sweep and elf are not meant to be seen, and the mouse puts away her broom and apron during a party. Ultimately, by interrogating how humans maintain homes, Kingsley, Carroll, Potter, Grahame, and Rowling ask fundamental ethical questions of how one should live. These questions, and their answers, reveal the changing political, social, and economic concerns of their times.

THE WATER-BABIES

In 1832, thirteen-year-old Charles Kingsley may have missed some of the significance of the Reform Act passed that year, but in 1848, after the collapse of the Chartist movement, Kingsley (now twenty-nine) vigorously protested poor working-class conditions (Jones 171–72). Between 1832 and 1848 important legislation had passed in Victorian England with respect to the working class: the Factory Act (limited working hours), the Poor Law Amendment Act in 1834, the Registration Act in 1837 (complemented the Factory Act), the repeal of the Corn Laws in 1846, and the Public Health Act in 1848. The next decade provided new and important milestones: cycles of economic prosperity and recession (with Britain being the richest nation in the world in 1851), an appreciable rise in wages, and changing demographics with the majority of the population living in cities (Steinbach xvii). During this time, Kingsley, an Anglican priest, became a key figure in the Christian socialist movement, and this interest continued in the writing of *The Water-Babies*. In his fantasy of a chimney sweep transformed into a water baby (a tiny, amphibious human-like creature), Kingsley threads together diverse issues of child labor, Darwinism, and education.[3] Accordingly, *The Water-Babies* depicts Tom, the working-class chimney sweep, evolving both morally and physically out of his class and profession into a scientist. By choosing the social issue of chimney sweeps, Kingsley acknowledges the particular difficulty and cruelty of this form of domestic labor because throughout the narrative, Kingsley values reasonable amounts of work (including domestic cleaning) and ties it in with moral formation.[4] To this mix of physical/moral formation and moral work/immoral overwork Kingsley also celebrates the machine. Colin Manlove perceptively demonstrates Kingsley's fascination with the "mechanical" at various levels including the Godhead; Manlove states that "the whole natural order works as one great engine, driven ultimately by God" (217). Although Manlove notes that Kingsley largely celebrates the mechanical in the natural world and not necessarily in its industrial forms in cities, understanding Kingsley's positive associations with machines and technology helps analyze his discourse on domestic work.

The Water-Babies demonstrates what can go wrong with the mechanical: chimneys with narrow flues that need cleaning, and greedy master sweeps, who use and ill-treat young boys to clean these chimneys and make a profit. In reviewing the situation of chimney sweeps, George Phillips notes that narrowed flues reveal both the technological advances in using coal for heating and also the level of domestic comfort that could now be expected and desired (445). Phillips observes that the first responses to the plight of these boys championed better treatment of them or the invention of machines to replace them (447–50). Kingsley's portrayal of Tom's reluctance in entering the chimney of a large wealthy home and becoming disoriented in the flues reflects the experiences of sweeps documented in newspapers and pamphlets of the period.[5] Instead of coming to an unfortunate end, however, Tom has a crucial moment of self-awareness when he comes down the wrong chimney of the Harthover estate into the pristine bedroom of a little girl, Ellie. The narrator explains: "Tom had never seen the like. He had never been in gentlefolks' rooms but when the carpets were all up, and the curtains down [. . .] and he had often enough wondered what the rooms were like when they were all ready for the quality to sit in [. . .] and now he saw, and he thought the sight very pretty" (Kingsley 17). Tom then catches sight of himself in a mirror and sees "a little black ape" (19), sadly out of place in this aesthetically pleasing room, and in one fell swoop, Kingsley integrates ideas of evolution, moral formation, education, and housework.[6] From the outset of the narrative, Kingsley connects Tom's lack of ability to read and pray with his inability to wash and become either physically or morally clean (1), and when Tom sees himself as an ape, he has almost regressed evolutionarily and crossed the line between human and animal. This moment firms Tom's desire to be clean, and this desire materializes shortly afterwards when Tom tumbles into a stream and appears to drown. Tom, however, has left his human shell and transformed into a water baby and embarks on a series of moral lessons.

Undoubtedly Kingsley differs from his contemporaries in his "solution" to the problem of chimney sweeps. Although the master sweep of the narrative receives his just punishment, Kingsley focuses on Tom, instead of machines to replace sweeps or reforming the treatment of sweeps. Kingsley so deeply integrates the machine with nature, science, and religious belief that Tom becomes the machine, and he becomes a very advanced machine when he evolves into a scientist. As a result, Kingsley closely ties domestic work with technological advances which, while true to the history of domestic work, creates problems of its moral worth and value. In "recreating" Tom, Kingsley portrays the abusive nature of this type of domestic labor and the depraved effects this lifestyle has on Tom's moral being. Tom cries "when he had to climb the dark flues, rubbing his poor knees and elbows raw [. . .] and when his master beat him, which he did every day in the week; and when he had not enough to eat, which happened every day in the week likewise" (1). The physical deprivation and abuse Tom experiences shape what he enjoys. Tom's pleasures stem from playing with the other sweeps, teasing animals, and acting like a master sweep and bullying his imaginary apprentices (2). Tom's domestic labor damages his body and soul when he teases animals, and his skewed imagination sees no wrong in perpetuating this lifestyle on other boys. Kingsley corrects these moral inclinations of his machine, Tom, through his education in the water. This moral evolution culminates in the figure of a scientist and seemingly provides a solution for the issue of chimney sweeps and societal abuse because it places Tom in a better position in terms of class and profession.

Kingsley's integration of the physical environment and moral formation, however, gives rise to some problematic elements. The moral cleanliness and superiority both in the physical space and occupants of Harthover (Ellie is Tom's moral tutor in the water) occurs before Tom's moral re-formation, and Ellie's pristine bedroom depends on various types of domestic work and workers (including the un-evolved Tom) to retain its purity. Ironically, Kingsley's "great fairy science" (with its advances of the flues and heating) creates the need for sweeps because Kingsley does not seek to limit technology or the standards of comfort. By not seeing the problematic nature of the mechanical and the scientific, but only its positives, and by not seeing the difficulties his aesthetic standard creates, Kingsley creates tension and irresolution in the very solution he offers. The connection between Tom's impurity and Ellie's purity creates ambiguity at the end of the narrative, for chimneys still need sweeping, and bedrooms need cleaning. The answer of science—more machinery—is one possibility the narrative opens up, but a tension between domestic labor and science occurs. Kingsley cannot escape the possibility that in creating a "machine" for chimney sweeps, different issues of injustice could arise.

Kingsley's problematic "technological" solution to the ethical concerns that housework raises captures the mid-Victorian confidence in the progress of science and technology; the ills that might occur over the course of this progress would eventually be worked out. As problematic as Kingsley's solution of seeing Tom as the "machine" is, one crucial element makes it vastly different from the typical Victorian discourse on chimney sweeps. Whether Kingsley's contemporaries saw the solution for chimney sweeps lying in better treatment of the sweeps or in the invention of machinery to replace sweeps, sweeps would remain in the working class. In striking contrast, *The Water-Babies* portrays room for upward class mobility. Tom can start out as a working-class domestic laborer and end as a scientist without creating societal anxiety or unease. In spite of Kingsley's various racial, religious, and class prejudices, he portrays an ordered class mobility reflecting the mechanical order of the universe. Kingsley's structuring of domestic work and moral formation also provides agency for the individual subject, whether morally formed or not. Tom has agency in creating Harthover's pure space, and Tom has the agency to evolve into the superior human machine of the scientist. Kingsley's didacticism in *The Water-Babies* may seem strange and unappealing to modern audiences, but *The Water-Babies* did have a noteworthy effect in its own time. With respect to the 1864 Act for the Regulation of Chimney Sweepers, Heather Shore observes that "[t]his immensely popular children's novel was arguably instrumental in increasing public support for Lord Shaftesbury's campaign. The plight of the sweep Tom did much to engage the sympathies of the Victorian reading public" (567). Although this Act achieved mixed results, Kingsley played his part.

ALICE'S ADVENTURES IN WONDERLAND

If *The Water-Babies* presents a world where the natural order made sense, two years later, in 1865, *Alice's Adventures in Wonderland* offers a world where disorder reigns supreme, and Alice's attempts to create meaning out of this chaos prove futile. Whereas Kingsley saw the potential for social injustice to "evolve out" of society, Charles Dodgson/Lewis Carroll presents a different response to evolution, one in which housework does not create order or virtue and where the possibility of working-class mobility (the franchise for working-class men would occur with the Second Reform Act, 1867) generates deep unease. Donald Rackin points out that through disorder/chaos Carroll mocks "wishful progressive evolutionism" (94).[7] Ruth Jenkins, also commenting on the theme of disorder, sets Carroll's work in a context of broad cultural change and notes that "[e]fforts to stabilize Victorian identity took many forms" (67), and argues that Carroll ultimately "undermines any stability" (79). Rackin and Jenkins point to the darker elements that the consistent disorder of Wonderland creates, and Nina Auerbach suggests that Alice, the dreamer, represents this disorder in the most intimate of ways: "the dainty child carries the threatening kingdom of Wonderland within her" (32).[8] In the midst of the instability of Wonderland, Carroll presents three scenes depicting housework: the first in which the Rabbit mistakes Alice for a maid, the second in which Alice witnesses a bizarre and violent exchange between a duchess and her cook, and the third in which Alice joins a tea party which is punitive for the participants. Through Alice's expectations and behavior in each of these incidents, the text reveals slippage between appearance and reality and raises questions about the middle-class subject and ethical behavior. Initially, for instance, Alice's ramblings through Wonderland may appear innocuous, but placed against Victorian understandings of gender and the *flâneur*, her ambling produces several transgressive elements. Susie Steinbach notes that "[n]ot everyone could take on the role of *flâneur*: the leisure to spend the day walking and observing, the courage to begin conversations with strangers [. . .] and the ability to enter into unfamiliar neighborhoods with impunity, were all reserved for the middle- to upper-class gentleman" (16). Whereas Wonderland does not resemble the city, the typical domain of the *flâneur*, it does represent public space, and Steinbach argues that "[t]he *flâneuse* was, in many ways, an impossibility because women did not enjoy men's freedom to enjoy public space" (17). Steinbach does observe that over time women did gain "urban freedoms" to shop or to observe the living conditions of the poor (neither of which Alice does), but the fact that Alice is a child masks some of her *flâneuse* qualities. Certainly Alice, like the *flâneur*, has leisure time: she enters homes and gardens brashly and freely converses with strangers. Her observations of domestic work as a *flâneuse*, however, do not edify either the reader or herself, and consequently, become a conduit for Carroll's censure.

In his depictions of housework, Carroll presents its functions: A maid helps make her employer's life easier, a cook provides wholesome food that nourishes an employer's family, a mother/nurse nurtures a child, and an outdoor tea party (which requires a domestic staff to make it possible) facilitates pleasant fellowship. Through the disorder of Wonderland, the ethical qualities of these functions become apparent. Before the Rabbit mistakes her for a maid, Alice good-naturedly tries to help him; when the Rabbit orders her about angrily, Alice becomes frightened. Rackin astutely argues that this fear lies in the "anxious vision of an entire middle-class world turned upside down; two topsy-turvy, 'backwards' places where the sensible child of the master class acts as servant, and the crazy servants act as masters" (8). Although Kingsley alludes to the degeneration of the race in his reference to the Doasyoulikes, he does not particularly tie it to class in *The Water-Babies*; however, the Victorian middle class did connect fears of degeneration with the working class, and Carroll reflects some of this unease. When Alice has one of her sudden changes in size inside the Rabbit's house (the proper domestic space for a middle-class woman), her assumed working-class identity has gained monstrous agency; Alice, no longer afraid of the "master," physically threatens the Rabbit. This class anxiety of degeneration resurfaces in the scene where Alice witnesses the cook's disrespect of rank and her sudden violence toward the Duchess and her baby (once again in the domestic space of the home). Alice's middle-class expectations of cooks and mothers are of nurture, but both Alice and the baby are unwelcome and in danger.

In this instance, Alice steps into the role of a nurse, and while her behavior appears ethical, the text reveals Alice's own double standards in attaching more value to the baby's looks than its character.[9] The ethical disconnect between appearance and worth, consequently, has its links to the world outside of Wonderland. Auerbach's observation of Alice's intimacy with Wonderland is important; Alice's insincerity undermines her middle-class propriety more severely because the ethical problem is intrinsic to Alice and not caused by location. Public space does not contaminate Alice; her desire to appropriate the *flâneuse* comes from within her. Alice's final encounter with housework occurs at the mad tea party. The reasonable expectations of housework providing pleasure, food, drink, and a clean place to sit are thwarted, and Alice learns that the Hatter, guilty of murdering time, now faces the punishment of being stuck in time. The Hatter's comment—"It's always tea-time, and we've no time to wash the things between whiles" (Carroll 74)—reveals a tedium of meals and housework, of the basics of living. If cleanliness is next to godliness, the participants of the tea party will never attain virtue. Alice's behavior once again demonstrates the ethical predicament that her character consistently faces. Although she leaves the table in disgust, Carroll portrays her looking back, "half hoping that they would call after her" (77), even though the tea party does not offer the most basic of emotional or intellectual companionship. When the guise of housework is stripped away, the relationships between Alice, the Hatter, and the Hare (all members of the middle class) also prove hollow: Alice settles for the lowest quality of friendship and personal interaction—all that is available to humanity.

By the juxtaposition of contemporary expectations of housework with the disorder of Wonderland and the innate double standards of "civilized" life, housekeeping becomes a thin Victorian veneer which barely covers up the class anger displayed by the working class and the disorder, tedium, and purposelessness of daily living experienced by all classes. Significantly, the semblance of order does not amount to anything morally. Despite being written so closely together and the similarity of visible housework, *The Water-Babies* and *Alice's Adventures in Wonderland* not only reflect the spectrum of responses Darwin provoked, but the texts also capture the transition from Victorian confidence to Victorian anxiety and despair. *The Water-Babies* demonstrates confidence in individual agency; Tom can master the world if he makes the right ethical choices. Wonderland, on the other hand, strips Alice of agency; Alice has no control of her body, let alone immediate or future action. Wonderland also reveals the upcoming generation for all classes at stake, with mothers and nurses unwilling and unable to take care of the young, and the young themselves degenerating into pigs. Whereas *The Water-Babies* portrays a wondrous world spread before Tom, Wonderland only offers the tedium of the tea party. Even if the working class (with its ostensible angry agency) were to rise, the text seems to suggest that they too, at some point, would face the dreariness of the tea party where Carroll strips the veneer of domestic service to the fullest. Carroll's representations of housekeeping and domestic laborers demonstrate the shift from Victorian confidence to despair at the loss of societal stability.

THE TALE OF TWO BAD MICE (1906) AND THE TALE OF MRS. TITTLEMOUSE (1910)

While issues of sanitation and the treatment of domestic workers are key to housework, an aesthetic value also plays a part. In *The Water-Babies*, the beauty of Harthover is a part of its moral purity, and Kingsley celebrates the beauty of the sea anemones (the cleaners of the sea), representing their importance to the natural/social order. Carroll depicts the smoke-filled kitchen of the Duchess and the messy table at the mad tea party to express the thin layer of outward show that hides disorder. In a manner similar to Kingsley, Potter explores what the aesthetic quality of a home, the cleanliness that goes beyond hygiene, has to reveal about the morals of its owners. Whereas Potter does depict intruders invading these abodes, these invasions do not exhibit the extreme disorder of Wonderland. Potter, however, does not reflect Kingsley's Victorian optimism either, but offers an Edwardian perspective of the ethical connections between housework and moral formation.[10]

In Potter's animal fantasies, human characters typically interact with animals directly; in *Two Bad Mice*, however, Hunca Munca and Tom Thumb interact with the humans of the house through the intermediary of a doll house. When the humans and two dolls, Lucinda and Jane (the cook), are away from the doll house, the mice enter the house, damaging some items and stealing others. This invasion has mixed results: The mice benefit from what they have taken, yet pay for the damage they have created both monetarily (Tom Thumb) and with housework (Hunca Munca).[11] In separate readings, Suzanne Rahn and Daphne Kutzer provide two contexts for the narrative, one political (recent riots over unemployment), the other biographical (Potter's parents viewed her fiancé as working class).[12] Kutzer insightfully points out that the middle-class girl who owns the doll house is "being encouraged through childhood play to look forward to running an adult household of her own with cooks and servants" (67).[13] What the little girl learns about housework through her play is revealing. Potter's illustrations and text portray the doll house having an abundance of objects that in a real home would create intense labor. Decorative items would need dusting and polishing, the variety of food would require time in the kitchen and scullery, and Jane would have to change clothes to appear clean after all this labor. Tellingly, the girl sees none of this time or labor because all the objects *only represent a real home*. Domestic work seems easy and becomes invisible for girls privileged by class; the expectation of a certain aesthetic level for the home combined with the ease of achieving it and the seeming happiness of Jane (with her painted smile) create a false reality for the girl. Consequently, the female mouse Hunca Munca's voluntary punishment proves confusing. As Kutzer rightly points out, Hunca Munca will have very little work to do (76), so what purpose does this housekeeping serve? Although Hunca Munca cannot physically manipulate the dolls in the manner the little girl can, the female mouse does play with the house in a similar fashion to the girl. The girl can play at dusting and cleaning; likewise, Hunca Munca can appropriate the house in her own pretense of housekeeping. This appropriation is indeed a part of the class unrest that Rahn and Kutzer see in the text, but it also shows a change in the type of community that Potter depicts. Potter's creatures come into direct contact with each other by choice, accident, or trespass. The little girl and the mice, however, can avoid each other even though they all "play" with the doll house; the oddly communal house offers the means for separating the spheres of their existence to individual use. [14] If the way homes are maintained reveals ethical values, two aspects of the text stand out: middle-class desire values a pleasing exterior obtained through the work of others, and the home begins to display the individualism of its occupants. A pleasing appearance at the expense of others is not unique to the Edwardian period, but this growing individualism that the text associates with domesticity marks a shift from the societal significance housework took in Kingsley and Carroll. [15]

This idea of individualism and control of the home becomes pronounced in Potter's *Mrs. Tittlemouse*. Like the doll house, Mrs. Tittlemouse's home faces invasion, but by denizens of the hedge. Potter emphasizes Mrs. Tittlemouse's particular animosity toward "dirty little feet" (12, 20) and depicts the mouse constantly cleaning. Mrs. Tittlemouse turns away creatures because of the dirt they will bring into her house, and when she discovers bees in a storeroom, she knows she will need help but decides not to ask Mr. Jackson (a toad) because "he never wipes his feet" (27). When the toad does turn up, the mouse follows him around to wipe up his mess (31, 36). During the toad's encounter with the bees, the mouse almost has a breakdown at the disorder and locks herself into the cellar. After the departure of the unwelcome guests, Potter describes the cleaning that ensues which lasts a "fortnight": "[Mrs. Tittlemouse] swept, and scrubbed, and dusted; and she rubbed up the furniture with beeswax, and polished her little tin spoons" (52). [16] The final scenes reveal Mrs. Tittlemouse throwing a party for five other mice and handing honey-dew through the window to Mr. Jackson (who can no longer enter the house because the mouse narrowed the entrance).

In *Mrs. Tittlemouse*, the immense amount of control the mouse desires over her house and her selection of company based on the cleanliness of the guests receives no moral censure, unlike characters in other tales whom the narrator labels bad (Peter Rabbit, Hunca Munca, and Tom Thumb) or careless (Jemima Puddle-Duck).[17] Potter's immense popularity during her lifetime with both adults and children and a transatlantic and wide European audience emphasizes the problematic nature of this exclusive community and the moral questions it poses. Mrs. Tittlemouse's standards of cleanliness do not have any link to moral choices or moral formation as seen in Kingsley. Instead of housekeeping offering an inclusive social order as seen in *The Water-Babies*, or a grim predicament faced by all of humanity as seen in Wonderland, *Mrs. Tittlemouse* privileges personal taste over all else, and the exclusive, "clean" community of mice that results remains unproblematic in the text. Kingsley's optimism and Carroll's despair may present opposing viewpoints in the possibilities of domestic labor, but they share an understanding of housekeeping being a societal issue. While housekeeping still requires thought and reflection, and clearly raises ethical questions, in *Two Bad Mice* and *Mrs. Tittlemouse*, issues of housekeeping have moved to the realm of the individual.

THE WIND IN THE WILLOWS

Potter and Grahame, to a certain extent, share similar ideas. Both authors offer depictions of housekeeping that reveal increasing individualism, and the ethical *questions* they raise through domestic labor still focus on issues of aesthetic standards, levels of comfort, class, and gender, but the scale of these questions has been reduced from the societal to the individual. The class insurrections that occur in Potter and Grahame are easily put down, and the stability of middle-class order is never seriously at risk in these narratives. Grahame, however, displays a different type of instability through his depictions of housekeeping; his nostalgia for a home lost indicates the instability of the Edwardian home.

A primary tension in *The Wind in the Willows* occurs between the call of open spaces and the maintenance of a home. The story begins with the Mole vigorously cleaning his house until he has "an aching back and weary arms" (Grahame 1) and then abandoning his home (and cleaning) for the freedom of open spaces. Likewise, the narrative ends with a different adventurer, the Toad, returning to his home to reclaim it and *clean* it. The text consistently connects the cleanliness of a home to the pleasure it can provide for its owner, and this pleasure typically takes the form of meals shared by friends. The moral value of clean homes has the positive value of hospitality; stray creatures can be taken in and comforted (such as the young hedgehogs in Badger's home), and the community can become close-knit (like the caroling mice being entertained at Mole's home). Yet the call of open spaces remains, and one of the reasons why this call is so persistent is because of the *type* of housekeeping this hospitality requires. At Toad Hall, the Badger, for instance, asks the Mole to see to the cleaning: "See that they sweep *under* the beds, and put clean sheets and pillowcases on, and turn down one corner of the bedclothes, just as you know it ought to be done; and have a can of hot water, and clean towels, and fresh cakes of soap, put in each room" (194). The comforts of home require work and responsibility, and when this work becomes stifling, characters like the Mole and Toad flee.

Ironically, although at some point all four of the main characters—Mole, Rat, Badger, and Toad—do some of the housekeeping that they find so burdensome, these characters would not have the amount of leisure time they do without some form of domestic help. In this context, Lois Kuznets states, "although the invisible hands of the servant class are never alluded to, even Mole, who seems to live under the most humble circumstances, can leave his spring-cleaning and return to find his house ship-shape" (106). The text reveals how this domestic workforce is valued and treated through the character of the Mole. Mole's particular role in housework appears repeatedly: Mole spring cleans; at Badger's home the Otter asks Mole to cook (59–60); Rat provides the leadership in cleaning Mole's home (73–81); Mole takes care of household matters in Rat's house (146); and Mole has the bedrooms cleaned at Toad Hall (194–95). Initially, Mole does much of the work directly, while at Badger's house Mole delegates young hedgehogs to cook, and at the end of the narrative Badger gives Mole a workforce to supervise.[18] During the late Victorian and Edwardian periods, in middle-class residences, women performed the types of housework Mole does (cleaning, cooking, making beds) either with a female servant or supervising female servants who did these tasks. Whether or not readers take the position of seeing the animals as genderless or as a tight-knit male community, Mole's subservient role represents the feminine, domestic sphere.[19] This subservience becomes complicated when Mole takes leadership in the battle to take back Toad Hall; Badger, the patriarch of the narrative, commends Mole's intelligence and resourcefulness and rewards him with more responsibility and servants. Housework, while being the means of offering hospitality, is, nevertheless, of lesser value, and those who perform housework also take on lesser value even if some (like the Mole) have upward mobility. Mole's "servants" display this best; they are upstart ferrets who invaded Toad Hall and now receive their punishment by doing housework.

The narrative's valuing of the end result of housework—convivial hospitality—but not the work itself has its parallel structure in the tension between desiring the pleasures of home (fellowship) and the call of the open spaces (*leaving* the responsibilities of housework). Kuznets remarks that "*The Wind in the Willows* is a book full of longing" (128), and Seth Lerer convincingly demonstrates that the "aesthetics of domestic life" (53) in the book place the

Badger's and Mole's homes firmly in the late Victorian period. These two homes are linked with the most intense forms of hospitality in the narrative. Badger's home offers warm, joyous refuge from the terrors of the Wild Wood, and Mole's home is the site for a cheery Dickensian Christmastide dinner. This nostalgia for an earlier period indicates a lack within the present, and the text's consistent delineation of the "anchorage" (Grahame 82) of these homes suggests that what is longed for in the past and lacking in the present is stability. This dichotomy between the moral devaluing of housework and nostalgia for the ideal, stable home again marks a shift in thinking about housework. Although Carroll questions the stability and purpose of the home, the instability of the home was a part of society's general disorder (seen across the spectrum of Darwinism, working-class agitation for improved conditions, and the beginnings of imperial anxiety as other world powers contested colonial space) and not particular to it. Kingsley portrays the stability of Harthover, and Potter, Grahame's close contemporary, depicts homes as stable in the midst of intruders, homes so stable that characters need to, at times, escape. With Grahame, however, the modern instability of the home enters, and housework proves to be a strange irritant. Housework is the key to an aesthetic and pleasurable ideal, but its burden makes those who accomplish it of lesser value.

Although Arlie Hochschild's *The Second Shift* would make its appearance eighty years later, both Potter's Hunca Munca and Grahame's Mole resemble, at times, the working woman who finishes a job outside the home and then returns to her house to do unpaid domestic labor. Hunca Munca works at the doll's house and then cares for her family; Mole fights a battle and then supervises the cleaning of Toad Hall. Ironically neither Hunca Munca nor Mole receive pay for work done outside their homes (apart from the pleasure they receive), and this double shift proves unproblematic in these works. Unpaid labor would not remain in this unquestioned position; J. K. Rowling, for instance, takes a very different stance on this issue.

THE *HARRY POTTER* SERIES

Although J. K. Rowling's final book in the *Harry Potter* series comes almost a hundred years after *The Wind in the Willows* (*Harry Potter and the Deathly Hallows*, 2007), the ethical concerns Rowling raises over housework are very similar to Kingsley's. The series repeatedly points out that the ill-treatment of the magical domestic workforce can only adversely affect the moral formation of individuals and society as a whole. The narrative across the books also makes housework a societal issue despite various characters (good and bad) arguing that the treatment of the elves is the individual owner's concern and part of the private/personal domain. Unlike Kingsley, Rowling does not depict an easy solution to the predicament of house-elves or even an end to the subjugation of the elves at the close of the series. The complexity of the situation comes across in Hermione's involvement with the elves. In her initial outrage over the labor of the house-elves at Hogwarts, Hermione stops eating her dinner in order to not benefit from what she terms later as "slave labor" (Rowling, *Goblet of Fire* 191). This boycott lasts until the next morning, and when Hermione eats breakfast, her friend Ron understands the reason behind the short-lived venture; he points out, "You were hungry" (194). This telling comment reveals the conundrum Hermione faces: Hermione cannot exist on her own at Hogwarts without using the services of the elves. Rowling has Hermione use the unjust system, the services of the elves, while she fights to remove the injustice of it. [20]

Hermione's problem connects to both second-wave feminist discourse on viewing domestic work as unpaid labor and/or the second shift for working women, and current feminist discourse on the service class (particularly migrant women) who provide domestic service/child care for middle-class women. Jenny Turner speaks of the need for feminism to address multiple contexts (such as race, class, colonialism globalization) and points out the inconsistencies that can arise when women ignore these contexts. Turner notes: "Betty Friedan made the epoch-defining suggestion that middle-class American women should dump the housework on 'full-time help.' There are so many examples of this sort that it would be funny if it weren't such a waste" (11–15). In some ways, Hermione might appear to take Friedan's stance because Hermione does not wish to do the type of work that the elves do—she wishes to *pay* them. Rowling's subtle inclusion of Hermione's goals of paying the elves, eliminating the abuse, and raising their social standing, however, places economic value on domestic work (even if it remains undesirable) and shifts moral value from the labor itself to the *laborer*. Rowling's personal life while she wrote the first book, a young single mother on welfare in Britain in the 1990s after a decade of Thatcherism, resonates with the position of the elves: Rowling's labor in the eyes of the state had yet to have economic value.

This depreciation of house-elves raises ethical questions about the individual and society. At several instances in the series, the text associates the indifference/cruelty of a wizard/witch to an elf being detrimental to the moral formation of the wizard/witch. Rowling does not polarize this issue by depicting only dark wizards mistreating elves; wizards like Sirius who demonstrate courage and tolerance can still treat elves poorly. This unethical behavior seen in the individual has its ramifications on society at large because the relationship between wizards and elves is one of domination and subjugation, and domination lies at the heart of the villain Voldemort's evil behavior, detrimental to the entire wizarding community. The domination of the house-elves echoes the theme of the main story and complicates it: In his arrogance

Voldemort overlooks an elf, Kreacher, who holds information crucial to Voldemort's defeat.

Yet despite the defeat of evil, the position of house-elves seems to remain unchanged at the end of the series. Jackie Horne points out that "in the very last line of penultimate chapter [*sic*], Harry wonders 'whether Kreacher might bring him a sandwich'" (97), suggesting that the status quo still remains. Many critics see ambivalence in Rowling's portrayal of the societal abuse of the house-elves, particularly in the unfortunate acronym for Hermione's organization—S.P.E.W—which seems to poke fun at the entire endeavor.[21] Brycchan Carey, however, argues that Rowling offers a positive range of models for political action (from Harry's personal action to Hermione's public organization). By juxtaposing Rowling with Kingsley a useful insight can be gained. Both Kingsley and Rowling focus on individuals to model change: Kingsley has Tom morally evolve, while Rowling depicts significant moral changes in Harry and Ron's attitudes toward house-elves. For instance, Harry initially holds Kreacher responsible for Sirius's death, but then begins to develop a more mature understanding of Sirius's moral flaws in treating the elf. Harry changes his attitude and behavior toward Kreacher and demonstrates genuine concern for him. When Harry is unexpectedly on the run, he feels regret that Kreacher does not know of this change in plans and later worries that Kreacher may be tortured (Rowling, *Deathly Hallows* 271, 278). Likewise, at a dangerous moment in the battle for Hogwarts, Ron feels genuine concern for the safety of the elves and does not wish to use them to fight (625). Harry does call on Kreacher at the end of the series, but his attitude has changed significantly.

Whereas *The Water-Babies* does not answer the question of what should be done with chimneys and sweeps until a solution can be implemented, the *Harry Potter* series acknowledges the limits of action—that in the midst of finding the answer for a societal problem, aspects of the problem will not go away. Even more nuanced is the understanding that other aspects of the problem will emerge. The series offers a realist aesthetic of the ethical concerns created by domestic labor, which presents an interesting complement to Kingsley's confident optimism. The series may demonstrate the realities of ongoing problems while trying to effect a solution, but the books display the optimism that evil/unethical practices can be defeated, that solutions can be found. Rowling, certainly, does not reflect Carroll's despair. Rowling also demonstrates a shift from Potter and Grahame's portrayals of growing individualism; instead, the individual's moral formation and the ethical/unethical practices of society are deeply integrated. In the midst of the instability that Rowling structures into her magical world (parents and peers are murdered, governments collapse), the story does not search for a home lost; it battles for the home that exists, both by defeating evil wizards and re-forming domestic labor.

Ultimately, this new attention to housework seen in Kingsley, Carroll, Potter, Grahame, and Rowling reflects the changing values of these different periods particularly in terms of aesthetic standards, gender, and class. This repeated attention to housework at a formative stage in children's literature reveals that housework not only becomes a *thinkable* concept in children's literature, but also offers a means to explore profound ethical questions of how one should live. Kingsley and Carroll begin this new discourse on domestic work by making it exceedingly visible, but for very different purposes. Tom's visibility foregrounds societal abuse and offers successful, rejuvenating change, whereas the unappealing dirty homes of Wonderland point to the degeneration of the species. Potter and Grahame, on the other hand, offer a complicated balance between visible and invisible housework which reflects a growing individualism. Potter's texts depict visible and invisible housework offering pleasure and control of the home to the individual female subject. The visibility of housework in Grahame invariably indicates discontent; when characters can pass on domestic chores to others (thus making it invisible for themselves and devaluing the worker), they regain their idyllic contentment. Rowling offers an interesting close to this discourse, reflecting Kingsley and Carroll's societal concerns of housework and moral formation and moving away from Potter and Grahame's emphasis on the individual. While Rowling does not see intrinsic worth in housework, she emphasizes the value of the worker by making house-elves visible and integral to the plot (and by engaging contemporary feminist discourse). Displaying optimism similar to Kingsley's, Rowling offers a solution to the ethical problems of domestic work, but understands the limits to action. British children's fantasy literature's marked attention to housework and moral worth reflects the changing place domestic labor holds in culture, at times problematic, at times uneasy, but always of interest.

NOTES

1. Mrs. Beeton, the paragon of Victorian household management, emphasizes cleanliness as well; she states, "Cleanliness is also indispensable to health, and must be studied both in regard to the person and the house, and all that it contains" (8).

2. Davidson notes the paradoxical nature of British women in the late 1800s continuing to do their laundry despite their well-expressed antipathy toward this domestic chore and the options available for having someone else do the washing. Davidson suggests that "women wanted to create that moral worth with their own hands, or if this was not feasible, at least in their own homes" (163). Judith Flanders observes that "housekeeping was a source of strength for women, through which they could somehow mystically influence their husbands" (16).

3. Jessica Straley, Ruth Y. Jenkins, Jonathan Padley, and Christopher Hamlin offer separate readings that see the diverse aspects of *The Water-Babies* presenting a unified argument. Straley argues that Kingsley uses an evolutionary model of recapitulation and Christianizes it. Jenkins sees Tom representing the "abject" and consequently a disruptive force against dominant cultural values, and Padley understands the various subtexts as consistently presenting Tom as marginalized. Hamlin, examining Kingsley's oeuvre, observes Kingsley taking a strong

environmental position throughout his work. These readings demonstrate the complexity of Kingsley's discourse on these various issues.

4. His characters, the "Doasyoulikes," for instance, regress evolutionarily because of their physical and moral indolence.

5. Thomas Jordan states that for chimney sweeps, "abrasions, falls, and burns were their lot, and occasionally death" (36), and Ginger Frost notes that "master sweeps were often brutal" (68).

6. Comparing Tom to a "black ape" definitely has racial implications, but it should also be noted that Jordan documents that sweeps sometimes "went unwashed for years" (37).

7. Jan Gordon also sees a Darwinian influence on the text and places the story's questioning of identity and origins with other Victorian fiction written after Darwin, particularly fiction depicting children.

8. Christine Roth suggests that Alice functions as a median between adulthood and childhood and views childhood as part of the postcolonial paradigm of native/other (26–30).

9. Terry Otten perceptively notes that Alice's "compassion coexists with her 'civilized' nature" (53), that Carroll juxtaposes a moral element (to prevent the baby's demise) with civility, the reluctance to take on the responsibilities of the baby.

10. Katherine Chandler also notes that in Potter a shift toward the modern appears. Chandler observes that Potter's books "quietly challenge Victorian mores and literary styles" and are "harbingers of modernism" (287).

11. Carole Scott argues that clothing in Potter's work represents the relationship between the individual and society, and sees Hunca Munca's cleaning service as a direct result of her stealing the dolls' clothing (197).

12. Ruth McDonald observes that Potter's parents saw Potter's fiancé (and publisher) Norman Warne as inferior because of his profession (16).

13. Kutzer then moves on to a reading which excels in bringing out the "sterility" (76) of the dolls' lives in contrast to the mice's liveliness.

14. The play, however, maintains gender roles and the invisibility of housework; Tom Thumb does not do housework but offers money to the dolls—a "crooked sixpence" that he finds under a carpet (Potter, *Two Bad Mice* 56), and Hunca Munca cleans the doll house before the dolls and their owner stir.

15. Potter's well-documented interest in maintaining the quality and appearance of her books ties in with the aesthetic values represented by the dolls' house. The size and appearance of her books made them toy-like, and Potter also tapped into the market with toys and other items based on her characters.

16. *Mrs. Beeton's Book of Household Management* (while not directed toward mice) offers guidelines and formulas for polishes and cleaning agents.

17. Kutzer reads *Mrs. Tittlemouse* in the context of Potter's new experience of home ownership and the constant interruptions she faced from visitors (121–23), but there are similarities between Mrs. Tittlemouse's home and the doll house. Mrs. Tittlemouse's house in the hedge has the familiar rooms of a middle-class home: a kitchen, parlor, pantry, larder, and multiple storerooms and cellars (Potter 8–11). Likewise, the high level of cleanliness that the mouse presents *as necessary* also reveals a desired aesthetic level; Mrs. Tittlemouse's house resembles the doll house in the aesthetic level desired by the occupants and the sterility that ensues. In both tales, Potter portrays the formation of a middle-class female subject who desires an aesthetic level of the home that necessitates labor-intensive housework. Since Mrs. Tittlemouse does the labor herself, her standards for company become exclusive.

18. Peter Hunt suggests one way of understanding Grahame's work is to see it as the "Mole's bildungsroman" in which Mole experiences "multiple development from outsider to insider, of child to adult, of lower class to middle class" (116). Although Hunt does not factor Mole's housekeeping in this assessment, Mole clearly "develops" in this aspect as well.

19. Bonnie Gaarden and Cynthia Marshall provide different ways to understand the issue of gender in *The Wind in the Willows*. Gaarden sees the four main characters as genderless and taking on male and female roles in the family; consequently, male and female figures can take on either a masculine or a feminine role. Marshall, on the other hand, argues that the animals are male and that the book offers a misogynistic viewpoint.

20. Tom Morris makes an interesting point when he argues that Hermione (who knows that house-elves can be freed when given clothes by wizards and witches) is ethically wrong when she deliberately leaves items of clothing lying around for the house-elves to accidentally pick up and inadvertently set themselves free (143–45). Morris argues that however much the house-elves deserve freedom they should also desire it and be willing participants in achieving it.

21. Horne, in her reading of the series, notes that Rowling presents two strategies of anti-racism—social justice antiracism, which attempts to battle institutional oppression (Hermione's founding of a society), and multicultural antiracism, which tries to root out racism by the appreciation of diversity. Although Horne sees potential drawbacks in both approaches, she privileges the social justice approach over the appreciation of diversity and sees the failure of the latter approach contributing to Harry "maintaining the wizard/elf hierarchy" at the end of the final book (97). Rivka Temima Kellner equates house-elves with women and argues that Rowling displays an ambivalent stance toward feminism. Suman Gupta, on the other hand, does not equate house-elves with women but finds it problematic that rational creatures can accept servitude without resentment; consequently, Gupta finds the presentation of house-elves in the narrative as flawed.

WORKS CITED

Auerbach, Nina. "Alice and Wonderland: A Curious Child." *Lewis Carroll*. Ed. Harold Bloom. New York: Chelsea House Publishers, 1987. 31–44. Print.

Beeton, Mrs. *Mrs. Beeton's Book of Household Management*. Ed. Nicola Humble. Oxford World Classics, Abridged Edition. Oxford: Oxford University Press, 2000. Print.

Carey, Brycchan. "Hermione and the House-Elves: The Literary and Historical Context of J. K. Rowling's Antislavery Camaign." *Reading Harry Potter: Critical Essays*. Ed. Giselle Liza Anatol. Westport, CT: Praeger, 2003. 103–15. Print.

Carroll, Lewis. *The Annotated Alice*. Martin Gardner (introduction and notes). New York: Norton, 2000. Print.

Chandler, Katherine R. "Thoroughly Post-Victorian, Pre-Modern Beatrix." *Children's Literature Association Quarterly* 32.4 (Winter 2007): 287–307. *Project Muse*. Web. 4 Jan. 2013.

Davidson, Caroline. *A Woman's Work Is Never Done: A History of Housework in the British Isles 1650–1950*. London: Chatto & Windus, 1982. Print.

Flanders, Judith. *Inside the Victorian Home: A Portrait of Domestic Life in Victorian England*. New York: Norton, 2003. Print.

Frost, Ginger. *Victorian Childhoods*. Victorian Life and Times Series. Westport, CT: Praeger, 2009. Print.

Gaarden, Bonnie. "The Inner Family of *The Wind in the Willows*." *Children's Literature* 22 (1994): 43–56. *Project Muse*. Web. 4 Jan. 2013.

Gordon, Jan B. "The Alice Books and the Metaphors of Victorian Childhood." *Aspects of Alice: Lewis Carroll's Dreamchild as Seen through the Critics' Looking-Glasses, 1865–1971*. Ed. Robert Phillips. New York: Vintage, 1971, 1977: 93–113. Print.

Grahame, Kenneth. *The Wind in the Willows*. New York: Henry Holt, 1980. Print.

Gupta, Suman. *Re-Reading Harry Potter*. New York: Palgrave Macmillan, 2003. Print.

Hamlin, Christopher. "Charles Kingsley: From Being Green to Green Being." *Victorian Studies* 54.2 (Winter 2012): 255–81. *Project Muse*. Web. 25 Nov. 2012.

Hochschild, Arlie. *The Second Shift: Working Families and the Revolution at Home*. Rev. ed. New York: Penguin, 2012. Print.

Horne, Jackie C. "Harry and the Other: Answering the Race Question in J. K. Rowling's *Harry Potter*." *The Lion and the Unicorn* 34.1 (Jan. 2010): 76–104. *Project Muse*. Web. 4 Jan. 2013.

Hunt, Peter. "Necessary Misreadings: Directions in Narrative Theory for Children's Literature." *Studies in the Literary Imagination* 18 (1985): 107–21. *Cengage Learning, Inc*. Web. 15 Oct. 2012.

Jackson, Rosemary. *Fantasy: The Literature of Subversion*. London: Methuen, 1981. Print.

Jenkins, Ruth Y. "Imagining the Abject in Kingsley, MacDonald, and Carroll: Disrupting Dominant Values and Cultural Identity in Children's Literature." *The Lion and the Unicorn* 35. 1 (Jan. 2011): 67–87. *Project Muse.* Web. 25 Nov. 2012.

Jones, Tod E. *The Broad Church: A Biography of a Movement.* Lanham, MD: Lexington Books, 2003. Print.

Jordan, Thomas E. *Victorian Childhood: Themes and Variations.* Albany: SUNY Press, 1987. Print.

Kellner, Rivka Temima. "J. K. Rowling's Ambivalence Towards Feminism: House Elves— Women in Disguise—in the *Harry Potter* Books." *The Midwest Quarterly* 51.4 (Summer 2010): 367–85. *EBSCO.* Web. 12 Oct. 2012.

Kingsley, Charles. *The Water-Babies: A Fairytale for a Land Baby.* Hertfordshire: Wordsworth Editions, 1994. Print.

Kutzer, M. Daphne. *Beatrix Potter: Writing in Code.* New York: Routledge, 2003. Print.

Kuznets, Lois R. *Kenneth Grahame.* Twayne's English Authors Series. Boston: Twayne, 1987. Print.

Lerer, Seth. "Style and the Mole: Domestic Aesthetics in *The Wind in the Willows.*" *The Journal of Aesthetic Education* 43.2 (Summer 2009): 51–63. *Project Muse.* Web. 12 Oct. 2012.

Manlove, Colin. "Charles Kingsley, H. G. Wells, and the Machine in Victorian Fiction." *Nineteenth Century Literature* 48.2 (1993): 212–39. *JSTOR.* Web. 8 June 2013.

Marshall, Cynthia. "Bodies and Pleasures in *The Wind in the Willows.*" *Children's Literature* 22 (1994): 58–68. *Project Muse.* Web. 4 Jan. 2013.

McDonald, Ruth. *Beatrix Potter.* Twayne's English Authors Series. Boston: Twayne, 1986. Print.

Morris, Tom. *If Harry Potter Ran General Electric: Leadership Wisdom from the World of the Wizards.* New York: Currency, Doubleday, 2006. Print.

Nikolajeva, Maria. "The Development of Children's Fantasy." *The Cambridge Companion to Fantasy Literature.* Ed. Edward James and Farah Mendlesohn. Cambridge: Cambridge University Press, 2012. Print.

Otten, Terry. "After Innocence: Alice in the Garden." *Lewis Carroll: A Celebration. Essays on the Occasion of the 150th Anniversary of the Birth of Charles Lutwidge Dodgson.* Ed. Edward Guiliano. New York: Clarkson N. Potter, 1982: 50–61. Print.

Padley, Jonathan. "Marginal(ized) Demarcator: (Mis)Reading *The Water-Babies,*" *Children's Literature Association Quarterly* 34.1 (Spring 2009): 51–64. *Project Muse.* Web. 25 Nov. 2012.

Phillips, George L. "The Abolition of Climbing Boys." *The American Journal of Economics and Sociology* 9.4 (July 1950): 445–62. *EBSCO.* Web. 4 Jan. 2013.

Potter, Beatrix. *The Tale of Mrs. Tittlemouse.* London: Penguin, 2002. Print.

———. *The Tale of Two Bad Mice.* London: Penguin, 2002. Print.

Rackin, Donald. *Alice's Adventures in Wonderland and Through the Looking-Glass: Nonsense, Sense, and Meaning.* New York: Twayne, 1991. Print.

Rahn, Suzanne. Tailpiece: The Tale of Two Bad Mice. *Children's Literature* 12 (1984): 78–91. *Project Muse.* 4 January 2013. Print.

Roth, Christine. "Looking through the Spyglass." *Alice beyond Wonderland: Essays for the Twenty-First Century.* Ed. Cristopher Hollingsworth. Iowa City: University of Iowa Press, 2009: 23–35. Print.

Rowling, J. K. *Harry Potter and the Deathly Hallows.* New York: Arthur Levine Books, 2007. Print.

———. *Harry Potter and the Goblet of Fire.* New York: Arthur Levine Books, 2000. Print.

Scott, Carole. "Between Me and the World: Clothes as Mediator between Self and Society in the Work of Beatrix Potter." *The Lion and the Unicorn* 16.2 (Dec. 1992): 192–98. *Project Muse.* Web. 4 Jan. 2013.

Shore, Heather. "Chimney Sweep—Cultural Icon." *The World of Child Labor: An Historical and Regional Survey.* Ed. Hugh D. Hindman. New York: M. E. Sharpe, 2009: 567–68. Print.

Steinbach, Susie. *Understanding the Victorians: Politics, Culture and Society in Nineteenth-Century Britain.* London, New York: Routledge, 2012. Print.

Straley, Jessica. "Of Beasts and Boys: Kingsley, Spenser, and the Theory of Recapitulation." *Victorian Studies* (Summer 2007): 583–609. *Project Muse.* Web. 25 Nov. 2012.

Turner, Jenny. "As Many Pairs of Shoes as She Likes." *London Review of Books* 33.24 (Dec. 2011): 11–15. Web. 24 April 2013.

Chapter Four

Appliance Reliance

Domestic Technologies and the Depersonalization of Housework in Postwar American Speculative Fiction

Andrea Krafft

During the postwar era, advances in domestic technologies dramatically altered the nature of housework for the majority of American women.[1] Although electrical home appliances existed prior to World War II, they became widespread when economic prosperity after the war led to increased home ownership.[2] As Karal Ann Marling notes in *As Seen on TV: The Visual Culture of Everyday Life in the 1950s* (1994), appliances became central features of postwar American homes, representing "a sense of freedom, of effortless ease, of technological mastery, modernity, and access to conveniences" (255). This celebratory image of the technologically enhanced home recurs throughout advertising imagery of this era, most notably in General Electric's "Live Better Electrically" campaign (which began in the mid-1950s). The jingle for this campaign touts this message:

> You can make your family's life much brighter.
> You will find your work much lighter.
> It's as easy as can be,
> When you live better electrically!

This peppy advertisement positions housewives as the primary beneficiaries of domestic technology, claiming that they will "have more time for fun and pleasure" because gadgets can take over tasks that formerly required extensive manual labor ("Live Better Electrically"). Furthermore, the dancing, apron-clad woman at the center of this advertisement (see figure 4.1), ensconced in a kitchen that contains a blender, oven, and electric mixer, reflects

69

a glamorized vision of technologically enhanced housework, in which, according to Betty Friedan, "the American housewife—freed by science and labor-saving appliances from the drudgery" of the home would find "true feminine fulfillment" (18).[3]

Despite this widespread image of appliance-enhanced ease, domestic burdens paradoxically increased after World War II as a result of the mechanization of the home. In *More Work for Mother: The Ironies of Household Technology from the Open Hearth to the Microwave* (1983), Ruth Schwartz Cowan observes that appliances not only created "new needs" but also "eliminated the chores that men and children used to do" (11, 201). Although the entire family prior to World War II shared some household chores (such as doing dishes), the mechanization of the home ultimately returned such tasks to the housewife's hands. While it seems that the rise of appliances would simplify housework, Friedan observes how domestic technologies "imposed new drudgery," raising standards of cleanliness so that a housewife, rather than doing laundry once a week, for example, would instead run "her washing machine and dryer every day" (241). Thus, the housewife, no longer aided in her work by other members of her family, often found herself con-

Figure 4.1.   This still image from General Electric's "Live Better Electrically" television campaign encapsulates the postwar image of appliance-enhanced housework. Source: "Retro Classic TV Commercial—1950s—Live Better Electrically (GE Theater)." Musicom Productions. YouTube, 27 Dec. 2008.

tinually operating appliances in a never-ending cycle of household maintenance.

Given that speculative fiction (SF) "concern[s] itself with problems of power" in "a technological age," it is not surprising that writers of fantasy and science fiction such as Shirley Jackson, Ray Bradbury, and Ira Levin confronted how postwar household technologies altered domestic relationships (Aldiss 14).[4] In fact, Lisa Yaszek argues in *Galactic Suburbia: Recovering Women's Science Fiction* (2008) that women writers in the postwar era "turned to SF to explore the relations of gender and technology after World War II" (8). I want to build on Yaszek's claim by demonstrating how multiple authors of speculative fiction, regardless of their gender identities, consistently interrogated the postwar image of effortless housework.[5] In this essay, I will examine how Shirley Jackson, Ray Bradbury, and Ira Levin demonstrate uneasiness about the filtering of housework through domestic technologies, marking how an influx of appliances threatens to displace and even replace the female subject.

"FAMILY MAGICIAN": THE FANTASY OF DOMESTIC WITCHCRAFT

As a frequent contributor to women's magazines who was reluctant to identify as a housewife, Shirley Jackson often focused on domestic issues ranging from representations of female anxiety in Gothic stories through more comical depictions of housework and child rearing.[6] Her short story "Family Magician," initially published in *Woman's Home Companion* in September 1949, reflects her ambivalent relationship to how postwar culture often elevated what Marsha Bryant identifies as the "magician status [of] the 1950s housewife" (184).[7] In this story, Jackson describes Mallie, a supernaturally gifted maid who becomes a domestic fairy godmother for two children (Jerry and Dottie) and their mother (Mrs. Livingston). While Mallie is not a housewife, her role as a servant echoes how the popular media of the postwar era often envisioned appliances as "electronic servants" that "operated via magical rather than mechanical principles," a pattern that Laura Scott Holliday describes in "Kitchen Technologies: Promises and Alibis: 1944–1966" (108, 112). Mallie likewise embodies idealized domestic technologies as she can "straighten a room just by standing in the doorway" (Jackson, "Family Magician" 217), automatically enabling Mrs. Livingston to live the popular fantasy of "the good life without sweat" (Halberstam 496). Although "Family Magician" at first appears to affirm a vision of easy and entertaining housework, Mallie's abilities often remind the reader about Mrs. Livingston's relative incompetence within the home. Jackson wavers between affirming a vision of magical housework and critiquing housework's dependence on (electronically) supernatural objects that can create an estranging experience for the human housewife.

On one hand, the magical maid helps to relieve stress within the home, as the narrator (Jerry) says, "Mother was working herself nearly crazy trying to make the house and everything go smoothly for us kids" (212). Because Mrs. Livingston, a widow, has to balance her roles as a household manager and the family's primary breadwinner, she does not have adequate time to complete her domestic labor. Mallie appears, seemingly out of fairyland, and according to Mrs. Livingston "just said she had come to help" and "took the mop away from me" (216). Similar to how appliances work in the "Live Better Electrically" campaign, the maid provides the mother with crucial leisure time, telling her to "go to a movie, maybe, or do some shopping" (213). Yet, Mallie is also a potentially terrifying invader, as Mrs. Livingston acknowledges that she "was scared for a minute" at the appearance of the supernatural stranger (216). The domestic helper is never a fully frightening figure in this story, yet this fleeting moment of strangeness marks how appliance culture does not occur without some degree of alienation for the housewife. Though such an ambiguous representation of technological housework may seem out of place in a domestic magazine such as *Woman's Home Companion*, Jackson speaks to a wider tendency within postwar publications to "see the domestic as a contested and negotiated concept rather than a proscribed and stable one" (Walker vii). Writing during a transitional moment when women were returning from factory jobs to domestic roles, Jackson scrutinized the increasing social emphasis on housework, vacillating between reinforcing and subverting the housewife role.

Much of "Family Magician" specifically reacts against a stereotype of the housewife as someone who no longer understands the processes behind domestic technologies, which appear to be mystifying and foreign to her. As Jenny Wosk observes in *Women and the Machine: Representations from the Spinning Wheel to the Electronic Age* (2001), postwar ads tended to turn away from imagining the woman as an engineer or a worker with mechanical knowledge in favor of representations of the housewife "as blissfully unconcerned with mechanical details" in a kitchen where the push of a button could produce fully cooked food, as in "Live Better Electrically" (230). Mrs. Livingston in Jackson's story is no exception to this pattern of the mystified female consumer, as she does not understand how her magical helper completes her housework. For example, she cannot explain how the maid transforms a ladybug, dandelions, a box of starch, and curtains into an elaborate party dress for her daughter, Dottie. She is similarly baffled when Mallie creates "broiled squab with cherry sauce" and wild rice from a hat trimmed with fake birds and handfuls of gravel (219). The only explanation that Mallie ever provides is that she has "magic," which, the narrator observes, is "the only answer she'd give, no matter what we asked her" (217). Excluded from learning Mallie's domestic magic, Mrs. Livingston seems akin to the smiling women of postwar advertisements who remove perfectly pressed clothing and delicious meals from appliances without understanding "the physical principles by which machines and tools operate" (Benston 34). Yet, the fact that Mrs. Livingston is often troubled when she tries to fathom the method behind Mallie's supernatural achievements indicates her tension with a turn toward an "industrialization of the home [. . .] over which the house-holders can be said to have no control at all, or certainly very little control" (Cowan 14). Anxiously relinquishing her home to an embodied appliance, she reflects the discomfort of women for whom domestic technologies marked a loss of agency and a turn away from the independent "New Women" of the late 1930s toward the passivity of "Operation: Housewife" (Friedan 38, 41). [8]

Though supernatural housework mystifies and often frustrates Mrs. Livingston, Shirley Jackson indicates how some women enthusiastically embraced the possibility of domestic magic, eagerly jumping into the housewife role. Specifically, Dottie (Mrs. Livingston's daughter) becomes a sorceress's apprentice, asking Mallie to "teach *me* some of that magic" (217). Though Dottie neither produces meals from inedible objects nor arranges rooms with a glance, she does become an expert pie baker and transforms into someone "sweet-tempered and polite," gaining the knowledge of how to behave as a future housewife (217). Mallie repeatedly gives Dottie cooking lessons and simultaneously enhances her personal appearance, telling her "that's all the magic *you'll* ever need" (218). [9] While the young male narrator of the story (Jerry) depicts Dottie's increased skill and gracefulness as a positive metamorphosis, his sister's domestic achievements occur alongside her increased passivity. Dottie becomes a marginal figure in the narrative as she begins to transform into an embodied appliance whose main task is to practice a highly constrained form of domestic magic. Although "Family Magician" seems to affirm how personal appliances ensured happier, more satisfied families, it is important to remember that Jackson filters this narrative through the voice of the male child, whose celebratory tone reflects the desire of a postwar patriarchal culture to reclaim the public sphere as a male domain.

Indeed, Jerry is all too pleased with how Mallie, beyond helping his mother and sister complete housework, bolsters heteronormative romance for both Mrs. Livingston and Dottie, effectively returning both women to positions within the home. For example, following her domestic training, Dottie becomes wildly successful at securing boyfriends, indicating that she will have no problems eventually starting her own nuclear family. More importantly, Mrs. Livingston, freed from her duties at home, finds a new husband by the end of the story, enabling her to exit the workforce and once again focus on her domestic role. It seems that the women in the story reflect the media stereotype of postwar American femininity in which a housewife

"kept her house spotless and efficient, got dinner ready on time, and remained attractive and optimistic" (Halberstam 590). Even Mallie reflects
these values, as she can make herself appear younger and is always amiable
in her housework, as "she never stopped smiling" (213). She leaves the
Livingstons with a constant reminder of their idealized domestic roles, sending them a magic mirror that reflects a dream image of its viewers. In providing the household with this enchanted object, she ensures that they will
always strive to imitate a "glossy image of the perfect family in its well-kept
house" (Ogden ix). Yet, the "funny old-fashioned" style of Mallie's mirror
suggests that the transformation of the family at the end of the story is a step
back into archaic values rather than a progressive turn for domestic relations
(222).

Although Jackson ends "Family Magician" on an optimistic note of domestic union, she repeatedly critiques how the postwar vision of the appliance-enhanced American family retreats into the stuff of fantasy. Her presentation of Mallie as a domestic witch warps housework into something other-
worldly, a "conflation of the domestic with the uncanny" that she also explores in her later novels (Murphy 13). As Lynn Spigel observes in her
discussion of television shows such as *I Dream of Jeannie* and *Bewitched*,
such blending of fantasy with domesticity destabilizes "the conventionality
of the everyday" (123). Jackson, while apparently supporting the message of
postwar domesticity, suggests that only a supernaturally empowered individual could handle the overwhelming nature of housework, thereby critiquing
the notion of technologically enhanced ease. Furthermore, it is notable that
when the embodied appliance takes over the task of housework, the mother
becomes virtually invisible, just as Dottie becomes voiceless when she at-
tains the role of embodied appliance. Mallie, while freeing Mrs. Livingston
from domestic labor, also highlights that the housewife might eventually
become obsolete (or at least replaceable in some way). "Family Magician"
thus presages darker speculative fictions in which the embodied appliance
becomes the emotional center of the nuclear family.

"I SING THE BODY ELECTRIC!" EMBODYING
THE PERSONAL APPLIANCE

While Shirley Jackson warns against the potentially disempowering effects
of an idealized vision of magical housework, Ray Bradbury, in "I Sing the
Body Electric!" (1969), considers the implications of another supernatural
appliance fantasy—the robot.[10] The figure of the robotic grandmother, whom
the narrator describes as a "dear and wondrous electric dream," fantastically
embodies the ultimate personal appliance (115). In her role as a cook and a
housekeeper, she demonstrates "the penetration of [. . .] technology into the

surfaces of the kitchen," resembling similar robot-maids of postwar popular culture, such as Rosie from *The Jetsons* (Holliday 115). Yet, the robot in this story is more than an appliance, as she becomes both a love object and a caretaker for Timothy, Tom, and Agatha, three children who have recently lost their mother. In the way that she provides an emotional center for this broken family, the electric grandmother exemplifies what Roland Marchand, in *Advertising the American Dream* (1985), calls "re-personalization." Marchand argues that mid-twentieth-century advertisers offered "personalities for consumption," positioning products as solutions for consumers who "craved a sense of personal contact" (357, 353). Advertisements frequently envisioned consumer goods as being agentive or willful, and the robot of Bradbury's story is the culmination of this vision, as she works to please her "grandchildren" and to fill the place of the lost parent.

Bradbury ties the electric grandmother directly to advertising language, as the children in the story read a pamphlet from "Fantoccini Ltd." about "the first humanoid-genre mini-circuited, rechargeable AC-DC Mark V Electrical Grandmother" ("Body Electric" 117). This advertisement, with the authority of its technological jargon, presents the robotic grandmother as "the answer to all your most grievous problems," an appliance that "is built with loving precision to give the incredible precision of love to your children" (117). Although Bradbury parodies the features of advertising language, he emphasizes that the appliance fills an emotional need on the part of the consumer. The children even recognize that they are the targets for this advertisement, but they still admire the product for its promises of "Love" and "Care" (118). As Marchand argues, the consumer's consciousness of repersonalization does not necessarily lessen its effects, as "most experiments in personalizing products brought a favorable public response, no matter how transparent the pretense of intimacy" (358). The children know from the beginning of this story that the grandmother is "a Toy" who only seems to be human, but this knowledge neither makes her any less appealing as a love object nor reduces the need for an appliance that can supplement their incomplete family (117).

Though the electric grandmother is in many ways a mundane appliance, Bradbury highlights the fantastical elements that make her more appealing to the consumer, mirroring how "fifties ads transformed domestic space into a dreamscape of daily miracles" (Bryant 180). The grandmother's selling point is that she is a "Miraculous Companion," anticipating consumer needs through her association with the supernatural (Bradbury, "Body Electric" 118). From the moment of her arrival, the grandmother appears as if out of a dream. Tom, the narrator, compares the helicopter that delivers her to "Apollo driving his chariot across mythological skies" (123). While she appears as a goddess of modern convenience, the grandmother also seems to be timeless and immortal, suggesting that she is a literally indispensable product. Specifically, she arrives, packaged like a mummy, in a sarcophagus of "real gold" with "real hieroglyphs [. . .] just like in the museums" (124). This repetition of the word "real" suggests that the appliance has some kind of authentic personality or core, which makes her virtually (or even better than) human.

Moreover, the fact that the word "mummy" recalls the image of the "mommy" is difficult to ignore, especially considering that this female-coded robot steps into the family to replace the absent mother. While the children certainly mourn their mother's death, the way in which they describe her makes her seem like another lost domestic convenience rather than an individual. Tom describes his mother as "the soft, the warm, the main piece of lovely furniture" that "was gone forever" (116). It seems that, in the appliance-centered home, the mother might be just another interchangeable and replaceable domestic product. While the Fantoccini Company insists that "nothing can replace the parent in the home," the story suggests otherwise, as the children's love for the robot quickly overshadows their memory of their mother (118). As Wayne L. Johnson argues, "I Sing the Body Electric!" sometimes reads as "a commercial for robots as human substitutes" (78). Other ads from this time similarly oppose domestic technologies with the mother, such as a Magnavox television advertisement. This ad, published in *Life* in 1951, touts a television that "like mother, makes the whole family happy" (Magnavox). While the ad insists on a domestic hierarchy in which technology is subordinate to family members, the television, with its offer of "the breathtaking intimacy of a personal appearance," becomes a very real threat to the mother's domestic dominion (Magnavox).

The electric grandmother's power to replace the mother derives from her hyperfemininity and her hyperbolic homemaking skills. Ordinary women, given their material constraints, simply cannot compete with appliances that are positioned as "hard-working mechanical brides" (Wosk 229). Beauty is integral to the grandmother, who, even before she is fully built at the Fantoccini factory, speaks the word "Nefertiti," which is "Egyptian for the Beautiful One Is Here" ("Body Electric" 121).[11] When the children receive their electric grandmother in her sarcophagus, they find that this "true mummy" wears a golden mask that is simultaneously young and wise (124). She may be a grandmother, but it seems that she is ageless, like the media image of femininity that the August 1969 issue of *McCall's* presents to its readers. Countless ads in this issue (in which Bradbury published his story) rely on the myth of permanent youth, such as a Dacron polyester campaign whose tagline is "forever young" and a Sears advertisement that celebrates "the new agelessness." Because the grandmother is an appliance, she can reproduce this beauty myth effortlessly, becoming a kind of perfect woman to unify a family that lacks a female caretaker.

Furthermore, the electric grandmother successfully surpasses the mother not only because she is a beautiful thing but also because she is a domestic wizard whose skills, like those of Mallie in "The Family Magician," again extend beyond those of a real person. The grandmother performs numerous magical feats, such as manifesting a kite string from her fingertips and producing fresh baked fortune cookies from her chassis. Most notably, she is able to cook meals that are "always something new, yet, wisely [. . .] seemed old and familiar" ("Body Electric" 134). Her meals are not only delicious, but also elicit emotional responses from the family, especially from the (nameless) father. He weeps after the grandmother produces a meal identical to one that he had "in a small French restaurant over near Les Deux Magots in Paris, twenty, oh, twenty-five years ago" (135). Her ability to transform memories into domestic actions suggests that she is psychically connected to the family, making her the ultimate "empathy machine" (Eller and Touponce 22). Although she acknowledges that she will never be a real woman, the grandmother is far more than a mere appliance. Agatha voices this best when she tells the electric grandmother that she has "always been alive" in the eyes of her "grandchildren" ("Body Electric" 143).

While the electric grandmother repeatedly insists that she is, at best, an honorary person, she often transcends the abilities of the ordinary appliance and blurs the line between the machine and human, an ambiguity that Bradbury embraces. The robot repeatedly describes herself as an empty vessel that "can neither touch nor taste nor feel on any level" (138). She clearly remains functional as an appliance, as she identifies herself as a living photo album whose purpose is to reflect "us back to ourselves just a trifle better than we had dared to hope or dream" (138). Just as Mallie leaves the Livingston family with a mirror that reflects their ideal selves, the electric grandmother is a distorting and selective mirror that comprises the ideal consumer product. Here, the appliance becomes the new affective center of the family, speaking to Bradbury's desire to imagine machines that "embody humanity" (Bradbury, "On Hitchcock" 71). Although the father refuses to see any emotional agency at the heart of the electric grandmother, telling her, "Good God, woman, you, you're not *in* there," he does identify the appliance as a woman, hinting at her ability to step into the role of the lost housewife (138).

As an explicitly *feminized* embodiment of the personal appliance, this "wondrous toy" (135) reveals how the discourse of domestic devotion in appliance culture threatens to mechanize housewives. The electric grandmother, with her continuous emphasis on self-sacrificing love, recalls how postwar America elevated motherhood as "the primary source of a woman's identity" (May 135). The method with which the Fantoccini Company assembles the grandmother further connects her with a model of housewifery in which fulfillment can only come through a series of sacrifices on behalf of the family. When designing the robot's voice, for example, Mr. Fantoccini asks the three children to speak, and he runs their voices through a machine that produces "three oscillograph patterns" ("Body Electric" 121). This process suggests that the robot lacks a voice of her own, as she becomes an amalgamation of the children's voices and echoes their needs on a daily basis. In addition to being essentially voiceless, the robot grandmother is faceless, as Tom (the narrator and oldest son) notices that her appearance shifts to mirror others, changing slightly depending on whom she is near. Bradbury never fully describes the grandmother's body either, suggesting that she is only significant when she is in the presence of a human family member. Her appeal does not stem from an original personality: she is only "human shaped," not fully human (125). Though Eller and Touponce argue that Bradbury elevates this mode of sacrifice, the robotic grandmother brings to mind Betty Friedan's description of American housewives who "have forfeited their own being" on the altar of ideal womanhood (311).

Although the electric grandmother will always retain her identity as an appliance, it seems that she is not completely different from the human caretaker on whom she is modeled. She is morally pure, taps into a mystical femininity, and, most importantly, is eternally available to her children. In fact, she surpasses the children's biological mother by virtue of her electronic immortality, which allows her to simultaneously sacrifice herself for the child yet also continue to provide maternal love. This occurs when she flings herself in front of an oncoming car to shield Agatha, yet emerges unscathed with the promise that "I shall always, always be here" (141). The appliance-centered family becomes a domestic fairy tale, as Tom notes that he, Timothy, Agatha, their father, and Grandma "lived happily ever after" (142). Like "Family Magician," "I Sing the Body Electric!" concludes in a way that sentimentally elevates the familial unit.

While scholars such as M. Keith Booker dismiss "I Sing the Body Electric!" on the grounds of its "rather puerile sentimentalism" (171), such readings ignore how the electric grandmother effectively replaces the human mother and speaks to growing anxieties about technological domination within the home. As in "Family Magician," the woman who unifies the family through effortless housework and sacrificial love often evacuates herself of any essential identity and agency. The robotic grandmother, always happily performing according to her programming, is the technological counterpart of the desperate housewife who anxiously tells Friedan, "I begin to feel that I have no personality" (Friedan 21). Moreover, the grandmother, as an idealized model of technological womanhood, represents how the demands of the feminine mystique encouraged postwar women to become embodied appliances, "to live according to an image that makes them deny their minds" (66). The fact that Bradbury published "I Sing the Body Electric!" only three years prior to Ira Levin's *The Stepford Wives* marks the beginning of a resistance to the positive fantasy of domestic technoculture, as both Bradbury and Levin depict appliances as ominous replacements of the housewife, rather than bastions of ease.

THE STEPFORD WIVES: ELECTRIFYING THE HOUSEWIFE

While Bradbury's "I Sing the Body Electric!" often echoes elements of the domestic fairy tale, Ira Levin's *The Stepford Wives* (1972) infamously transforms Joanna Eberhart and the other female inhabitants of a suburban Connecticut neighborhood into the victims of a science-fictional nightmare.[12] Writing nearly ten years after the publication of Betty Friedan's *The Feminine Mystique* (1963), Levin captures the emergent tensions between the postwar women who scrutinized housework and those men who resisted the rise of second-wave feminism. In fact, he quotes a passage from *The Second Sex* (1949) as an epigraph for his novel, citing Simone de Beauvoir's warning about men who resist women's attempt to "escape" from their domestic prisons into "the light of transcendence" (qtd. in Levin 401). Levin envisions a dark world of masculinist control that, as Anna Krugovoy Silver has astutely observed, involves the literal transformation of "women from individuals with goals and ambitions into cleaning appliances" (66). Friedan warns about this kind of depersonalization when she writes that housework and the cult of motherhood lead to "a stunting or evasion of growth" for American women (77). She draws on the language of science fiction when, speaking of the inescapability of the feminine mystique, she notes that magazine editors are "Frankensteins" who "no longer have the power to stop the feminine monster they have created" (66). Even positive representations of housework from the postwar era point to the monstrous and robotic nature of the housewife. For example, *Management in the Home: Happier Living Through Saving Time and Energy* (1954), a domestic science manual, describes the female body as a "machine" (Gilbreth, Thomas, and Clymer 103). Responding to this widespread image of the mechanized domestic worker, Ira Levin envisions how the female body becomes an extension of the home via the machinations of a patriarchal technoculture.

The robotic nature of the Stepford women is immediately apparent to Joanna Eberhart after she moves to the community from New York City with her husband, Walter. Joanna, as both "a semi-professional photographer" and an active participant "in the Women's Liberation movement," stands apart from the Stepford women, as she enters the narrative from a position of agency and relative freedom from housework (Levin 406).[13] To this disciple of Betty Friedan, the passive Stepford women appear to be metaphorical robots due to their extreme, mindless commitment to housework (though she does not suspect until later that the women are literal automatons). In a parodic poem describing the Stepford women, she writes, "They never stop, these Stepford wives [. . .] They work like robots all their lives" (444). Specifically, they mechanically obey idealized media depictions of femininity in which women appear "fluffy and feminine [. . .] gaily content in a world of bedroom and kitchen, sex, babies, and home" (Friedan 36). Much like June Cleaver and Harriet Nelson, the Stepford women embody "homogenized, romanticized views of contented Moms who never knew as much as Dad" (De Hart 126). In fact, Joanna, producing a counter-discourse to the tropes of popular culture, explicitly confronts the language of ladies' magazines and commercial advertising when she compares the Stepford wives to "actresses in commercials" (Levin 430). Something about the women in her community strikes her as "too nicey-nice to be real," as they primarily talk about which cleaning supplies are the most effective and live in perfectly organized homes (430). Joanna's principal anxiety is a fear of conformity, of becoming "a compulsive hausfrau" in a world that defines women through housework (410).

Though Joanna critiques Kit Sundersen and the other Stepford women for what she perceives to be their radically backwards way of life, their domestic efficiency reveals her own anxieties surrounding housework and her role within the home, suggesting that the feminine mystique retains a degree of power over the liberated woman. On one hand, Joanna wants to maintain a sense of gender equality, as she splits housework with her husband and boycotts cleaning when Walter joins the Stepford Men's Association. On the other hand, she acknowledges that there is always "plenty [of work] to do" at home "and some that she actually *wanted* to do" (412). Living among picture-perfect women makes Joanna hyperconscious of her own limitations, such as when seeing the organized grocery carts of her fellow shoppers, she feels "a guilty impulse to put [hers] in order" (418). Similarly, she compares her difficult housework to the Stepford wives' apparent ease, imagining that they "would sail through it all very calmly and efficiently," easily manipulating bulky appliances (455). Joanna's anxious guilt about her domestic disorderliness highlights how the choice between the Stepford model and second-wave feminist values is not clear-cut, as choosing to embrace "a messy kitchen" effectively leads to alienation from the community at large (415). Though Joanna does befriend Bobbie Markowe, another member of the National Organization for Women, the assimilation of her closest friend to the Stepford way of life cynically suggests that conformity to the feminine mystique will outweigh feminist resistance. Levin underscores how the Stepford image presents women with an impossible choice: they can either assimilate and lose their sense of agency or, live with the constant knowledge of their deviance from domestic norms. While this binaristic view obscures the diversity of female experience, in the world of *The Stepford Wives*, the Stepford Men's Association effectively establishes a discourse in which women can be either passive angels or dangerous outsiders.

Levin emphasizes that Joanna becomes mentally unstable when confronted with this uncomfortable choice, and he even refuses to clarify whether Stepford is actually a haven for robotic wives or if this is just a housewife's paranoid delusion. The movie famously removes this psychological ambiguity by presenting us with the image of Joanna's robotic double, "a perfect replication [. . .] save for dark voids instead of eyes" (Johnston and Sears 89). In the film, no hope exists for Joanna's escape from the Stepford model of womanhood, as the director Bryan Forbes transforms Levin's novel into a horror story on the level of *Invasion of the Body Snatchers* (1956). Yet, the robotic other never directly appears in Levin's novel, although Joanna's friends do change overnight from sexual and domestic rebels into obedient, attractive caretakers. It is unclear how much of the novel is a product of Joanna's potential breakdown, as even Dr. Fancher, her psychologist, acknowledges that "any move is traumatic to a degree [. . .] particularly the city-to-the-suburbs move for a woman who doesn't find her housewife's role totally fulfilling" (Levin 464). In moments like this, Joanna fits Betty Friedan's characterization of American homemakers as "virtual schizophrenics" who are unable to deal with a constant sense of domestic dissatisfaction (67). Whether or not the robots exist, Levin demonstrates how the demands of housework and domesticity are "achieved at enormous cost to the wife," leading to mental illness and a need for tranquilizers (Coontz 36). Even though she is not yet a Stepford wife, Joanna suffers from the psychological impact of this model of womanhood, suggesting that she lacks the agency to break out of the demands of housework and domesticity.

In addition to the psychological ambiguity that shapes Levin's narrative, technology and science undoubtedly haunt the Stepford community and affect the lives of its residents (at least in an economic sense). Joanna, driving outside of Stepford with her friend Bobbie Markowe, notices a group of "neat low modern buildings" that include businesses such as "Ulitz Optics," "CompuTech," "Haig-Darling Computers," and "Instatron" (Levin 440). Joanna and Bobbie initially blame these businesses for the strange conditions in Stepford, speculating that the women are becoming tranquilized through toxic chemical runoff that turns the town into "Zombieville" (439). Yet, in *The Stepford Wives*, technology is not something that runs amok but is always under the control of human agents. Specifically, the men of Stepford all work in varying fields of technological development, most notably, Dale Coba (also known as Diz), who "worked in 'audioanimatronics' at Disneyland" before joining "Burnham-Massey-Microtech" (468). Within the novel, gender determines one's relation to technology, affirming Kirkup and Keller's claim that "men kept technology, at both the craft and the professional level, to themselves" (3).

If the Stepford wives are indeed robots, then their design specifications meet the gendered expectations of male creators who seek to maintain a system that depersonalizes women, transforming them into submissive domestic servants. Most of the wives repeat variations of the same script, as they assure Joanna that they are "living a very full life," and that their former independence was "lazy and selfish" (431, 436). They not only attest to extreme levels of domestic obedience but also embody the beauty myth, as all of the Stepford women appear to be youthful, well dressed, and well endowed with secondary sexual characteristics. Furthermore, Levin emphasizes how the popular media determines the lives of these women, as Ike Mazzard, a former women's magazine illustrator, works with Dale Coba in designing the robotic replacement wives (163). In this system, "every girl's an Ike Mazzard girl," transforming into a "hyper-real version" of herself for the purposes of entertaining and satisfying her husband/owner (421; Johnston and Sears 89). Like postwar appliances covered in "gorp" (i.e., excessive chrome décor), the Stepford wives become ornamental extensions of the home, sapped of their ability to exist outside of housework.

In writing about a male conspiracy to replace and apparently kill women in favor of obedient and docile robots, Levin demonstrates the depersonalizing nature of housework during the postwar era. The fact that he never reveals whether the robots are real only heightens the alienating vision of the story, as the only other motivation for the Stepford wives to behave as they do is because domestic stability requires it of them (lest they lose their secure homes). Joanna Eberhart's transformation at the end of *The Stepford Wives* is of course the most radical case of this change, as she enters the novel as a radical feminist and leaves it as a devoted housewife who reflects the values of the feminine mystique. In Levin's universe, the only women who can perform housework are embodied appliances. This novel ultimately provides a dark view of how technology might not only displace women in the home but also destroy them completely. Joanna's question of "what happens to the real ones" haunts the text, as we never know whether the Stepford wives are human women or if their technological doppelgangers have replaced the biological originals (471).

"THE VELDT" AND "THERE WILL COME SOFT RAINS": (DE)PERSONAL(IZING) APPLIANCES

Ira Levin is not alone in imagining the technologies of housework as depersonalizing, as Ray Bradbury envisions homes in which appliances threaten to displace their inhabitants. In both "The Veldt" (1950) and "There Will Come Soft Rains" (1950), Bradbury responds to how the postwar American home had become "the fundamental unit of technoculture," critiquing how automated appliances invade housework and damage family relations (Yaszek 9). While scholars such as Wayne Johnson and Edward J. Gallagher read these stories in relation to Bradbury's technophobic anxieties, such interpretations fail to address that he specifically comments on domestic technologies. Unlike the robotic grandmother of "I Sing the Body Electric," who is capable of sentiment and empathy, the technologies in these stories completely oppose human values and only lead to apocalyptic disaster. This runs counter to the image of the "home of tomorrow" whose "'mechanical servants' [. . .] promised to liberate housewives from chores while also orchestrating daily activities" (Spigel 383). Unlike such popular fantasies as General Electric's Carousel of Progress, Bradbury's techno-homes are sites of anxiety and mortality, in which fantastically electrified or technologically alive objects displace human beings and highlight the housewife's anxiety about the increasing prevalence of appliances. He grates against the notion that domestic technology provides security, instead describing how it literally depersonalizes the home.

In "The Veldt," an extreme overreliance on appliances renders the housewife and caretaker obsolete, as two children murder their parents in order to continue living in a fully automated "Happylife Home" (13). Just as the husbands in *The Stepford Wives* choose appliances over authentic romantic companionship, Wendy and Peter Hadley abandon their parents for a house "which clothed and fed and rocked them to sleep and played and sang and was good to them" (13). The intense irony of the story is that the automated home is meant to ensure the family's security and happiness, entertaining them and making it so that they "wouldn't have to do anything" (16). However, the promise of ease is insidious here because the house, especially the technological nursery that cares for the Hadley children, becomes "their mother and father, far more important in their lives than their real parents" (24). Though the personal appliance is benevolent in "I Sing the Body Electric!," it here displaces the real parents, as the children treat the home as a living thing rather than as a tool to shape their daily lives. Darkly reflecting Wendy and Peter of *Peter Pan*, the Hadley children are not so much "devotees of never-never land" as they are the apostles of a form of appliance culture that submerges them in a fantasy of imaginative independence from their parents (Diskin 152).

Long before Wendy and Peter murder their parents, Lydia Hadley recognizes her own domestic obsolescence, as she tells her husband (George), "I feel like I don't belong here" because "the house is wife and mother now, and nursemaid" (16). Bradbury suggests that technology leads not to the housewife's liberation, but rather to her increased anxiety about her loss of relevance in the face of increasing mechanization. Appliances do free Lydia Hadley from her housework, yet they also turn her into a useless spectator in her own home, as she "watched the stove busy humming to itself, making supper for four" (13). The issue at this moment is not that the Happylife Home has taken over domestic tasks so much as the fact that the Hadley children prefer the appliances to their own mother, as Bradbury suggests, "that machines cannot successfully replace human love and affection" (Mengeling 93). Unlike "I Sing the Body Electric!" in which the electric grandmother steps in to replace the dead mother, "The Veldt" illustrates the tense relationship between the living mother and the superior capabilities of the electric home. It is only fitting that the Hadley children transform the mechanism of the home into their murder weapon, turning to their new technological mother to replace the obsolete housewife.

Bradbury continues this pattern of technology replacing the homemaker in "There Will Come Soft Rains," which features a techno-home that carries on with housework in a post-apocalyptic landscape that is devoid of human residents. He discourages the reader from taking "pleasure in seeing inanimate things come alive," instead presenting the home as a grotesquely warped space (Marchand 358). The automated home constantly repeats its domestic routine, becoming increasingly absurd as the stove serves breakfast to an empty kitchen, only to clean the uneaten meal soon afterward (Bradbury, "Soft Rains" 322). Gadgets haunt the house but appear to be frightening rather than comforting, especially the "tiny robot mice" which scour the carpets "like mysterious invaders" and look out from the walls with "pink electric eyes" (323). Although the house enters the narrative as a fantasy space in which "the dinner dishes manipulated like magic tricks," it quickly devolves into something that appears to be "surreal" (326; Eller and Touponce 155).

Just as the house's domestic magic becomes a source of terror for the reader, the home appears to live in a state of anxiety, as the gadgetry continuously anticipates a human presence. For example, "the garage chimed and lifted its door," only closing "after a long wait" ("Soft Rains" 323). In this constant struggle between activity and the silence of its surrounding environment, the house becomes neurotic. Bradbury describes how the house has "an old-maidenly preoccupation with self-protection which bordered on a mechanical paranoia" (324). The window shades slap away birds and animals, as the home obsessively preserves itself for the return of its inhabitants. Although the increasingly unstable home positions itself as "an altar," the story reminds us that "the gods had gone away, and the ritual of the religion continued senselessly, uselessly" (324).

In describing people as the gods of domestic space, Bradbury emphasizes technology's subservient role to its creators, suggesting, as Gallagher aptly notes, that "it has no function without humanity" (80). Yet, the house's situation is strangely analogous to that of the postwar American housewife, whom popular magazines and experts such as Benjamin Spock encouraged to find fulfillment "in childbearing and in serving other people" (Miller and Nowak 151–52). In representing the home as hysterical and helpless, Bradbury symbolically feminizes this domestic space. The female home here is not a comforting vision of domestic wholeness but rather a barren and psychotic space, suggesting that appliance culture disempowers and destabilizes the housewife. As the home begins "announcing the time, playing music, cutting the lawn, or setting an umbrella frantically out and in" ("Soft Rains"

328) it resembles a woman on the verge of a breakdown. These activities only accelerate as the house begins to burn down, as "the stove could be seen making breakfast at a *psychopathic* rate, ten dozen eggs, six loaves of toast, twenty dozen bacon strips" (328; emphasis added). This excessively manic production recalls the kind of "kitchen craziness" that magazines publishing contemporaneously with Bradbury encouraged their readers to embrace (Bryant 182). For example, a Frigidaire Electric Range advertisement from a 1952 issue of *Life* illustrates an oven popping out cakes, golden-brown turkeys, and steaks, "a money-saving dream" in which "it all happens at once." Yet, in "There Will Come Soft Rains," this positive image of domestic plenty fails to stave off destruction, as the story culminates with the frantic failure of the appliances to preserve the home. That even a techno-home fails to meet the demands of housework demonstrates the shortcomings of a culture that encouraged high levels of appliance reliance.

CONCLUSION: CAN WE LIVE BETTER ELECTRICALLY?

Shirley Jackson, Ray Bradbury, and Ira Levin, in their speculative fictions about technologically enhanced housework, all critique the extent to which the postwar American reliance on appliances reshaped the nature of housework. Jackson and Bradbury's elevation of magically and electronically empowered caretakers suggests that ordinary women cannot fulfill the demands of housework unless they too have supernatural abilities or become living appliances. Ira Levin similarly explores how appliance culture and the feminine mystique mechanize housewives, marking a need to rethink the gendered implications of technoculture. Levin in particular sparked a critical reassessment of the housewife, as the term "Stepford wife" continues to circulate in popular parlance as a means of critiquing artificial, passive, or eerily obedient women. Although the 2004 Frank Oz remake of *The Stepford Wives* was a box office failure, the attempt to remake the classic 1975 film indicates that anxieties about domestic technologies and housework still have relevance. As Sidney Eve Matrix notes, Oz's campy adaptation of Forbes's film failed to entertain its audiences because "the discourses of the feminine mystique are not so outdated that they have lost their cultural currency" (117). Yet, Oz's film is about more than the feminine mystique, as it considers how technology and appliances disrupt domestic relationships, speaking to a continued cultural investment in how technology relates to gendered power dynamics. In brief, the critical voices of Jackson, Bradbury, and Levin only mark the beginning of a resistant strain in postwar American culture to the dominance of domesticity, as producers of contemporary speculative fiction continue to undercut the idealized image of appliance reliance.

NOTES

1. Some people did not experience mechanization until much later, as "a full 25 percent of Americans, forty to fifty million people, were poor in the mid-1950s" (Coontz 29). However, given that I am talking about mainstream and middle-class white writers, I will not be discussing matters of economic disparity at length here.

2. Miller and Nowak observe that "between 1950 and 1960 the number of U.S. homeowners increased by over nine million, reaching an incredible 32.8 million" (7).

3. David Halberstam similarly describes how "the pictures of" housewives "in magazines showed them as relentlessly happy, liberated from endless household tasks by wondrous new machines they had just bought" (588).

4. A note on terminology: I use the term "speculative fiction" rather than "science fiction" because Jackson, Bradbury, and Levin all blend their stories of technology with features of fantasy, horror, and detective fiction.

5. While I focus my analysis on Jackson, Bradbury, and Levin, other authors such as Judith Merril, Joanna Russ, and James Tiptree Jr. also critically re-examine domestic power in their speculative fiction.

6. For a classic example of Jackson's uneasiness with the "housewife" label, see her domestic memoir *Life Among the Savages* (1952). In an episode about the birth of her third child, she describes an argument with a hospital nurse over whether her occupation is "writer" or "housewife" (426).

7. For further discussion of the magical housewife figure, see Kristi Rowan Humphreys's chapter in this collection entitled "Supernatural Housework: Magic and Domesticity in 1960s Television."

8. In her study of twenty years of women's magazine, Betty Friedan argues that magazines depicted women in the late 1930s as "New Women, creating with a gay determined spirit a new identity for women—a life of their own" (38). However, she observes that, beginning in 1949, magazines started printing "innumerable paeans to 'Operation Housewife'" and preaching a return to the home.

9. Magic is solely a feminine realm in this story, as Mallie jokes that she "can't use magic on boys" because it "just wears away on their tough hides" (Jackson, "Family Magician" 220).

10. "I Sing the Body Electric!" existed as a teleplay in 1958 and Bradbury adapted it for *The Twilight Zone* in 1962 (Eller and Touponce 382–83).

11. When Bradbury published the story in *McCall's*, he titled it "The Beautiful One Is Here," again marking the centrality of beauty to the figure of the electric grandmother.

12. I want to emphasize that I will be discussing the popular novel rather than the 1975 Bryan Forbes or 2004 Frank Oz film adaptations.

13. Joanna even notes her division of housework with her husband, observing that "it was Walter's turn to do the dishes" (Levin 407).

WORKS CITED

Aldiss, Brian. *Trillion Year Spree: The History of Science Fiction*. New York: Atheneum, 1986. Print.

Benston, Margaret Lowe. "Women's Voices / Men's Voices: Technology as Language." *Inventing Women: Science, Technology and Gender*. Eds. Gill Kirkup and Laurie Smith Keller. Cambridge, MA: Polity Press, 1992. 33–41. Print.

Booker, M. Keith. *Monsters, Mushroom Clouds, and the Cold War: American Science Fiction and the Roots of Postmodernism, 1946–1964*. Westport, CT: Greenwood Press, 2001. Print.

Bradbury, Ray. "I Sing the Body Electric!" 1969. *I Sing the Body Electric, and Other Stories*. New York: Harper, 1976. 115–44. Print.

———. "Ray Bradbury: On Hitchcock and Other Magic of the Screen." 1972. *Conversations with Ray Bradbury*. Ed. Stephen L. Aggelis. Jackson: University Press of Mississippi, 2004. 54–79. Print.

———. "There Will Come Soft Rains." 1950. *The Vintage Bradbury*. New York: Vintage, 1990. 322–29. Print.

———. "The Veldt." 1950. *The Vintage Bradbury*. New York: Vintage, 1990. 13–28. Print.

Bryant, Marsha. "Plath, Domesticity, and the Art of Advertising." 2002. *Critical Insights: The Bell Jar by Sylvia Plath*. Ed. Janet McCann. Pasadena: Salem, 2012. 180–200. Print.

Coontz, Stephanie. *The Way We Never Were: American Families and the Nostalgia Trap*. New York: Basic, 1992. Print.

Cowan, Ruth Schwartz. *More Work for Mother: The Ironies of Household Technology from the Open Hearth to the Microwave*. New York: Basic, 1983. Print.

Dacron. Advertisement. *McCall's* Aug. 1969: 9, 11. Print.

De Hart, Jane Sherron. "Containment at Home: Gender, Sexuality, and National Identity in Cold War America." *Rethinking Cold War Culture*. Ed. Peter J. Kuznick and James Gilbert. Washington, DC: Smithsonian Institution Press, 2001. 124–55. Print.

Diskin, Lahna. "Bradbury on Children." *Ray Bradbury*. Eds. Martin Harry Greenberg and Joseph D. Olander. New York: Taplinger, 1980. 127–55. Print.

Eller, Jonathan R., and William F. Touponce. *Ray Bradbury: The Life of Fiction*. Kent, OH: Kent State University Press, 2004. Print.

Friedan, Betty. *The Feminine Mystique*. New York: Norton, 1963. Print.

Frigidaire Electric Ranges. Advertisement. *Life* 3 Nov. 1952: 74. *Google Books*. Web. 1 May 2013.

Gallagher, Edward J. "The Thematic Structure of *The Martian Chronicles*." *Ray Bradbury*. Eds. Martin Harry Greenberg and Joseph D. Olander. New York: Taplinger, 1980. 55–82. Print.

Gilbreth, Lillian M., Orpha Mae Thomas, and Eleanor Clymer. *Management in the Home: Happier Living through Saving Time and Energy*. New York: Dodd, Mead, 1954. Print.

Halberstam, David. *The Fifties*. New York: Villard Books, 1993. Print.

Holliday, Laura Scott. "Kitchen Technologies: Promises and Alibis: 1944–1966." *Camera Obscura* 16.2 (2001): 79–131. *Project Muse*. Web. 15 Oct. 2012.

Jackson, Shirley. "Family Magician." 1949. *Just an Ordinary Day*. Eds. Laurence Jackson Hyman and Sarah Hyman Stewart. New York: Bantam, 1996. 212–22. Print.

———. *Life Among the Savages*. 1952. *The Magic of Shirley Jackson*. Ed. Stanley Edgar Hyman. New York: Farrar, 1966. 383–530. Print.

Johnson, Wayne L. *Ray Bradbury*. New York: Frederick Ungar, 1980. Print.

Johnston, Jessica, and Cornelia Sears. "*The Stepford Wives* and the Technoscientific Imaginary." *Extrapolation* 52.1 (2001): 75–93. *General OneFile*. Web. 5 Dec. 2012.

Kirkup, Gill, and Laurie Smith Keller. "Introduction." *Inventing Women: Science, Technology and Gender*. Eds. Gill Kirkup and Laurie Smith Keller. Cambridge, MA: Polity Press, 1992. 1–4. Print.

Levin, Ira. *The Stepford Wives*. 1972. *Three by Ira Levin: Rosemary's Baby, This Perfect Day, The Stepford Wives*. New York: Random House, 1985. 401–85. Print.

"Live Better Electrically—1961.wmv." YouTube, 3 May 2012. Web. 31 July 2013.

Magnavox. Advertisement. *Life* 1951. Ad Access, 2007. Duke University Libraries. Web. 28 Apr. 2012.

Marchand, Roland. *Advertising the American Dream: Making Way for Modernity, 1920–1940*. Berkeley: University of California Press, 1985. Print.

Marling, Karal Ann. *As Seen on TV: The Visual Culture of Everyday Life in the 1950s*. Cambridge, MA: Harvard University Press, 1994. Print.

Matrix, Sidney Eve. "Behind the Idyllic Façade, a Terrible Secret: Technologies of Gender and Discourses of Domesticity in *The Stepford Wives*." *Storytelling* 6.2 (2007): 109–19. *ProQuest*. Web. 26 Nov. 2012.

May, Elaine Tyler. *Homeward Bound: American Families in the Cold War Era*. New York: Basic, 1988. Print.

Mengeling, Marvin E. "The Machineries of Joy and Despair: Bradbury's Attitudes toward Science and Technology." *Ray Bradbury*. Eds. Martin Harry Greenberg and Joseph D. Olander. New York: Taplinger, 1980. 83–109. Print.

Miller, Douglas T., and Marion Nowak. *The Fifties: The Way We Really Were*. Garden City, NY: Doubleday, 1977. Print.

Murphy, Bernice. "Introduction: 'Do You Know Who I Am?' Reconsidering Shirley Jackson." *Shirley Jackson: Essays on the Literary Legacy*. Ed. Bernice Murphy. Jefferson, NC: McFarland, 2005. 1–21. Print.

Ogden, Annegret S. *The Great American Housewife: From Helpmate to Wage Earner, 1776–1986*. Contributions in Women's Studies 61. Westport, CT: Greenwood Press, 1986. Print.

Sears. Advertisement. *McCall's* Aug. 1969: 29. Print.

Silver, Anna Krugovoy. "The Cyborg Mystique: *The Stepford Wives* and Second Wave Feminism." *Women's Studies Quarterly* 30.1–2 (2002): 60–76. *ProQuest*. Web. 8 Dec. 2012.

Spigel, Lynn. *Welcome to the Dreamhouse: Popular Media and Postwar Suburbs*. Durham, NC: Duke University Press, 2001. Print.

Walker, Nancy A. *Shaping Our Mothers' World: American Women's Magazines*. Jackson: University Press of Mississippi, 2000. Print.

Wosk, Jenny. *Women and the Machine: Representations from the Spinning Wheel to the Electronic Age*. Baltimore: Johns Hopkins University Press, 2001. *eBook Collection (EBSCOhost)*. Web. 8 Dec. 2012.

Yaszek, Lisa. *Galactic Suburbia: Recovering Women's Science Fiction*. Columbus: Ohio State University Press, 2008. Print.

Chapter Five

Making Easier the Lives of Our Housewives

Visions of Domestic Technology in the Kitchen Debate

Nicole Williams Barnes

In the summer of 1959, U.S. Vice President Richard Nixon visited the Soviet Union as part of a cultural exchange program aimed at improving relations between the two countries. During Nixon's visit, he and Soviet premier Nikita Khrushchev toured the American National Exhibition in Moscow together. The key draw of the Exhibition for the Russian public was the Model Home exhibit, which purported to show its Russian visitors how the typical American family lived. While touring this exhibit, the two leaders sparred over the relative merits of capitalism and communism through debating each country's technological strengths. Throughout this argument, now known as the Kitchen Debate because it purportedly took place in the kitchen of the exhibit,[1] Nixon focused on modern American technological advances on the home front, from vacuum cleaners and washing machines to dishwashers and color television.

Faced with Sputnik and Soviet intercontinental ballistic missiles, America at this moment trailed Soviet technological superiority. As the prototypical (and stereotypical) debate between men attempting to out-macho each other often goes, when one loses the size battle, he changes the parameters of the argument to quality. Nixon, who could not compete with Khrushchev when it came to the size of his arsenal, instead argued for American superiority in the Cold War based on the American way of life and the standard of living of its citizens. Khrushchev, arguing from the position of arrogance possible only when superiority in one arena is well established, graciously agreed to argue on Nixon's terms, confident the Soviet standard of living was adequate to win the debate. Thus leaders of the two embattled superpowers toured a model home exhibit and discussed the relative merits of dishwashers and vacuum cleaners.

As the first cultural exchange between the two embattled nations, the Kitchen Debate represents one of the few times that the cultural battleground of the Cold War materialized. The ideological struggle of the Cold War, which had focused on militaristic technological and economic battles, instead at this moment centered on housewives and their housework. Throughout the Kitchen Debate, Nixon pivoted the discussion from satellites to vacuum cleaners and dishwashers, from missiles to washing machines and color television. In doing so, Nixon shifted the front lines of the battle for technological superiority from the space race and the military to the home front, wherein domestic appliances become the metric of evaluation. An analysis of this visit not only defines attitudes toward housework in the Cold War era but also explores the ways housework came to represent the essence of the American way of life, placing the ideological battlefield of the Cold War within the American home. Housework, then, comes to represent the strength of a nation.

The Kitchen Debate's discussion of housework as the suburban housewife's primary responsibility is therefore informative of the ways housework and gender roles were valued and idealized in the Cold War era. Since Nixon's purpose in the debate was to define the American way of life for an international audience, it serves as an excellent representation by which to interpret both the ways women's work in the American home was understood during the Cold War and the cultural valuation of that work. An analysis of the Kitchen Debate, then, explores the ways in which the American Cold War woman's roles as wife and mother were defined by housework through an examination of dominant cultural gendered narratives of the 1950s.

A rhetorical study of this debate analyzes the ways Nixon defined his gendered American way of life to understand how housework continues to reaffirm the home as a woman's place. Nixon, faced with a Soviet opponent whose aerospace and military technology far outstripped America's own, utilized Cold War gendered narratives of housework to redefine the role of the technological realm as one of provision through consumerism. New domestic technology commodified housework by developing household appliances Nixon argued made "easier the life of our housewives" (Nixon 1), and thus created a femininized technological space within the home. These appliances created a new market for suburban women and thus were integral to the commodification of the expectations of their role as wives and their domestic labor. Structuring both the space of the home and the woman's relationship to it, these technological advances interpolated women into specific gender roles defined by technology both created by and provided by men. Rather than the feminine sphere providing a new metric by which to evaluate the strength of a nation, this analysis of the Kitchen Debate demonstrates that Nixon's argument instead serves to increase masculine control over the feminine space of the home.

GENDER, TECHNOLOGY, AND THE SUBURBS

The suburbs came to define success and the American Dream at this time, as well as the gender roles that accompany that dream. The development of a credit culture, rooted in the GI bill that lowered down payments necessary to obtain a mortgage, stabilized interest rates and extended other sources of credit to veterans, opened home ownership to millions of families previously unable to purchase their own home, increasing the percentage of homeowners and decreasing the number of rental properties in the suburbs (Kelly 73–74). The changes to mortgage laws also reaffirmed the expectations that families should start younger and maintain their own homes apart from extended family members (Coontz 26). The ease of home ownership lowered both the average age at marriage and the average age of parenthood; men felt prepared to support a family with less help from their parents at an earlier age (May 1–3). The suburbs provided the space for these new families to establish themselves as "nuclear families," so named for the newfound ability to split the atom, and individual family units became the norm for American culture. As more and more families aspired to this suburban lifestyle, the suburbs began to represent the American family, as well as the American way of life.

The expansion of the credit culture encouraged these middle-class suburban families to increase their perceived income status by purchasing status symbols, like houses and cars, and increasing personal debt (Jackson 216–18; 246–48). These visual markers of status culminated in the ultimate middle-class luxury of one-earner families: stay-at-home wives as a status symbol demonstrating their husband's success. Therefore, while most middle-class suburban women in the fifties had some form of job (see May 74–80), when asked, they defined themselves as wives and mothers and not by their occupation (Friedan 44). These middle-class, white, suburban women at the time thus understood their identity completely within the private sphere of the home. The suburbs became a gendered feminine space.

This suburban American way of life and its consumerism came to define American capitalism as the counterpart to Soviet communism and became a motivating factor in the fight against the Soviet Union. In order to understand how Nixon's stance in the Kitchen Debate focused attention on the gendered feminine sphere of technology while increasing masculine control over this space, we must next examine the technological battle in the masculine sphere of the military. Before the Soviets tested their first atomic weapon, the American public imagination was awash with the potential of atomic energy to improve their lifestyle in visions of atomic-fueled lawnmowers and cars (Boyer 109–14). The Soviet nuclear tests in August of 1949 instigated a fear of the bomb and the resulting technology, and suddenly this public imagination focused on mutually assured destruction and nuclear annihilation instead of atomic benefits. The "Sputnik Crisis," as the Soviet Union charged into the final frontier, brought new terrors to the American imagination as the threat of intercontinental ballistic missiles (ICBMs) and spy satellites combined. Senator Henry Jackson described the Sputnik launch as "a devastating blow to the prestige of the United States as the leader in the scientific and technical world" and claimed that Sputnik confirmed Soviet claims that they had launched an ICBM the previous August (as qtd. in Goldman 308). The Soviets thus possessed the technology to launch weapons of mass destruction against the United States as well as an eye in the sky to monitor their actions and response. The failure of the first two attempts at an American satellite cemented Soviet superiority in the space race (see Dickson 155–67). With the combined threat of Sputnik and ICBMs, the Soviet Union quickly overtook the United States at the front of both the arms and space races.

The American public, paralyzed by these fears, felt technological progress should focus on facing these threats and therefore derided domestic and consumer technology. The day after the announcement of the launch of Sputnik, news of a new hydrogen weapon reached Washington and began to spread through the nation; the American public then wondered why recent American technological developments included the Princess phone, 3-D movies, and dishwashers (Dickson 108). After Sputnik, the American public assumed Soviet technological superiority.

Nixon's position in the Kitchen Debate, then, was one of weakness. He faced a Soviet public winning both Soviet and American minds in the battle for technological superiority, and an American public at home derisive of American technological advances and behind in the Cold War. A focus on domestic technology would seem a feeble solution to this position of weakness. The historical importance of the Kitchen Debate as a watershed moment in the Cold War benefits heavily from hindsight; at this point, Khrushchev's arrogance at the strength of his arsenal provoked a desire to compete with the United States on an expanded technological battlefield,[2] and therefore historical discussions of the importance of consumer technology provide a history of the winners. Laura Holliday argues that technological exhibitions like the Kitchen Debate created a "hegemonic vision of the American Way of Life" (104) through uniting consumerism, technology, and nationalism in the fight against Soviet communism; she states that this exhibit was "hurled at the Soviet Union like a cold war missile" to demonstrate the United States' "superior use of technology toward ends that mattered to its citizenry, and thus [its] superiority over the Soviet Union" (105). Consumerism and commercialism become a civic duty of responsible citizenry and affirmed American capitalism as superior to Soviet communism.[3] This strategy could only work if Khrushchev agreed to debate on Nixon's terms.

Because household technology was derided as superfluous extravagance at the time of the Kitchen Debate, Nixon's primary job in the debate was to convince both Soviet and American audiences that this domestic technology was vital to national interests and security. A gendered and technological contextual lens demonstrates the usefulness of the Kitchen Debate in understanding American gender constructs of the postwar era and the ways consumer technology was used to fight communism. We can thus use the debate to analyze the ways these consumer technologies manipulated gender constructs to combat a changing American culture as well as functioned as ammunition on the ideological battlefield of the Cold War.

THE ROLE OF THE HUSBAND: PROTECTION TO PROVISION

Nixon's focus on domestic technology distracted from Soviet superiority on other fronts and eased the mind of the American audience by concentrating on the "good life" of the American people. This good life assumed a husband who worked to support his family while the wife maintained the house and raised the children. The gendered division of labor between the husband's employment in the public sphere and his wife's domestic responsibilities in the private sphere helps explain how Nixon's argument functioned to exert masculine control over the feminine private sphere.

Feminist theories of the public sphere focus on distinctions between the public and the private, strategically defined to place men in positions of power (Weintraub and Kumar 27–28). These theories examine how "private" includes traditionally feminine occupations to maintain the patriarchal structure of society. The creation of a public space of political deliberation distinct from a feminized private sphere consigns women to the home and prevents them from entering the public sphere of political influence (Arendt and Canovan 40–43). The distinction of this political sphere from the private sphere functions to demarcate the boundaries of the public in ways that are detrimental to subordinate social groups (Fraser 134–36). Distinguishing between the spheres thus serves to maintain masculine power in both realms, as men define the parameters of the spheres and qualifications for entry into the public sphere; the domestic sphere, then, prevents women from entering the public, political sphere of influence by defining social and cultural gender roles within this public/private distinction. This distinction is hierarchical, repressing and filtering those things considered private by creating what appears to be natural distinctions that are closely tied to ideas of gender, masculinity, and femininity as the "language of private feeling" (Warner 24). Traditional gender roles supported by the distinction between the public and private spheres locate power within the masculine realm and define men's position of power over the household as one of protection. The role of the husband as protector is tied to the submissive housewife raising children.[4] The Cold War home was perceived as a haven from the fear of Soviet superiority and therefore came to represent stability and security (May 19–21) and distracted from these militarized dangers. The age of anxiety created by the threat of mutually assured destruction led both genders to seek comfort within the stability of the home, encouraging women who had made strides in employment equality during the war effort to embrace a new life within the suburbs. Stephanie Coontz argues that during the 1950s both men and women rooted their identity in the family; men were breadwinners while women, even if they did work outside the home, were expected to exert the majority of their energy in the domestic front (27).[5] During the atomic age both genders were encouraged to define themselves within the family; stay-at-home mothers redefined motherhood as the protector of the children and opened the way for new interpretations of the responsibilities of the father (Griswold 194–97). Defining gender norms within the home capitalizes on the home as a safe haven to create a sense of security within these gender roles.

Nixon's shift from the masculine sphere of the political to the feminine sphere of the home, then, positions his arguments within the private feminine sphere and would seem to be a disadvantage in the debate against the dominant, masculine public, since political power resides in the masculine public realm. However, the Kitchen Debate reinforces this upheaval in assumed gender roles; as the mother assumes protective duties, the father must redefine his position in the family. Before the Kitchen Debate, the role of the military mirrors the role of the husband as the protector of the household. Thus, Nixon's first step must be to redefine power outside of this militaristic public sphere. As the new masculine role included being the breadwinner, the father's position shifted from one of protection to one of provision, earning money to provide for the needs of his wife and children. Nixon's focus on domestic technology within the Kitchen Debate linked the concept of consumerism to power by reinforcing the father figure as breadwinner and provider.

Nixon redefined the sphere of power and influence by expanding the competition of the Cold War to the domestic, evaluating the relative merits and strength of household technology and downplaying the importance of the arms and space races. Nixon justified a shift away from militarism: "[w]ith modern weapons it does not make any difference if war comes [. . .] My point was that in today's world it is immaterial which of the two great countries at any particular moment has the advantage. In war, these advantages are illusory" ("Khrushchev-Nixon Debate" 5, 6).[6] If military power was deceptive, then the Soviet Union was not in fact the superior superpower. While warfare will always define a country's strength on the battlefield, Nixon painting military strategy and advantage as illusory was the first move away from defining a nation's strength on the field of battle. Since the two superpowers were not at war on a physical battlefield, the strength of each participating nation could not be defined by that battlefield.

Nixon's shift from the military to the home is possible only if Khrushchev agrees on the importance of cultural exchange and competition. Khrushchev's government came to power with the promise of raising the standard of living, and his counterparts in the Soviet bloc even nicknamed his economics "refrigerator communism" or "consumer communism" (Reid 212). The shift to a focus on domestic technology, then, paralleled a shift in the Soviet Union. Khrushchev felt Russian developments in household technology were progressing rapidly and presumed Soviet technology would outstrip its American counterparts within seven years (Nixon 3). Khrushchev's role in the Kitchen Debate reinforces this shift to a domestic focus wherein American technology is superior to Soviet technology, allowing the American audience to change their attitude toward technological progress in appliances and establishing the United States as a cultural hegemon.

Twice in the debate, Khrushchev agreed that the Soviet Union wanted to compete against the United States in color televisions, washing machines, dishwashers, and other household technologies. When Khrushchev agreed that the Soviet Union wanted to compete on the appliances front, Nixon solidified the move from the military to the domestic. Nixon posited: "Would it not be better to compete in the relative merits of washing machines than in the strength of rockets?" ("Khrushchev-Nixon Debate" 5). The concept that it would be "better" to compete on the home front rather than the military front placed housework at the center of the Cold War battlefield. Once Nixon established that both nations should evaluate the merits of capitalism and communism through the lens of consumer products instead of military technology, the Kitchen Debate was able to demonstrate America's prominence as the preeminent superpower.

MEASURING A NATION'S STRENGTH

A *Christian Science Monitor* reporter who attended the American National Exhibition described the exhibit as a "heartwarming" breakthrough in cultural relations between the United States and Soviet Union (see Richmond 45). The Exhibition and Nixon's role in the Kitchen Debate defined American culture in the feminine sphere with this focus on domestic appliances. The technological focus of the Kitchen Debate was on housework and its newest technologies: a washing machine, a dishwasher, a color television, a vacuum cleaner. Nixon proudly pointed to each appliance as increasing the quality of life for women and therefore placing the strength of his nation on the shoulders of its housewives. Nixon's rhetoric in the Kitchen Debate was provisionary, and emphasized consumerism as the best way to provide for one's family. For Nixon, the Exhibition demonstrated the role of the husband as provider of the family's monetary and material needs. In redefining the man's position in the household, Nixon was able to change the prevailing derision of household appliances and shifted the measure of a superpower from militaristic to domestic.

Nixon's first move to define the man as provider was an emphasis on the status of the woman as "housewife." At the introduction to the kitchen of the model home, Nixon stated that "in America, we like to make life easier for our women" (Nixon 1). When Khrushchev protested Nixon's "capitalist attitude," Nixon refused to engage Khrushchev on this question and instead claimed his views as universal: "I think that this attitude toward women is universal. What we want to do is make easier the life of our housewives" (Nixon 1). The parallel structure of Nixon's sentences conflates "woman" and "housewife," implying the terms are interchangeable. Nixon structured "housewives" as the clarifying term and blurred the distinction between "women" and "housewives" to define the typical American woman as housewife. His claims to the universality of this gendered narrative defines the American way of life as suburban gender roles and the narrative of provision.

Khrushchev attempted to argue against this gendered narrative by labeling it a "capitalist attitude towards women" (Nixon 1) while simultaneously arguing for his country's abilities at provision. However, ignoring the gendered aspect of this narrative negates the power of the narrative. In arguing that Soviet women could work and provide for themselves, Khrushchev robbed them of the position of weakness that necessitates provision in the first place. Thus provision defines the power of the husband through an emphasis on the dependency intrinsic to the role of housewife.

Continuing to refer to the "housewife" alludes to a husband whose earnings provide for the household, and therefore the wife does not have to work outside of the home. Focusing on the man's earnings as the gateway to the lifestyle on display establishes the husband as provider, as well as emphasizing housework as the defining aspect of the housewife. Nixon explained the accessibility of the home and appliances on display to establish the Exhibition as representative of prototypical Americana and demonstrated the typical American father's ability to provide this lifestyle to his family. The lifestyle on display was available to all Americans: "Any steelworker could buy this house. They earn $3 an hour" (Nixon 1). Steelworkers as prototypical blue-collar workers establish that the average American family can afford this lifestyle. When Khrushchev questioned Nixon's claims, Nixon merely provided another example: "Most American [vets from World War II] can buy a home in the bracket of $10,000 to $15,000" (Nixon 1).[7] Since the display could be purchased in America for $14,000, Nixon's examples of steelworkers and veterans argued implicitly that the majority of Americans could afford to purchase everything on display. Nixon portrayed the exhibit as the standard for the majority of American homes and emphasized the typical man's ability to provide the displayed appliances for his wife and family to demonstrate America's provisionary strength through its prototypical family man.

The husband's provision defines the housewife as consumer and her housework as the focus of that consumption. Once these gendered expectations establish the housewife as consumer, choice becomes key to demonstrating the strength of the nation's technology: choice necessarily favors the capitalist mindset. Nixon continuously referred to the market's competitive nature as proof of this strength. "Diversity, the right to choose, the fact that we have 1,000 builders building 1,000 different houses is the most important thing" (Nixon 2). He persistently derided Soviet technology that refused its consumers a choice and emphasized the importance of competition to ensure superiority of technology and product. The importance of choice also boiled down to each individual housewife: "We have many different manufacturers and many different kinds of washing machines so that the housewives have a choice" ("Khrushchev-Nixon Debate" 5). While the women are here the consumers, emphasizing their position as a housewife implies that they can have choices only if their husband can provide the money necessary to supply and replace the appliances in the first place.

The ability for Americans to fulfill their desire for the newest and therefore "best" technology is dependent upon the husband as breadwinner, and therefore Nixon cemented the man as provider on his side of the debate through his emphasis on the newness of the appliances. Nixon stressed the newness of the technology, as opposed to the obsolescence of older models, throughout his discussion with Khrushchev. He pointed specifically to the "newest model" or "newest technology" five times in the debate, discussing the "latest technology" an additional three times. The American lifestyle is "designed to take advantage of new inventions and new techniques" (Nixon 2). The "built-in panel-controlled washing machine" ("Khrushchev-Nixon Debate" 3), which Khrushchev explained was also available in the Soviet Union, was the "newest model." The ability to constantly replace older technology with its newest derivative necessitates an income that can afford to supply the house with the latest and newest technological developments. Men's ability to continuously replace outdated appliances with the newest model demonstrates their position as breadwinner and provider to their family, and is Nixon's measure of the strength of a family.

While choice and innovation imply that women have the right to choose which technology is in their house to assist in their duties as housewife, Nixon's phrasing demonstrates the control of the masculine over this feminine technology. It is not up to the housewife to decide which technology is necessary to assist her around the house; Nixon's choice focuses on manufacturer and style and ignores the housewife's ability to decide which technology is necessary. In Nixon's explication of the exhibit, the man provides a washing machine, and the woman chooses the brand and style. The husband therefore controls both the wife's spending and her housework by defining which technology she will have to assist her; her consumerism is driven by aesthetics alone. Nixon placed America's strength in the housework he deemed most important, based on the technology that assisted in that housework. Through drawing attention to particular aspects of housework and ignoring housework that was unaided by technology, Nixon defined which housework was important. In so doing, Nixon exerted control over the feminine domestic sphere to define provisionary strength.

Defining housework through these technologies serves to commodify the role of the housewife, as well as her housework. Provision is consumerism in that it creates a technology market where one previously did not exist. A woman's desire to update an "obsolete" kitchen defines this technology, not by function but by consumer trend. Therefore the work Nixon emphasizes throughout the debate is commodified work; more than providing essentials, husbands as providers supply technology that enables a "life of leisure" that focuses on housework and children. The technology becomes a marker of lifestyle and wealth, and housework becomes a product that can be purchased, not through servant labor but through appliances. As these products define the work women do within the home, they commodify that work.

As Nixon shifted the debate from military technology to domestic technology, he defined consumer technology and the housework of the women who use it through masculine terms. He thus solidified the masculine position as the head of housework by emphasizing men's position as the providers of this technology. Through his discussion of this technology, he demonstrated the ways men control women's work in the home through defining what that work is and how it should be done. Nixon's gender ideology continued to constrain women's choices by keeping them in the techno-kitchen (Holliday 82), and provision defined which tools and accessories were available to assist in their housework. Nixon's American husband alleviates the burden of housework by purchasing these domestic technologies and therefore controls the housework through its purchase. Each technological development Nixon pointed to as the newest pinnacle of American superiority would be made obsolete by the next model that would only increase the efficiency of the technology and therefore the housewife's leisure time, "mak[ing] life more easy for our housewives" (Nixon 1). In making life easier, the husband provides a better life for his wife.

Domestic technological advances claim to lighten the load for women in order to grant access to a life of leisure available to those in higher income brackets who can afford servants,[8] yet only serve to lighten the load of housework that the men who provide the technology deem important. The technology that Nixon discussed also served to emphasize the housework that American culture deemed necessary and important for the housewife to complete, and in this way functioned to define the occupation of housewife. When Nixon jokingly pointed to a self-propelled vacuum cleaner and said, "you don't need a wife" ("Khrushchev-Nixon Debate" 5), he implied that the technology alleviated housework to the point of oblivion. The sheer amount of technology present, however, undermined his joke. Nixon's vision was of a woman who no longer needed to worry about the wifely duties of cleaning, and ignored the women in the Model Home demonstrating the technology for male tourists, who could not use the technology themselves (Oldenziel and Zachmann 2). This technology created the expectation that since whatever chore under consideration is easier to complete, it should always be done. While a washing machine does ease the hassle of laundry, it also raises the expectations of cleanliness for clothing and household washables. Women can easily wash more clothes at once, so clothes should always be clean and ready to wear. Vacuum cleaners replaced brooms as the primary method of cleaning carpets, thereby increasing expectations of the cleanliness of carpets: since it is easier to clean, it should always be clean. While Nixon could joke that wives were no longer necessary when vacuum cleaners can self-propel, his argument defines the housework of the wife as never complete.

Claims that these technologies provide women a life of leisure are undermined by Nixon's emphasis, first, on the wifely duties the technology implies and second, in his focus on the importance of the role of the mother. Raising children therefore becomes the most important aspect of housework. The newest technology in ranges, convection ovens, and microwave ovens emphasized the importance of preparing a meal to be waiting for the husband when he returned from work, as well as meals for the children, while decreasing the amount of time these meals took to create. Provision thus allays the duties of the wife so that instead she can focus on the important job of motherhood; it ensures that mothers have the time and energy to raise their children. The strength of the American domestic technology guaranteed American children were being raised properly and under a watchful eye, ensuring the strength of the future America. The father provided the technology that secures America's future.

Key to this reading of the Kitchen Debate is the Soviet counterargument. The Soviet side of this debate defined domestic technology not through gendered terms, but through a focus on the family as a unit, and their argument serves as an example of how this technology can be understood outside of gendered divisions of housework. In the debate on provision, the Soviet Union provided for their children and grandchildren, while the American provided for his wife. Khrushchev extolled the virtue of houses built "firmly [. . .] for our children and grandchildren" (Nixon 1). Nixon responded that while American houses will also last for more than twenty years, "[t]heir kitchen is obsolete by that time [. . .] The American system is designed to take advantage of new inventions and new techniques" (Nixon 2). While Khrushchev focused on the home itself as the site of protection and provision for a family unit that includes multiple generations, Nixon substituted the kitchen for the home. He stated that "after twenty years, many Americans want a new house or a new kitchen" (Nixon 1–2), stipulating that their kitchen will be "obsolete" twenty years later. The kitchen is the site of provision, shifting the provisionary duty from the children to the wife. Once provision focuses on the wife, housework becomes her duty as repayment. Her husband has provided her assistance in her housework, and therefore, through provision, has defined which housework is necessary to her duties, and which superfluous. This process of provision functions to interpolate women into the gendered ideology of the time.

An unexpected technological advance demonstrates the importance of technology in protecting children and enforcing motherhood as the primary occupation of the housewife. Throughout the Kitchen Debate, Nixon returned to one technological symbol of American greatness: the color television.[9] Nixon explained to Khrushchev: "There are some instances where you may be ahead of us—for example in the development of the thrust of your rockets for the investigation of outer space. There may be some instances, for example, color television, where we're ahead of you" (Nixon 3–4). This discussion of color television first and foremost reminded Khrushchev of American technological superiority in this arena. While Khrushchev denied Nixon's claim that American color televisions and color television broadcast technology was more advanced than in the Soviet Union, the distribution of the filmed Kitchen Debate demonstrated Nixon's point. The Kitchen Debate was one of the first color television recordings, and Nixon and Khrushchev agreed that the debate should be broadcast simultaneously in both the USSR and the United States to demonstrate the willingness of the heads of state to debate on the important issues of the time. The debate, however, was taped using American color film, and the tape had to be sent to a facility in Redwoods, California, to be formatted to be compatible with Soviet technology. The Soviet Union at the time did not have sophisticated enough broadcast technology to distribute the Kitchen Debate in color. Nixon's references to color television, then, reinforced his commitment to focus attention on American technological superiority.

Color television is at first glance a diversion from the household appliances that "make easier the life of our housewives." While this technology today is one of entertainment and relaxation, Nixon discussed instead the utility of the television and closed circuit feeds for aiding women in raising children. Nixon pointed to a television screen and explained: "We can see here what is happening in other parts of the home" ("Khrushchev-Nixon Debate" 4). For Nixon, the television here was surveillance instead of just entertainment and enabled mothers to observe their children from a different room of the house. The television made child rearing easier by providing the ability for constant supervision while the mother worked in other areas of the house. The ability for mothers to keep a constant eye on their children also reinforces their role as protector of the children and emphasizes child rearing as the most important household responsibility. Since children can be supervised continuously, the mother was always expected to be aware of where her children were and what they were doing. This constant supervision implied that if her children needed her, she could drop whatever else she was doing and help or protect them. By providing the means to watch over her children, then, the husband reminds her of her duty to protect the future of her family.

Nixon's ability to shift the debate over technological superiority from the space race to domestic appliances relied upon redefining the role of the husband as provider instead of protector of the household. As protector, the man must rely on military superiority to ensure the safety of his wife and children; as provider, the man must earn enough to ensure his wife enjoys the lifestyle he believes she deserves and prefers. While the woman becomes the consumer, her housework becomes the commodity. This shift from protector to provider created a feminized technological sphere within the home through focusing on women's use of technology while maintaining the gendered nature of both public and private spheres. As a provider, the husband therefore defines and controls his wife's occupation as housewife by focusing her attention on specific housework through the purchase of technology to accomplish that housework. The provision of this technology also serves to commodify the husband's expectations; housework as a woman's responsibility must fit within the parameters of the man's vision of what needs to be done.

CONCLUSION

Throughout the debate, the relationship between the government and its people mirrors the relationship between the husband and his family. Khrushchev's focus on military and space technology protected his people from outside threats; while he attempted to argue that the Communist government provided for its people, Nixon argued that choice and access are primary components of provision. An American government that encouraged competition was therefore providing the American people access to the best technology available. Nixon shaped the debate around provision to argue both that American husbands best provided for their families and the American government best provided for its people. The wife's housework was then vital to the strength of a nation.

Cold War containment narratives began as an ideological struggle between two superpowers; as the privileged narrative throughout the Cold War, "containment" became a sort of national motto to suppress communism within the United States (Nadel 3). This containment narrative also served to tie gender identity to national security through encouraging homogeneity (Corber 8). An analysis of this debate illuminates ways in which national narratives define gender and social identity in instances of supreme national anxiety. Analyses of instances in which national narratives seek to confine gendered roles and expectations demonstrate the circumstances necessary for national audiences to fully interpolate the subject position proffered by these narratives. The act of recognition at being addressed in these instances creates an audience that acknowledges and therefore accepts the status, culture, and history the narrative constructs; this constitutive act positions the audience toward political, social, and/or economic action that serves to strengthen a national community (Charland 87). In the case of the Kitchen Debate, interpolation affirmed women's subject position within the narrative of containment as a domestic labor force confined to a gendered private sphere by accepting Nixon's premise that the subject position is natural and essential to gender. This discussion provides insight into the ways patriarchal interests, in this case, in the guise of national security, attempt to guide women to interpolate subordinate subject positions and thus implicitly accept masculine control over their lives and their work.

NOTES

1. One purported transcript of the Kitchen Debate appeared in the *New York Times* on July 25, 1959, the day after the leaders visited the model home exhibit. However, several versions of transcripts exist for this debate, and the 16-minute video that aired in both the United States and the Soviet Union adds to these transcripts. Stories in the *New York Times* from July 24–27 suggest that these transcripts vary because the "Kitchen Debate" actually took place throughout the duration of Nixon's visit. See these *New York Times* articles and a discussion of the filming of the Kitchen Debate (Lindner, *Abbey Newsletter*).

2. When Khrushchev rose to power in Russia, he made it clear that one of his goals was to expand Soviet technological developments in domestic and household equipment, prompting some to refer to him as the "Refrigerator Candidate." See Oldenziel and Zachmann, *Cold War Kitchen: Americanization, Technology, and European Users.*

3. Hill emphasizes the Whirlpool Corporation's sponsorship of the American National Exhibition to underline consumerism as the main motivation behind the event (50); Holliday refers to the exhibit as the "RCA/Whirlpool Miracle Kitchen of Tomorrow" in each reference

to the Debate in the article to emphasize this consumerist motivation (see page 105 as example). Whitfield rationalizes the power behind Nixon's argument for consumerism because "the images that resulted [. . .] seemed to confirm what many Americans believed [. . .] The way they lived, with their comforts and conveniences, was shown as an essential part of the American way of life. Not only was it worth defending, but it was a defense in itself because its richness challenged every other political system [. . .] to do the same for its citizenry" (75).

4. Griswold traces the history of the nurturing, protective father, and Coontz discusses how upper-class men viewed their ability to hire servants as necessary to protect their wife and children from housework (11).

5. For an in-depth discussion of the ways gendered work contributes to gender identity, see Abel and Nelson, *Circles of Care: Work and Identity in Women's Lives*; Cott, *The Bonds of Womanhood: "Woman's Sphere" in New England, 1780–1835*; DuVall, *Domestic Technology: A Chronology of Developments*; and Matthews, *"Just a Housewife": The Rise and Fall of Domesticity in America*.

6. Nixon and Khrushchev are here also arguing on Khrushchev's ultimatum over atomic testing. In the week before Nixon's visit, Khrushchev declared a moratorium on nuclear testing, threatening to resume testing almost immediately if the United States and Great Britain did not join in the moratorium. Nixon's proclamation that "in this day and age [ultimatum] misses the point" is a response to Khrushchev's declaration.

7. "Vets from World War II" is stipulated but not quoted in the *New York Times* transcripts; other transcripts stipulate "vets from World War II" in parentheses.

8. See DuVall, *Domestic Technology*; Leavitt, *From Catharine Beecher to Martha Stewart: A Cultural History of Domestic Advice*; Rutherford, *Selling Mrs. Consumer: Christine Frederick and the Rise of Household Efficiency*; Cowan, *More Work for Mother: The Ironies of Household Technology from the Open Hearth to the Microwave*.

9. At this time the major networks were debating the value of investing in color television. Most believed color television to be too expensive to develop, and so Nixon's focus on color television would have been against the grain of the current technology trend. NBC was the first network to broadcast fully in color in 1966; it took twenty-five years for color television to take a firm hold of television technology. See Abramson, *The History of Television, 1942 to 2000* and Burns, *Television: An International History of the Formative Years*.

WORKS CITED

Abel, Emily K., and Margaret K. Nelson. *Circles of Care: Work and Identity in Women's Lives.* Albany: SUNY Press, 1990. Print.

Abramson, Albert. *The History of Television, 1942 to 2000.* Jefferson, NC: McFarland, 2003. Web. 22 Oct 2012.

Arendt, Hannah, and Margaret Canovan. *The Human Condition.* Chicago: University of Chicago Press, 1998. Print.

Boyer, Paul S. *By the Bomb's Early Light: American Thought and Culture at the Dawn of the Atomic Age.* Chapel Hill: University of North Carolina Press, 1994. Print.

Burns, R. W. *Television: An International History of the Formative Years.* London: Institution of Electrical Engineers, 1998. Web. 22 Oct 2012.

Charland, Maurice. "Constitutive Rhetoric: The Case of the *Peuple Québécois.*" *Quarterly Journal of Speech* 73.2 (1987): 133–50. Print.

Coontz, Stephanie. *The Way We Never Were: American Families and the Nostalgia Trap.* New York: Basic, 1992. Print.

Corber, Robert. *In the Name of National Security: Hitchcock, Homophobia, and the Political Construction of Gender in Postwar America.* Durham, NC: Duke University Press, 1993. Print.

Cott, Nancy F. *The Bonds of Womanhood: "Woman's Sphere" in New England, 1780–1835.* New Haven, CT: Yale University Press, 1997. Print.

Cowan, Ruth. *More Work for Mother: The Ironies of Household Technology from the Open Hearth to the Microwave.* New York: Basic, 1999. Print.

Dickson, Paul. *Sputnik: The Shock of the Century.* New York: Walker, 2011. Print.

DuVall, Nell. *Domestic Technology: A Chronology of Developments.* Boston: G. K. Hall, 1988. Print.

Fraser, Nancy. "Rethinking the Public Sphere." *Habermas and the Public Sphere.* Ed. Craig Calhoun. Cambridge, MA: MIT Press, 1993. Print.

Friedan, Betty. *The Feminine Mystique.* 1963. New York: Norton, 2001. Print.

Goldman, Eric Frederick. *The Crucial Decade—and After: America, 1945–1960.* New York: Vintage, 1960. Print.

Griswold, Robert L. *Fatherhood in America: A History.* New York: Basic, 1993. Print.

Hill, Michelle. "My Kitchen's Better Than Yours." *Michigan History* 83.4 (1999): 50–53. Web. 29 Nov 2010.

Holliday, Laura S. "Kitchen Technologies: Promises and Alibis, 1944–1966." *Camera Obscura* 16.2 (2001): 79–131. Web. 15 Oct 2010.

Jackson, Kenneth T. "Race, Ethnicity and Real Estate Appraisal: The Home Owners Loan Corporation and the Federal Housing Administration." *The Journal of Urban History* 6.4 (1980): 419–52. Print.

Kelly, Barbara M. *Expanding the American Dream: Building and Rebuilding Levittown.* Albany: SUNY Press, 1993. Print.

"Khrushchev-Nixon Debate." *New York Times,* 24 July 1959. Web. 4 Oct 2010.

Leavitt, Sarah. *From Catharine Beecher to Martha Stewart: A Cultural History of Domestic Advice.* Chapel Hill: University of North Carolina Press, 2002. Print.

Lindner, Jim. *Abbey Newsletter,* 21.7 (1997). Web. 20 Oct 2010.

Matthews, Glenna. *"Just a Housewife": The Rise and Fall of Domesticity in America.* New York: Oxford University Press, 1987. Print.

May, Elaine Tyler. *Homeward Bound: American Families in the Cold War Era.* New York: Basic, 2008. Print.

Nadel, Alan. *Containment Culture: American Narratives, Postmodernism, and the Atomic Age.* Durham, NC: Duke University Press, 1995. Print.

Nixon, Richard M. "The Kitchen Debate." *Teaching American History.* Ashbrook Center for Public Affairs at Ashland University. Web. 4 Nov. 2012.

Oldenziel, Ruth, and Karin Zachmann. *Cold War Kitchen: Americanization, Technology, and European Users.* Cambridge, MA: MIT Press, 2011. Print.

Reid, Susan. "Our Kitchen is Just as Good: Soviet Responses to the American Kitchen." *Cold War Kitchen: Americanization, Technology, and European Users.* Ed. Ruth Oldenziel and Karin Zachmann. Cambridge, MA: MIT Press, 2011. Print.

Richmond, Yale. "The 1959 Kitchen Debate." *Russian Life* 52:4 (Jul/Aug 2009): 42–49. Web. 17 Apr 2011.

Rutherford, Janice Williams. *Selling Mrs. Consumer: Christine Frederick and the Rise of Household Efficiency.* Athens: University of Georgia Press, 2003. Print.

Warner, Michael. *Publics and Counterpublics.* New York and Cambridge, MA: Zone Books, Distributed by MIT Press, 2002. Print.

Weintraub, Jeff Alan, and Krishan Kumar. *Public and Private in Thought and Practice: Perspectives on a Grand Dichotomy.* Chicago: University of Chicago Press, 1997. Print.

Whitfield, Stephen. *The Culture of the Cold War.* Baltimore: Johns Hopkins University Press, 1996. Print.

Chapter Six

Supernatural Housework

Magic and Domesticity in 1960s Television

Kristi Rowan Humphreys

Television in the 1950s celebrated the all-American nuclear family, one typically featuring a professional father and a full-time housewife. As perhaps the greatest examples of this trend, sitcoms such as *Father Knows Best* (1954–1960), *Leave It to Beaver* (1957–1963), and *The Adventures of Ozzie and Harriet* (1952–1966) presented ideal concepts of traditional middle-class, white American domesticity. Television in the 1960s witnessed a trend to infuse housewife characters with supernatural abilities. In shows such as *Bewitched* (1964–1972), *I Dream of Jeannie* (1965–1970), and *The Addams Family* (1964–1966), women used magical powers to craft domestic spheres that are gilded in normalcy but are anything but traditional. Whereas various studies have examined how 1950s sitcoms presented gender systems defined by domesticity, in which the mothers often assume background, devalued positions,[1] and how 1960s sitcoms paralleled the changing social climate in America with characters that embodied women's emerging social and sexual powers,[2] few have focused on the function of housework within these models. In both decades, character development for sitcom housewives occurred through scenes involving domestic duties, and viewers witnessed idyllic models of household management based on various patterns of housework. In the sixties, though, "supernatural housework" became the mechanism by which television portrayed women who possessed the hidden powers to change men into dogs or to make storm clouds appear, but who often were unwilling to use these powers for much more than vacuuming the drapes. This study analyzes the evolution of "supernatural housework" in television shows of the 1960s—*Bewitched*, *I Dream of Jeannie*, and *The Addams Family*—as the embodiment of social response to the ideal concepts of housework and household management put forward by the June Cleavers, Harriet Nelsons, and Margaret Andersons of the 1950s. Furthermore, whereas popular interpretations of the supernatural qualities of 1960s television tend to view them as representations of the emerging female sexual and political energy of the decade, this study contends that through "supernatural housework," the sixties characters of Samantha Stephens (*Bewitched*), Jeannie (*I Dream of Jeannie*), and Morticia Addams (*The Addams Family*) actually furthered the dominant gender discourse of the fifties—one suggesting that fulfillment for women had only one definition: housewifery.[3]

GENDER REPRESENTATIONS IN 1950S TELEVISION

Postwar America witnessed great confusion regarding dominant and subordinate roles between husbands and wives, and many were left wondering who would "wear the pants" in the family (Douglas 51). During World War II, many women answered the call to abandon their domestic spheres, their academic pursuits, and their professional aspirations to go to work, and their large-scale entry into the workforce created competition for the men once the war ended. The 1950s witnessed a trend to return women to the home, where they were assured they would find ultimate fulfillment as females. This evolving sentiment maintained that women, regardless of educational levels, should celebrate their femininity by putting careers aside to focus on being wives and mothers. In *Where the Girls Are: Growing Up Female with the Mass Media*, Susan J. Douglas says this message claimed that "'real' women found fulfillment in diaper pails and macaroni recipes" instead of atom splitting and space travel (51). In other words, whereas women had proven they were capable of pursuing careers, the dominant gender discourse of the era encouraged them to believe they would be happiest serving their husbands.

Considering that almost thirty-five million families had television sets by 1956 (Leibman 3), television was quite possibly the most effective vehicle for spreading this message. In *Living Room Lectures: The Fifties Family in Film and Television*, Nina C. Leibman describes the process by which television programs worked "to re-channel careerist desires by extolling the virtues of being a good wife and mother" (195). Television shows of the 1950s promoted a version of housewifery and motherhood through female characters who happily and gracefully spent their days cooking and cleaning and being absent from most of the important family discussions. This message of "the feminine mystique," the term later coined by Betty Friedan in 1963, was received enthusiastically, as by the 1960s the representation of women had decreased to only 35 percent of the nation's workforce from about 50 percent in the 1930s, even though the number of females graduating from college had nearly tripled (242). Shows such as *Father Knows Best, Leave It to Beaver*, and *The Adventures of Ozzie and Harriet* promoted a particular vision of middle-class existence, offering fictional white families that functioned smoothly as a result of fathers who worked diligently to afford nice suburban homes, mothers who wore heels and pearls to serve their families, and children who happily sat down at the dinner table to discuss adolescent problems with the family.

There is no question that real American women were watching and learning from these characters. In fact, the American homemaker—the person deemed responsible for buying her household products—was the primary target of television advertisers during this decade (Leibman 86). But advertising and production executives were not just seeking to appeal to the American homemaker; through the presentation of a particular version of femininity in relation to housework, they were seeking to show her what she ought to be—to *create* her.[4] In these programs, female viewers witnessed homemakers who found joy in vacuuming the living room, who were stimulated by the excitement of finding a good bargain, and who found contentment in mending their husbands' buttons before heading to bed. They found an idealized version of their real-life mundane housework—one that might possibly earn them in time happiness, excitement, contentment. In fact, these fictional housewife characters were very real to viewers. Jane Wyatt, who played Margaret Anderson in *Father Knows Best*, recalled that females would frequently approach her to assess or criticize her homemaking abilities on the show (Leibman 88). The popularity of these housewife characters was largely due to the intentional use of strong actresses to play relatively passive roles. Whereas the reason for this casting involved executives believing that weak women made poor consumers, these characters conveyed the message to real housewives that even strong, intelligent women found the greatest fulfillment serving their men (Leibman 190, 192). Furthermore, these characters performed their housework managerially, in the same way a career woman ran her office. This depiction further convinced 1950s housewives struggling with the real-life drudgery of housework that, as Leibman puts it, this type of housewife "was a career woman after all; it's just that her career was the home and family" (193).

Despite the fact that assertive actresses brought appeal to these characters, it is nevertheless the case that the mother's function in these shows is often marginalized by her insubstantial domestic duties, as her "presence is signified only by the meals she prepares and the neatness of the house" (Leibman 205). Scenes present the mother filling candy dishes, arranging flowers, or spreading peanut butter on slices of bread, while the father is in the study solving the family crises and giving the kids real advice about school problems or the opposite sex. Episodes almost always feature at least one meal where family members gather at the table to discuss the day, while the mother's housework removes her from these important discussions. The children address their questions and answers to the father, while the mother floats upstage to serve or enters the kitchen to fetch more food and can be heard calling from the stove. As Leibman points out, "It is her very culinary duties that cause mother's familial exclusion" (129). For example, in the episode "Tutti Frutti Ice Cream" (1957) of *The Adventures of Ozzie and Harriet*, Ozzie and sons sit around the table talking and eating ice cream, while Harriet moves around upstage looking through kitchen cabinets. In the *Leave It to Beaver* episode "Beaver's Birthday" (1961), the males sit around the table discussing the lesson of saving money, as June is off screen preparing food. Similarly, in "Beaver's Cat Problem" (1961), June butters toast as the males talk around the table.

Repeatedly, the only time the mother is allowed to take part in discussions of family problems is when the husband helps her with her chores before or after dinner. Consequently, the kitchen is the second most filmed room in the 1950s television house, but the father rarely imparts his sage advice there (Leibman 129). Interestingly, whereas the mother characters are largely defined by their domestic duties, the duties themselves are often omitted, revealing only the final product of a finished meal or a clean house. The house cannot run efficiently without these tasks, but the omission of the tasks

Figure 6.1.   June prepares breakfast while Ward and Wally discuss important issues of the day. Source: *Leave It to Beaver* (CBS), 1958–1963

themselves implies that they are essentially valueless and that the secret to effective homemaking is the "invisibility" of the housework (Leibman 218). This emphasis on the invisibility of housework changed in the 1960s, as housework became the mechanism through which magical powers were revealed.

1960S TELEVISION AND *THE FEMININE MYSTIQUE*

When Friedan published *The Feminine Mystique* in 1963, she described what she called the "problem that has no name"—the widespread boredom and restlessness housewives were experiencing in the 1950s and 1960s. Many of these white middle-class housewives had been educated alongside the men but had given up their professional dreams for the promise of ultimate feminine fulfillment; women believed in this promise and found themselves bewildered by the actual boredom of homemaking. They had listened to the television shows of the fifties and early sixties, such as the *Leave It to Beaver* episode "Beaver's IQ" (1960) when Beaver says, "Girls have it lucky . . . they don't have to be smart; they don't have to get jobs or anything; all they got to do is get married." But after years of dirty diapers, bologna sandwiches, and PTA meetings, these women didn't feel so "lucky." And in the sixties, the "problem that has no name," the actual unhappiness of the American housewife, was finally being discussed, although as Friedan described, "almost everyone who talked about it found some superficial reason to dismiss it . . . some said it was the old problem—education: more and more women had education, which naturally made them unhappy in their roles as housewives" (22). Furthermore, Friedan argued that the more a woman's "intelligence exceeds [her] job requirements, the greater [her] boredom" (251). Regardless of the reason, housewife boredom had become a national issue in the sixties, and women's college presidents across the nation were delivering speeches that assured females that sixteen years of education was indeed proper preparation for housewifery (22). Friedan regarded the outcome of this boredom as unsurprising, when the reality remained that many women were using their sixteen years of education to perform the most menial of tasks—tasks that in the labor force would receive the lowest wages—only to feel guilty when those tasks did not fulfill them.

1960S TELEVISION AND THE BORED HOUSEWIFE

With regard to housewife boredom, *Bewitched, I Dream of Jeannie*, and *The Addams Family* answered the call. Whereas June Cleaver's life actually appeared boring, the lives of Samantha Stephens, Jeannie, and Morticia Addams did not. Just as housewives across the nation had sworn off their careerist aspirations to iron sheets and clean toilets, Samantha swears off her super-natural powers to marry Darrin, but the opportunity to use those powers, whether she does so or not, prevents her from becoming bored or from appearing boring. *Bewitched* and *Jeannie* address this issue directly. In the *Bewitched* episode "Fastest Gun on Madison Avenue" (1966), Samantha (Elizabeth Montgomery) tells Darrin (Dick York), "You know there's a lot more to running a house than most people think." Darrin replies, "Honey, I think it's wonderful the way you've adjusted," and Samantha claims, "I love being a housewife." Darrin then asks, "Are you sure you won't get bored once the novelty has worn off?" Confidently, Samantha says, "How could I be bored being married to someone like you?" *Jeannie* addresses boredom in the episode "The Yacht Murder Case" (1965), when after breakfast Tony (Larry Hagman) rushes off to work. Jeannie (Barbara Eden) chases after him, asking what she's supposed to do with herself all day. These shows reflect at the very least awareness that housewife boredom had entered the national discourse.

Friedan identified the essence of housewifery as the elimination of "wom-en's creative energy, rather than using it for some larger purpose in society" (254), but Samantha, along with Jeannie and Morticia, does not have to suppress her creative impulses because she has the power to act on them. For Douglas, it is this ability of Samantha's to act on her creative ideas that separates her from the real-life housewife: "Samantha has a more exciting destiny. While she claims that marriage to Darrin is what she wants, she gets to have it both ways, to have the reassurances of being a suburban wife and the adventures of being a more unconventional woman" (130). Furthermore, whereas the unimportance of 1950s television mothers is signified by their often meaningless and superfluous activities such as arranging flowers and polishing silver (Leibman 255), these tasks are the very moments in 1960s television when housewives are allowed to use their supernatural abilities. Scholars, such as Douglas, view this as "domesticating the monster"—ac-knowledging the "impending release of female sexual and political energy, while keeping it all safely in a straitjacket" (Douglas 126). Like Douglas, popular interpretations of these shows claim that the fear of these supernatu-ral powers, or sexual energy, remaining uncontained causes men to demand that their women not use their powers, and if they must, they should confine their powers to completing domestic chores within the private sphere.[5] The very aspects of the 1950s television housewife's life that are viewed as being mundane and boring—the cooking, the vacuuming, the ironing—are perhaps the most exciting moments for the 1960s television housewife, as these are the scenes when viewers see Samantha twitch her nose to clear the table, Jeannie nod her head to get Tony some coffee, or Morticia perform a spell to create party punch. The boring indeed is transformed into the thrilling. Out-side of the issue of boredom, though, these 1960s housewife characters actually use housework to continue the message of the 1950s sitcoms and further the main discourse put forth by the feminine mystique. They did so in four ways: through the expansion of domestic chores to fill the time, through the rejection of time-saving modern appliances, through the elevation of suburban living, and through the celebration of bargains and budgets.

1960S TELEVISION AND THE EXPANSION OF HOUSEWORK

With regard to housework, Friedan conceptualized what she called the "double deception" of the feminine mystique. The housewife's role is "dressed up" in an effort to make her housework appear equal to a man's work in society. According to Friedan, the housewife performs a much less "real" function, and the emptiness of this reality can be concealed only by "decorating" the function with superfluous activities. She identifies the "double deception" as follows:

1. The more a woman is deprived of her function in society at the level of her own ability, the more her housework . . . will expand—and the more she will resist finishing her housework or mother-work, and being without any function at all.

2. The time required to do the housework for any given woman varies inversely with the challenge of the other work to which she is committed. Without any outside interests, a woman is virtually forced to devote her every moment to the trivia of keeping house. (239)

In an effort to justify her existence, the housewife found herself expanding the housework to fill the time.[6] Mid-century studies, such as Theodore Caplow's book *The Sociology of Work* (1954) and the *Journal of Home Economics* article "Time: Resource or Utility" (1957), were reporting that even though housewives of the 1950s and 1960s had access to time-saving appliances, products, and methods, they were spending as many or more hours a day on housekeeping as women thirty years prior,[7] and that working women were accomplishing the same housework in half the time.[8] Many housewives sought the challenge of expansive housework because they were convinced that making their menial tasks more difficult, necessary, and creative would make their work seem more fulfilling and worthwhile. For example, the Wrights' 1950s *Guide to Easier Living* advises the fifties housewife to engage in expansive housework schedules that include daily carpet-sweeping of rugs and dry mopping of floors, as well as weekly floor waxing and range cleaning.

This is the first way in which 1960s television sitcoms actually further the issues exposed by 1950s television housewives. Samantha, Jeannie, and

Morticia have the ability to make the vacuum cleaner run on its own, while they perhaps read a book. But just as real mid-century housewives weren't choosing easier, time-saving methods for their housework, television house-wives with supernatural abilities weren't either. They were *choosing* to be typical housewives, and if typical housewives wash their own dishes and sew their own dresses, then they want to do the same, even if it takes all day. A high regard for normalcy and status quo is highlighted throughout these shows, whether it is through Samantha claiming, "All I want is a normal life of a normal housewife" in the episode "Witch or Wife" (1964), or Jeannie demanding, "No more presto . . . I want to be a typical woman" in the episode "The Americanization of Jeannie" (1965). For the television house-wives, their magic is acceptable only when it functions as a bandage for housework mistakes. Once they have attempted a domestic chore on their own and something goes wrong, they allow themselves to intervene with magic; this decision to manipulate typically leads to additional problems, thus implying that it is best for these women to stick to manual methods of housework and swear off magic altogether. Consequently, the message being sent to the real housewife viewer is that she is right to avoid the shortcuts: her more laborious methods do a much more effective job than "short-cut," time-saving methods, and *this* is the reason her place is in the home.

Bewitched abounds with examples of Samantha wanting to be "typical" and expand the housework to fill the time. In fact, of the three characters examined in this study, she is the most resistant to resorting to magic for housework. In the first episode of the first season, "I, Darrin, Take This Witch, Samantha" (1964), Samantha and Darrin have just married when she resolves to reveal herself as a witch. Darrin decides to keep her, if she promises not to perform any witchcraft. Darrin says, "Now, it's not going to be easy. You're going to have to learn to be a suburban housewife. You're going to have to learn to cook and keep house, and go to my mother's house every Friday night." Samantha replies, "Sounds wonderful." Samantha is a woman with the opportunity to be anything she wants to be, as she has the supernatural abilities literally to craft herself into anything, and yet she as-pires to be a typical suburban housewife—a view reinforced by 1950s televi-sion that the housewife is what every woman should *want* to be. Samantha's mother, Endora, often represents the voice that Friedan claims housewives suppress—"that voice within women that says: 'I want something more than my husband and my children and my home'" (32). Endora also represents that constant reminder to housewives that they *could* use short cuts to make domestic tasks easier, rather than expand the work to fill the time. In the episode "Be It Ever So Mortgaged" (1964), Samantha is icing a cake for Darrin and is doing a rather terrible job. Endora says, "No need to overdo this grubby little housewife role," and she fixes the cake with magic. Similarly, Samantha offers Endora coffee she made herself in the episode "Mother

Meets What's His Name" (1964). Endora does not want her homemade coffee because she prefers Turkish coffee, so she magically transforms it. Samantha reminds her that she wishes she wouldn't do that because she is trying to make this a "normal" household. Even though Darrin isn't aware of the magic, just as real husbands often are unaware of their wives' methods, Samantha is determined to obey Darrin's requests and perform her housework manually as well as possible. "Help, Help, Don't Save Me" (1964) opens with Samantha vacuuming. Suddenly, a horse's bridle appears around her neck. Endora reveals herself and says, "You enjoy working like a horse; I thought you might like looking like one." Samantha responds to her mother's insistence that she do something more exciting by saying, "I'm going to stay right here and I'm going to clean this house with my own two hands, and then I'm going to fix dinner. And then I'm going to take a bath and put on the sexiest dress I own." Samantha's insistence reflects a pride not only in her expansive housework schedule, but also the fact that she has the ability to accomplish it and still feel sexy for her husband.

Several episodes highlight expansive housework specifically. In the episode "Maid to Order" (1966), a very pregnant Samantha is reaching up to vacuum the drapes. Darrin rushes down the stairs and turns off the vacuum because he doesn't want her stretching in her condition. He tells her to sit down, but Samantha claims the drapes *need* to be vacuumed. Only then is she willing to use magic to finish the drapes, as magic is the only way she can obey her husband by sitting on the couch and still get the drapes cleaned. Darrin is bed-ridden in the episode "A is for Aardvark" (1965), and Samantha has been downstairs ironing when she checks on him with her arms full of sheets and towels. She tells him she is exhausted, but this is the last of the ironing. Ironing sheets and towels might be the most egregious example of expanding the work to fill the time, but it is matched by the episode "Pleasure O'Riley" (1965). Darrin gets a phone call on a Saturday with a request to play golf. Sam tells him very excitedly that he doesn't have to explain his abandoning her on a Saturday because she has closets to clean! Apparently, closets *must* be cleaned on a Saturday because every other day of the week surely is consumed by her daily housework. Each of these episodes highlights Samantha's determination to complete types of housework that are rarely necessary, yet performed regularly on the show. This aligns perfectly with Friedan's claim that housewives were expanding the work to fill the time. Of the thirty-six episodes in the first season alone, 90 percent contain scenes involving Samantha's housework, and 30 percent involve Samantha correcting her housework mistakes with magic. Whereas magic is present in every episode, Samantha almost always chooses to expand the work to fill the time by performing all of her domestic chores by herself in an effort to be the "typical suburban housewife."

Similarly, in *I Dream of Jeannie* and *The Addams Family*, Jeannie and Morticia cast aside their supernatural abilities in an effort to do things as normal housewives do them. In the earlier seasons of *I Dream of Jeannie*, Jeannie is more inclined to rely on magic for housework, but as she becomes increasingly domesticated and bored with the instantaneousness of magic, she longs to do things herself. For example, in the first season, Jeannie often is seen using magic to make Tony's breakfast appear, to pour coffee, or to dust the living room, but as her boredom increases (e.g., she is seen lounging around reading magazines while a rag magically dusts the room around her), she uses less magic for her domestic chores. This parallels Friedan's claim regarding mid-century housewives: Jeannie requires more of a challenge than her "supernatural housework" is providing, and she begins expanding her housework to fill the time. Even in the first season, though, Jeannie begins to attempt her housework without the help of magic. In the episode "My Hero" (1965), Tony finds groceries in the kitchen and asks Jeannie about them. She tells him she has been to the market to get groceries to make his dinner. Jeannie has the power to make dinner appear with a nod of her head, but instead, she not only shops for groceries, she intends to cook the dinner herself. In "The Marriage Caper" (1965), Tony asks her to make him a cheese sandwich. She uses magic to make a goat and pail appear, but she proceeds to make the cheese manually. The next scene shows her slicing the cheese block in the kitchen. In the same episode, Jeannie asks Tony why he is staring at his newly purchased groceries in the kitchen. When he tells her he is cooking dinner, she replies, "But cooking is woman's work." Tony asks, "Do you know anything about cooking?" Jeannie tells him she will take care of it and proceeds to start a fire by putting frozen foods on burners while they are still in their packages. Only after she has attempted the cooking herself does she use magic to transform the dinner. Similarly, in the episode "The Americanization of Jeannie" (1965), Jeannie is picking up after Tony, but she fails to remember where she has put everything, and in "Is There an Extra Jeannie in the House" (1966), Jeannie is unsuccessfully arranging flowers in a vase and eventually uses magic to fix her botched attempt.

Over the course of several seasons, Jeannie begins to move toward wanting more out of her life as a homemaker with supernatural abilities. In the episode "The Permanent House Guest" (1966), Tony yells, "Jeannie, would you come out please? I'd like my breakfast." Jeannie makes his breakfast appear magically and then disappointedly replies, "I'm being wasted. Anyone can make you one egg and two slices of bacon . . . I will be a laughingstock—a genie who can only bring her master bacon and eggs!" Eventually, Jeannie tempers her disappointment by doing more chores by herself. In "Too Many Tonys" (1965), Jeannie is sewing a dress, mixing icing for a cake, and making dinner. Doctor Alfred Bellows (Hayden Rorke) enters and asks, "Do you do this often?" Jeannie tells him she cooks every night. He mentions how good it smells, and Jeannie asks, "Which one? Bread, pie, or cake?" He is astonished that she is making all three when she says, "Yes, Captain Nelson loves my baking." Doctor Bellows replies, "With so many flighty young girls around, it's nice to meet a real old-fashioned home-body . . . I mean, *real* wife material." By the fifth season (1969), Jeannie is regularly seen performing housework manually. In "Never Put a Genie on a Budget," Tony asks Jeannie if he has a clean shirt. She says, "Yes, in the bottom drawer. I washed it myself!" She takes pride in accomplishing the tasks that make her a "typical" housewife, even though her tasks now are more laborious and consume more of her time. Although Jeannie's determination to complete her tasks manually without the help of magic is not as strong as Samantha's, in the first forty episodes of *Jeannie*, roughly 60 percent involve Jeannie doing some level of housework.

In *The Addams Family*, even though Morticia frequently uses magic to smoke or create punch, she is more often seen performing housework manually. In "The Addams Family Goes to School" (1964), Morticia knits regularly and claims to be fixing their favorite lunch—boiled eye of newt. Similarly, in "Morticia Joins the Ladies League" (1964), she demonstrates ironing for Lurch and then proceeds to hang curtains in an effort to impress her female guests from the Ladies League. Even though she appears to be less concerned with being "normal" than Samantha or Jeannie, she does strive to be a typical housewife through the expansion of housework; however, her idea of "typical" is not consistent with that of her fellow housewives.

1960S TELEVISION AND THE REJECTION OF MODERN APPLIANCES

In addition to validating the expansion of housework to fill the time, 1960s television uses housework to further the "feminine mystique" through the rejection of modern, time-saving appliances. Friedan described studies of mid-century housewives that assessed their attitudes regarding electrical appliances. In one study from a 1945 women's magazine, 51 percent of the women were considered "true housewives." These women largely rejected new devices because, as one woman claimed, it is not possible to make housework easier when a machine cannot replace hard work (208–9). In another study,[9] housewives were given four options regarding methods of cleaning, with one being completely automatic and four being completely manual. The majority chose the fourth option, as their very worth depended on a need for their housekeeping abilities. One woman claimed, "As for some magical push-button cleaning system, well, what would happen to my exercise, my feeling of accomplishment, and what would I do with my mornings?" (217). In other words, if an appliance saved the housewife time, she would have to create more work to fill the time saved by the appliance in order to justify her existence.

Television shows of the sixties reinforce the rejection of appliances, largely through the housewives' failure to use the appliances properly and then resorting to magic to fix what they could not do with the appliances. Even though the impetus is different, the rejection of the time-saving appliance is consistent with the attitudes Friedan identified for real mid-century housewives. At the beginning of the *Bewitched* episode "Be It Ever So Mortgaged" (1964), Samantha is cooking breakfast. The male narrator says, "Here you see the average, normal suburban housewife in one of her daily routine tasks—preparing breakfast for her husband. With a modern kitchen and all of the conveniences at her disposal, the capable housewife moves efficiently through her tasks." At this point, Samantha accidentally sets a pan aflame on the stove, spills her freshly squeezed orange juice on the floor because she is unable to use the juicer properly, and burns the toast in the toaster. The narrator continues, "Of course there are problems, especially if your husband expects breakfast before he goes to work." Samantha rejects the appliances and fixes her mess with magic so that Darrin may eat before work. Similarly, in the episode "How to Be a Genie in Ten Easy Lessons" (1966) of *I Dream of Jeannie*, Jeannie is attempting to do laundry using the washing machine for the first time. After dropping the clothes in the washer, she begins pushing buttons at random. When nothing happens, she gives up and nods her head. The shirts come out of the washer clean, dry, and folded. Again, Jeannie rejects the appliance and remedies her mistake with magic. In "The Americanization of Jeannie" (1965), Jeannie gets a job selling appliances. When she isn't able to get women to buy her oven, she begins demonstrations that involve the oven magically making food appear. Women gather around and become agitated. Jeannie's assumption that they want ovens capable of doing their jobs for them is perhaps incorrect, as she leaves the crowd of women admitting, "This would not have happened to a modern woman." Furthermore, along with the mid-century housewife's fear that modern appliances might negate the need for her existence, there also was the issue of men's perceptions of how these modern appliances made the housework "easy," thus furthering the "less real" function the housewife was already experiencing. For example, in "Help, Help, Don't Save Me" (1964) of *Bewitched*, Darrin accuses Samantha of using magic to get him to use her advertising ideas. Samantha tells him she hasn't been anywhere near him: "I've been right here at home. I vacuumed and scrubbed and cleaned, and I made dinner." When Darrin says, "Big deal," she asks, "What does that mean?" Darrin replies, "Well, I've seen the way you can wham, wash, and pow, clean and ring-a-ding up a dinner." Samantha says, "Well, I didn't wham, pow, or ring-a-ding up anything. These are bona fide dishpan hands!" Darrin responds, "Well, you could have whipped that up too for appearances." For the real mid-century housewife, part of justifying her existence involved thwarting misperceptions that time-saving appliances lessened her housework to the extent that she could spend her days filing her nails, and the rejection of magic by these supernatural housewives is a stand-in for the rejection of appliances by real housewives. Even though Darrin is referencing Samantha's magic in the previous example, the real housewife regarded modern appliances in the same way—capable of ring-a-dinging up a load of clothes in a way that removes the need for her manual labor.

1960S TELEVISION AND THE
ELEVATION OF SUBURBAN LIVING

These shows also glamorize the suburban lifestyle in the same way their 1950s predecessors did. Friedan claimed that housewives were driven by boredom to buy more spacious homes in the suburbs where there was more to clean and generally more work to be done, thus temporarily solving the emptiness. She argued that the open floor plans of suburban homes contributed to women expanding the housework to fill the time. For example, she states, "In one free-flowing room, continual messes continually need picking up" (246). This problem of the free-flowing floor plan is addressed in the episode "And Something Makes Three" (1964) of *Bewitched*. Samantha is dusting in the living room and the house is in general disarray. The open floor plan of the Stephens's house reveals her messes from the living room, through to the dining room and kitchen. She has couch cushions on the floor, laundry on the dining room table, and bagged groceries in the kitchen. Her friend Louise calls and says she needs to come over immediately. Samantha does not have time to clean all three rooms before Louise comes over, so she twitches her nose to make the messes disappear. Even though Samantha is willing to resort to magic in this emergency situation in order to maintain the "invisibility" of her housework, the scene still confirms for real housewives the value of open-floor plan, suburban homes, even if they create more housework.

Most of the other examples that elevate suburban living involve the addition of gardening to the 1960s television housewife's list of daily domestic duties. "Mother Meets What's His Name" (1964) presents Samantha planting flowers in the yard. The male narrator says, "Among the more soul-satisfying, suburban activities is that collaboration with nature that brings fragrance and beauty to the home-horticulture. Husbands are appreciative of their wives' efforts as they leave for their offices, secure in the knowledge that their mates are home digging rather than in town shopping." Samantha returns in the next scene to find all of her plants dead. Again, she uses magic to fix her mistake before Darrin comes outside. Similarly, Jeannie often is seen tending to her plants. In the episode "My Wild-Eyed Master" (1966), Tony surprises Jeannie at home to find her watering the plants using magic, while she reads a magazine. After being "caught," Jeannie begins to water the plants manually and seems to find it much more satisfying. And in *The Addams Family*, Morticia spends most of her time feeding her magical hamburger-eating African Strangler plant, Cleopatra, and generally addressing her garden. The suburban home represented in each of these shows increases the housewife's workload, thus further justifying the need for her existence.

1960S TELEVISION AND THE THRILL OF THE BARGAIN

Finally, these shows serve to further the "feminine mystique" by emphasizing the thrill these housewives experience when finding a bargain and while adhering to a budget. In an effort to fulfill a need for achievement, real housewives sought the challenge of finding a good deal or of accomplishing tasks with minimal expense. According to Friedan, for the housewife, finding a bargain allowed her to say, "I'm doing a good job as a housewife; I'm contributing to the welfare of the family just as my husband does when he works and brings home a paycheck" (224). The bargain was a way for housewives to feel less like they were *draining* the earnings of their husbands, and more like they were *saving* money for their husbands. Being mindful of bargains and budgets also was a way for the housewife to feel a sense of accomplishment by developing an expertise in something, thus taking a more professional approach to housekeeping. For example in *Bewitched*, "Fastest Gun on Madison Avenue" (1966) begins with Samantha on the phone with the grocer while Darrin eats breakfast behind her. She says to the grocer, "You can send me two pounds of onions, a pound of butter, a head of lettuce, and sixty cans of wax beans." After she hangs up, Darrin looks at her quizzically. She claims, "They're having a sale on wax beans! You know, by buying sixty cans, I save three cents a can!" Darrin replies, "Wonderful. And it also takes care of all your wax-bean buying needs for the next fifteen or sixteen years!" Despite Darrin making fun of her, Samantha is excited about the bargain and feels she has functioned as an effective household manager. Similarly, in the episode "Little Pitchers Have Big Fears" (1964), Samantha answers the door to find a salesman selling brooms, who condescendingly greets her with, "No housewife ever has enough brooms and brushes." But Samantha is too discerning for this act. After determining these brooms would not be good bargains, Samantha replies, "I have all the brooms and brushes I need," and she magically fills her living room with these items. In *I Dream of Jeannie*, the episode "Never Put a Genie on a Budget" (1969) depicts Tony telling Jeannie that they are going to have to learn to live on what he makes. "I don't want you to blink anything ever again. You are my wife, and you're going to have to learn to live on my salary." Tony puts her on a budget, and she finds the challenge of the budget thrilling. That evening, when they host a guest from Russia, Jeannie serves him a TV dinner and stale bread. She praises the deal she got on these items at the store and is quite proud of her ability to stay within the budget set by Tony. Later, Tony tells Jeannie they are throwing another party, but she claims they cannot because it is not in her budget. She is determined not to go over budget, regardless of the circumstances, as she believes that meeting the challenge of her budget will make her more valuable to Tony.

Whereas these 1960s characters promote housewifery in ways that paralleled 1950s characters, the mechanism through which the housewife-role is explored changed from the purported "natural" to the supernatural. By removing the veneer of perfection created by the housewife characters of the fifties, and by infusing the sixties characters with fallibility, it is likely that toward the end of the decade, many viewers were able to accept and relate to these supernatural housewives more easily than they could the June Cleavers of the fifties. In fact, Lynn Spigel confirms in *Welcome to the Dream House: Popular Media and Postwar Suburbs* that these characters "made people pause at what had once seemed natural and everyday" (133), as viewers began to regard the supernatural elements of the shows as being more "natural" than the traditional elements that echoed the ideal concepts put forward by the fifties. Spigel finds that these supernatural shows, which she calls "fantastic sitcoms," "provided a cultural space in which anxieties about everyday life could be addressed, albeit through a series of displacements and distortion" (117). In other words, the changing social climate of the sixties— one that involved the women's and the civil rights movements—was reflected in the new magical powers of these television housewives. But through housework, the message of the feminine mystique remained the same. The elevation of housewifery often was hidden behind the magic. At the same time, television housework in these shows made some changes from the fifties quite apparent. The 1960s kitchen was still one of the most filmed rooms in the house, as it was the optimal space for the housewife to reveal her supernatural housework, but also it was the place where the important discussions, the integral plot points, occurred. Rather than functioning as a space where the marginalized mother is given a replay of the evening's discussions, as it did in the fifties, the 1960s kitchen is where the woman serves as an active participant in her family's affairs. These types of changes signify a changing social climate—one grappling with old images of the past and the reality of the present—and as these shows improve the understanding of such transitions, they highlight the importance of television as a part of history.

NOTES

1. This idea is put forward by Nina C. Leibman in *Living Room Lectures*.
2. Susan J. Douglas reveals this interpretation in *Where the Girls Are*.
3. On page 44 of *The Feminine Mystique*, Betty Friedan claimed that after 1949, society determined that fulfillment for women could be achieved only through the role of the house-wife-mother. Furthermore, she mentioned the woman's loss of self-identity in society's rush for the security of togetherness.
4. Leibman discusses this creation of the housewife in *Living Room Lectures*.
5. An example of this popular interpretation is Susan J. Douglas's work, *Where the Girls Are*.
6. Friedan based her argument on the Parkinson effect, a term articulated by Cyril North-cote Parkinson in 1957, stating that work expands so as to fill the time available for its completion.
7. This comes from the study *The Sociology of Work* by Theodore Caplow (234, note 3 on p. 408 of Friedan).
8. This is based on the study "Time: Resource or Utility," *Journal of Home Economics*, 49 (Jan. 1957), note 3 on page 408 of Friedan's work.
9. Friedan claims (407) that these studies were performed by the Institute for Motivational Research, directed by Dr. Ernest Dichter.

WORKS CITED

Douglas, Susan J. *Where the Girls Are: Growing Up Female with the Mass Media*. New York: Three Rivers Press, 1995. Print.
Friedan, Betty. *The Feminine Mystique*. Tenth Anniversary Edition. New York: Norton, 1974. Print.
Leibman, Nina C. *Living Room Lectures: The Fifties Family in Film and Television*. Austin: University of Texas Press, 1995. Print.
Spigel, Lynn. *Welcome to the Dream House: Popular Media and Postwar Suburbs*. Durham, NC: Duke University Press, 2011. Print.
Wright, Mary, and Russel Wright. *Guide to Easier Living*. Salt Lake City: Gibbs Smith, 1950. Print.

VIDEOGRAPHY

"A Is for Aardvark." *Bewitched: Season One*. Writ. Earl Barret. Dir. Ida Lupino. Sony, 2005. DVD.
"The Addams Family Goes to School." *The Addams Family: Volume One*. Writ. Seaman Jacobs and Ed James. Dir. Arthur Hiller. MGM, 2006. DVD.
"The Americanization of Jeannie." *I Dream of Jeannie: The Complete Series Box Set*. Writ. Arnold Horwitt. Dir. Gene Nelson. Sony, 2008. DVD.
"And Something Makes Three." *Bewitched: Season One*. Writ. Danny Arnold. Dir. William Asher. Sony, 2005. DVD.
"Be It Ever So Mortgaged." *Bewitched: Season One*. Writ. Barbara Avedon. Dir. William Asher. Sony, 2005. DVD.
"Beaver's Birthday." *Leave It to Beaver: Season Five*. Writ. Bob Ross. Dir. Hugh Beaumont. MCA, 1961. *Netflix*. Web. 7 May 2013.
"Beaver's Cat Problem." *Leave It to Beaver: Season Five*. Writ. Joe Connelly and Bob Mosher. Dir. David Butler. MCA, 1961. *Netflix*. Web. 7 May 2013.
"Fastest Gun on Madison Avenue." *Bewitched: The Complete Second Season*. Writ. Lee Erwin. Dir. William Asher. Sony, 2005. DVD.

"Help, Help, Don't Save Me." *Bewitched: Season One*. Writ. Danny Arnold. Dir. William Asher. Sony, 2005. DVD.

"How to Be a Genie in Ten Easy Lessons." *I Dream of Jeannie: The Complete Series Box Set*. Writ. Sidney Sheldon. Dir. Hal Cooper. Sony, 2008. DVD.

"I, Darrin, Take This Witch, Samantha." *Bewitched: Season One*. Writ. Sol Saks. Dir. William Asher. Sony, 2005. DVD.

"Is There an Extra Jeannie in the House." *I Dream of Jeannie: The Complete Series Box Set*. Writ. Charles Tannen. Dir. Hal Cooper. Sony, 2008. DVD.

"Little Pitchers Have Big Fears." *Bewitched: Season One*. Writ. Barbara Avedon. Dir. William Asher. Sony, 2005. DVD.

"Maid to Order." *Bewitched: The Complete Second Season*. Writ. Richard Baer. Dir. William Asher. Sony, 2005. DVD.

"The Marriage Caper." *I Dream of Jeannie: The Complete Series Box Set*. Writ. Tom Waldman and Frank Waldman. Dir. Alan Rafkin. Sony, 2008. DVD.

"Morticia Joins the Ladies League." *The Addams Family: Volume One*. Writ. Phil Leslie and Keith Fowler. Dir. Jean Yarbrough. MGM, 2006. DVD.

"Mother Meets What's His Name." *Bewitched: Season One*. Writ. Danny Arnold. Dir. William Asher. Sony, 2005. DVD.

"My Hero." *I Dream of Jeannie: The Complete Series Box Set*. Writ. Sidney Sheldon. Dir. Gene Nelson. Sony, 2008. DVD.

"My Wild-Eyed Master." *I Dream of Jeannie: The Complete Series Box Set*. Writ. Sidney Sheldon. Dir. Hal Cooper. Sony, 2008. DVD.

"Never Put a Genie on a Budget." *I Dream of Jeannie: The Complete Series Box Set*. Writ. Sidney Sheldon. Dir. Oscar Rudolph. Sony, 2008. DVD.

"The Permanent House Guest." *I Dream of Jeannie: The Complete Series Box Set*. Writ. Sidney Sheldon. Dir. Hal Cooper. Sony, 2008. DVD.

"Pleasure O'Riley." *Bewitched: Season One*. Writ. Ken Englund. Dir. William D. Russell. Sony Pictures, 2005. DVD.

"Too Many Tonys." *I Dream of Jeannie: The Complete Series Box Set*. Writ. Bob Fisher and Arthur Alsberg. Dir. E. W. Swackhamer. Sony, 2008. DVD.

"Tutti Frutti Ice Cream." *The Adventures of Ozzie and Harriet: Season Six.* Writ. Dick Bensfield and Perry Grant. Dir. Ozzie Nelson. ABC, 1957. *Netflix*. Web. 7 May 2013.

"Witch or Wife." *Bewitched: Season One*. Writ. Bernard Slade. Dir. William Asher. Sony, 2005. DVD.

"The Yacht Murder Case." *I Dream of Jeannie: The Complete Series Box Set*. Writ. David Braverman and Bob Marcus. Dir. Gene Nelson. Sony, 2008. DVD.

Chapter Seven

Every Day Should Be Like Sunny Weather

Ayelet Waldman and Michael Chabon Channel Carol Channing to Resolve the Politics for a New Generation of Parents

Mimi Choi

"Your mommy hates housework, your daddy hates housework, I hate housework, and when you grow up, you'll hate housework, too." Those of a certain age will be able to summon up the inimitable voice of Carol Channing in "Housework" from *Free to Be . . . You and Me*, a best-selling record from 1972. Among Channing's early listeners were Ayelet Waldman and Michael Chabon, who grew up to become spouses and writers, including essays on parenthood that credit Channing and Marlo Thomas, creator of *Free to Be*,[1] for influencing their largely feminist approach to raising their four children and sharing domestic responsibilities. Through their essays, I examine the querulous issue of housework in domestic relationships and consider why the encouragement from Channing and Thomas, as well as some (but not all) second-wave feminists, to share domestic responsibilities remains an often perplexing issue forty years later. While *Free to Be* was popular and critically well received, as Waldman's *Bad Mother* (2009) and Chabon's *Manhood for Amateurs* (2009) affirm, the position of "Housework," both within the *Free to Be* project and its potential social value, is complicated and marginalized by critiques, omissions, and ambivalence. To some extent this challenged territory resembles the terrain of the women's movement of the last several decades. Through commentary by Waldman, Chabon, and others, including Betty Friedan, Arlie Hochschild, and Barbara Ehrenreich, we can see that this contested domestic issue is often aggravated, as well as occasionally redeemed, by politics both personal and public.

After "Housework" was included on the 1972 album conceived by Marlo Thomas, it was excluded from the television special, first broadcast on March 11, 1974, and passed over in some of the subsequent print and audio editions,[2] limiting its potentially resonating influence in the *Free to Be* history. This status is further circumscribed by the reticence and relative silence on this decision by Thomas, producer Carole Hart, and other participants in the project. This group includes several *Ms.* magazine (1971–) contributors, notably cofounder Gloria Steinem, who wrote one of the prefatory notes in the original 1974 text of *Free to Be*. As an advocate of feminist issues, *Ms.* has published numerous articles about or including housework, but the publication's editorial stance is more attenuated than others, such as those often labeled as "radical feminists," including the Redstockings, who were active around the same time as the formation of *Ms.* and the development of *Free to Be*. Redstockings argued against what they regarded as patriarchal oppression, and their position on housework was forcefully and satirically expressed in Pat Mainardi's 1970 essay, "The Politics of Housework."[3] In contrast, many *Ms.* contributors, particularly those who worked on *Free to Be*, tended to align with the National Organization for Women (NOW), cofounded by Betty Friedan in 1966. Both the Redstockings and NOW used confrontational tactics, but a priority of pragmatism, rather than ideology, evidently guided NOW, *Ms.* magazine, and the creators of *Free to Be*. While this strategy oriented to the mainstream has ensured cultural longevity for the more moderate activists,[4] our focus here examines aspects of their agendas and decisions that appear to have been neglected in their centrist objectives.

Shortly after the *Free to Be* album was released in the fall of 1972, the *New York Times* published a review written by Deborah Jowitt in which she commented of "Housework": "The skit, unintentionally, I'm sure, demeans those who accept the clean-up chores without fuss, and makes those who take pleasure in such chores sound like real suckers."[5] As well, notes Lori Rotskoff, who edited the anthology *When We Were Free to Be* (2012) with Laura L. Lovett, *Ms.* magazine received letters charging the skit "denigrated domestic labor and the women who perform it, either in their own homes or for pay in other people's homes."[6] Rotskoff also states that based on such responses, Thomas and her team decided to leave "Housework" out of the TV special because they "would not insult people who performed domestic work."[7] The creators' decision to leave "Housework" out of the TV special was coupled with textual alterations in the book published to coincide with the broadcast. The lines spoken by Carol Channing that appear at the beginning of this chapter, "Your mommy hates housework, your daddy hates housework," were not published in print but did remain when the skit was available in audio form. This decision may be viewed as appropriately sensitive to the criticism they received,[8] and Rotskoff interprets the situation as an opportunity for Thomas and her team "to have their consciousness raised unexpectedly."[9] But, intentionally or not, Thomas and her team created a vacuum and unanswered questions.

The decision makers behind the exclusion were also part of the same group of feminists who a few years earlier marched to commemorate the fiftieth anniversary of the passage of the Nineteenth Amendment (which gave women the vote), clashing with New York City police as their ranks swelled along Fifth Avenue.[10] And some went on to lobby vigorously for the passage of the ill-fated equal rights amendment (ERA) through the early and mid-1970s.[11] The decision to exclude "Housework" from the TV special and revise the text may illustrate a sensitive response, but still leaves the impression that they were reluctant or unwilling to fully engage with their critics on the issue.

As editorial consultant, Letty Cottin Pogrebin, a writer at *Ms.*, provided Thomas and Hart with an overview of responses to the album. This indirect contact may have been logistically practical, but it contrasts with Thomas's more direct engagement with letters she received during the production of her TV show *That Girl* (1966–1971). Along with playing the main character, Thomas served as producer and deliberately inserted aspects of feminism as her political consciousness developed and her awareness expanded of her audience and their issues. In her memoir, *Growing Up Laughing* (2010), Thomas recalls receiving letters from teenaged girls who felt despair upon discovering they were pregnant and women who were in abusive marriages and looked to Thomas for help (305–6). As someone who was raised in an intact, supportive, and affluent family, Thomas recounts feeling a visceral jolt to be asked for her advice based on her visibility rather than experience: "That mail politicized me. [. . . I]t was the seed for much of what I'd put my energy toward in the years ahead" (306). By the time *That Girl* finished production in 1971, Thomas did feel a measure of her power and influence that she could apply soon after to the *Free to Be* project. But having assembled a group that responded to her vision of the project, the implicit hierarchy may have also created detachment and insulation, in contrast to the firsthand sensibility as she had experienced through the letters a few years earlier.

The exclusion of "Housework" appears to be a case where Thomas and her team chose not to fully advocate or engage meaningfully with critics, both in the media and from the audience, on the issue of sharing domestic responsibilities. Whether the exclusion was a noble but essentially unvoiced support of those who felt subjugated by domestic labor or a concern by *Free to Be*'s creators not to be attacked with further criticism as experienced by more ideological groups like the Redstockings,[12] the net effect was to render mute, delay, or create a vacuum on a substantive discussion of sharing domestic responsibilities. By keeping "Housework" out of the TV special, *Free to Be*'s creators seemed to suggest that hewing closer to the status quo was essentially more palatable than trying to interrogate established conventions.

This apparent effect, however, demands further examination. The overall concept of the album was "to expand children's personal horizons [and . . .] challenge stereotypes," as well as to learn about "cooperation and friendship, and about mutual respect and personal dignity" (Pogrebin, in Thomas, *Free to Be* 1974, 12–13), and excluding "Housework" from the TV broadcast meant those objectives were undermined and the segment rendered a kind of invisible presence. As well, Carole Hart emphatically notes that "Housework" was specifically intended to target and satirize TV commercials, challenging their stereotypical and demeaning presentation of women. But by the time of the TV special two years later, they realized that the piece might also be seen, as Hart noted, "as denigrating to housework itself. So, we let it go."[13] As an experienced record and TV producer, Hart's perspective comes from determining whether material is best suited in an audio, visual, or combined format. But the text, with alterations, appears in the book accompanied with illustrations, similar to cartoon panels, depicting a woman tackling housework while a man reads a newspaper in an armchair and two children watch TV, both groups seemingly oblivious to the woman working. Two more frames follow which present the woman cleaning and becoming progressively exhausted. This tableau is followed by images of the man and children undertaking tasks around the house along with the woman. This visual corollary of the text of "Housework" presented essentially a storyboard, potentially useful for a TV broadcast. But this rendering went no further and neither the illustration nor the text, altered or original, appear in the most recent print edition published in 2008, suggesting that the decision to exclude "Housework" from the 1974 TV special carried enough weight to influence the content of subsequent print editions.

But other contested segments were staunchly defended. Thomas fondly remembers supporting "William's Doll" against fears of homophobia expressed by TV network executives before the program aired and then later feeling pride that the song, along with "It's All Right to Cry," written by Carol Hall and sung by Rosey Grier, a former professional football player, came to be embraced by gay men, particularly when they were young boys and who felt otherwise isolated in their closeted identity (Rotskoff and Lovett, *When We Were Free to Be* 13). This example of Thomas's active championing suggests a viable template on how to promote and validate specific segments and how to keep salient issues visible so that any possible dialogue is both initiated and encouraged to progress. Although this template was most likely developed on an *ad hoc* basis and Thomas's defense of "William's Doll" had to be formulated early, long before the TV special aired, it represents a set of structural guidelines that were available to be applied to "Housework." If the effect of Jowitt's review, published at the end of 1972, could be discernible to the *Free to Be* creators by early or mid-1973 when they were developing the TV special and book, an articulate and articulated defense of "Housework" could have been developed not that much later than a defense of "William's Doll."

In many ways, *Free to Be* is undeniably an artifact of a particular period and its unanticipated ubiquity today is enabled by YouTube and other by-products of advancements in digital technology that were unknown and unknowable in the 1970s. Prior to the twenty-first century, the material was consumed through CDs and DVDs, which had replaced the original vinyl recordings commercially available and 16 mm film of the TV special that was distributed to many schools. Although the unlimited access available today suggests that any orphaning of "Housework" in the past can be reclaimed, its limited availability through the first several decades essentially undermines any potential legacy. While some who are now middle-aged parents may remember hearing Carol Channing, many who are familiar with *Free to Be* through the 16 mm film or DVD have no awareness of the skit, or view it negatively, or do not view *Free to Be* as expressing any position on sharing housework, or its other objective of fostering media literacy.[14] As well, for many, the longevity of *Free to Be* faces resistance by those who relegate it as a relic of another time—Chabon recalls "William's Doll" as "a segment in that echt-seventies, ungrammatically titled [. . .] *Free to Be You and Me* [*sic*]" (16)—and for those who subscribe to progressivism, it is a cultural artifact to be left behind to tackle other issues.

Both Waldman and Chabon believe that they may be among the few fans who absorbed and actively practice *Free to Be*'s liberal philosophy. Both, especially Waldman, regard "Housework," which she writes that she remembers listening to numerous times along with other songs on the album, as a helpful guide for beleaguered parents seeking domestic sanity and even pleasure. While Chabon is less specific about "Housework" than Waldman, he too remembers listening to the record and recounts his developing consciousness, particularly in adolescence, of doing chores around the house. He was also charged with looking after his younger brother and regularly cooking dinner for the two of them while his mother, recently divorced and a newly minted lawyer, established her career far from home (139). Becoming accustomed to performing domestic tasks routinely from an early age ensured that Chabon transferred his sense of responsibility into adulthood with apparent ease, prompting Waldman to recall: "In the early days of our relationship, he used to say he was the only husband in the world who had to pick up his *wife's* socks" (43, original emphasis). But even if in sharing housework Waldman and Chabon regard themselves as somewhat unusual among their peers, they are nevertheless identifiable and articulate proxies growing up in the *Free to Be* generation.

"Housework" exhorts sharing chores—"Make sure you do it together!"
(Thomas, *Free to Be* 50, 46),[15] but Channing and Harnick do acknowledge it
is unpleasant—"Remember, nobody smiles doing housework" (36).[16] Although Deborah Jowitt criticized the characterization of drudgery, it is a
defining characteristic entrenched long before *Free to Be* was conceived. In
The Feminine Mystique (1963), Friedan summarizes surveys utilized by postwar manufacturers: Housekeeping "is not only endless, it is a task for which
society hires the lowliest, least-trained, most trod-upon individuals and
groups. . . . Anyone with a strong back (and a small enough brain) can do
these menial chores" (309). For Friedan, housework represents a modern
suburban trap that too many women expand to fill excessive time, wasting
their intellect and the college education they acquired (or were beginning to
acquire) and then relinquished upon marriage (122). For many readers, Friedan unleashed a rallying cry to throw off the shackles of housework, exit the
suburbs, and pursue a career in the city. As she recounts her disdain for
waxing floors and provoking suspicion and judgment from her neighbors
when she calls a taxi for her children instead of participating in the carpool,
Friedan would seem to condemn both the drudgery and the social obligation
of housework.

While this interpretation of Friedan's text effectively galvanized many
women to abandon their suffocating suburban circumstances and pursue formerly quashed ambitions, a deeper, and perhaps ahistorical, reading of *The
Feminine Mystique* reveals a more nuanced perspective of housework. In
extending the image of housework as a trap, Friedan encourages us to examine it as a metaphor that women have entered largely willingly, as enthusiastically as reciting their wedding vows and perhaps as naively.

In interviewing college undergraduates in the late 1950s, Friedan is struck
by their fixation on marriage that precludes career ambitions, personal autonomy, and, essentially, an identity beyond being their husband's wife or their
children's mother (125–27). Their "fear to face this terrifying blank which
makes them unable to see themselves after [the age] of twenty-one" (126),
compounded by a kind of industrial marketing complex "designed to sell
washing machines, cake mixes, deodorants, detergents, rejuvenating face
creams, hair tints" (126), produces a tendency towards self-infantilization
and self-abnegation across at least one generation of young women across the
United States and much of the Western world. The result, on a large scale,
were women who regarded themselves capable and worthy only of being "a
server of food and a putter-on of pants and a bedmaker, somebody who can
be called on when you want something" (64). In giving this condition a
name, the feminine mystique, Friedan essentially provided a key for many
women to search and define their own identities.

To that end, Friedan argues that "the unknown heart of woman's problem
in America for a long time [has been the] lack of a private image" (131).

While we can view her comments as specifically historical and therefore regard them as detached from our own era, the development of her argument provides an enduring relevance: "Public images that defy reason and have very little to do with women themselves have had the power to shape too much of their lives. These images would not have such power, if women were not suffering a crisis of identity" (131). Friedan's objective to redress this crisis through *The Feminine Mystique* can be seen as a model for Thomas's vision for *Free to Be*, for children to "invent their own futures without limitation," as Pogrebin wrote in the 1974 edition (12). While Thomas's idealistic aspirations have been widely applauded, this utopianism appears to be not so much worth celebrating than demanding continued scrutiny and dialogue when we recognize that she was initially motivated to develop the project because she regarded the books available for children in 1972 to be outdated and reinforcing gender stereotypes. In Thomas's assessment, the next generation of children were on their way to becoming encoded with the same sexist language and constricting social norms that Friedan had rebuked a decade earlier. But this time, Thomas implicitly argued, children needed to be liberated from a mystique that they had been born into, were being raised in and, because of their young age and inexperience, had no agency to throw off its restrictions as their mothers might have done a decade earlier.

"Housework" espouses the importance of sharing housework: "If you want all the days of your lives / To seem sunny as summer weather, / Make sure, when there's housework to do, / That you do it together!" (*Free to Be* 52–55; 48–51). But along with these closing lines, we can see an affinity with Friedan's critiques of the advertising industry: "Now, most of the time / it's a lady we see who's doing the housework on TV. [. . . A]nd she's doing her best / to make us think / that *her* soap / or detergent / or cleanser / or powder / [. . .] is the best kind of soap / (or detergent / or cleanser / [. . .] bleach) / that there is in the whole wide world!" (25–63; 21–59). This mocking of exaggerated marketing claims evokes Friedan's perspective that housewives were being encouraged to expand their housework time to fill out their entire day: "Somehow, somewhere, someone must have figured out that women will buy more things if they are kept in the underused, nameless-yearning, energy-to-get-rid-of state of being housewives" (299). This comment appears early in the chapter titled "The Sexual Sell," in which Friedan writes as a kind of journey into discovering the insidiously manipulative tactics routinely practiced by marketers. Guided by "a man who is paid approximately a million dollars a year for his professional services in manipulating the emotions of American women to serve the needs of business" (300), Friedan concludes that properly manipulated, "American housewives can be given the sense of identity, purpose, creativity, the self-realization, even the sexual joy they lack—by the buying of things" (301).

Harnick's lyrics in "Housework" provide a blunt summation of the same critique pitched in language more appropriate to children: "[T]hat lady is smiling / because she's an actress. / And she's earning money / for learning those speeches / that mention those wonderful / soaps / and detergents / and cleansers" (*Free to Be* 79–86). Pogrebin remembers advising Thomas, "We need to challenge the sex-typing of both paid jobs and household chores" (Rotskoff and Lovett, *When We Were Free to Be* 42), suggesting the connection between the *Free to Be* philosophy and Harnick's composition. If Thomas, who was familiar with *The Feminine Mystique* long before undertaking *Free to Be*,[17] wanted to promote media literacy in children and encourage them to regard the practices of the business with a critical eye, Harnick's text would seem to satisfy that part of the brief.

As a listener to the record, Waldman implicitly agrees. With *Free to Be*, her mother was exposing her to a feminist education as early as possible and, in the guise of music and stories, as attractively as she knew how. Young Ayelet quickly warmed to the messaging: "We took Marlo Thomas's lessons very seriously" (42), not just singing "lustily" to the record, but her mother, inspired by "William's Doll," bought her younger brother a doll, and Ayelet, the budding feminist, remembers incorporating lyrics and references to the record into her everyday speech.

"Housework" occupied a key position, as Waldman notes, "to the delight of both of our mothers, we are in many ways living out Carol Channing and Marlo Thomas's dream" (43). This importance in Waldman's childhood recollections provides a foundation for her influence on how to think about sharing domestic responsibilities as well as dating and choosing her future partner.

> My mother taught me [. . .] that I needed to be careful to structure my life in order to accommodate [ambition]. One of the keys to create the life she wanted for me was to find a mate who would be a willing foot soldier in my battle for equality. I needed a husband who would value my professional identity as much as his own, who would assume half the household and child-care duties. Who would, if anything, subsume his ambitions to mine. I needed, in short, a man different from my father. (24)

Waldman's perspective reflects a generation of children raised by women influenced by Friedan but who did not always feel they could change their lives significantly. This passage economically encompasses the stages of female experience that concerned Friedan in *The Feminine Mystique*. From her own magazine writing and research, Friedan believed women before and shortly after World War II pursued their ambition without constraints, implying that to reach for lofty goals, such as flying a plane (88–89), were admirable pursuits. But for Waldman and her generation raised with a different consciousness, ambition had to be planned more strategically. Her language in the passage above draws heavily on military imagery, suggesting that to fulfill the hopes her mother has seeded in her, Waldman would have to confront adversaries that her mother recognized but could not resist because of her marriage constraints. For Waldman, and perhaps other young girls also told by their mothers to be ambitious and seek an equal partner, the possibility that "Housework" could be patronizing or "denigrating" was not apparent or, at least, not remembered.

So it would seem to be the case for the creators of *Free to Be*. Thomas, the eldest child of successful comedian Danny Thomas (1912–1991), grew up in Beverly Hills, California, one of the most affluent areas in the United States. Although she recounts much of her family life in her memoir, little is conveyed of domestic responsibilities beyond slight references to a beloved couple who are suggested to be servants (58–59) and an "ever-rotating nanny" (59). Only after Thomas married and became stepmother to five children, including four teenaged boys living in the same house, did she feel the burden of domestic responsibility and its implicitly inescapable sexism:

> "Where are my shoes?" Phil would constantly ask.
> What is it about men? They think we women have a radar attached to our uterus. And the thing that killed me was that I knew where they were. I knew where Phil's shoes were. I knew where *all* four boys' shoes were.
> How did this happen? Had my mother secretly planted a chip in me at birth that would activate when I said "I do"? I was beginning to understand why there hadn't been a female Shakespeare or Mozart. There wasn't room in their heads for symphonies and sonnets—their brains were cluttered with where everyone's shoes were. (314)

Her marriage and this recognition occurred many years after she initiated *Free to Be*, and long after she and her team excluded "Housework" from the TV special. If she reflected on Harnick's text and perhaps a certain measure of irony in her circumstances, she does not express such thoughts in her memoir.

In the summer of 1972, as the content for the *Free to Be* album was taking shape, Letty Cottin Pogrebin decided to use her three young children as "canaries in the mine, our first focus group [. . .] listening to the tapes of the songs and stories that Marlo and Carole had commissioned" (Rotskoff and Lovett, *When We Were Free to Be* 43). Pogrebin cites specific segments that compel her children to laugh, cry, and dance, adding, "The record was a roaring success from the start, partly due to the wonderful writing by prominent creative talents and partly due to the performers who spoke or sang their lines in the recording studio" (43). Soon after, a listening party was organized at the offices of *Ms.* Carole Hart recalls, "Everyone on the staff and lots of guests who'd been involved with the process were there. I was so nervous that I couldn't stay in the room, so I sat outside in the hallway with the door slightly open. There was applause after the title song and lots of laughter [. . .] and both continued throughout, [. . .] with major cheers at the end" (Rotskoff and Lovett, *When We Were Free to Be* 38). Among these first listeners were some of the most discerning critics of gender inequity and class bias, and if anyone registered concern that "Housework" denigrated those who undertake domestic labor, such a view was not documented.

Were Thomas, Pogrebin, Hart, *Ms.* staffers and their guests oblivious to the possibility that "Housework" was "denigrating" housework?

In tracing the genesis and development of *Free to Be* relevant to "Housework," I am compelled to speculate that the creators subconsciously put this skit, in the term attributed to Jacques Derrida, under erasure. As Gayatri Chakravorty Spivak notes in the translator's preface to Derrida's *Of Grammatology* (1976, 1997), the term comes from her translation of Derrida's expression "sous rature," which Spivak explains, "is to write a word, cross it out, and then print both word and deletion. (Since the word is inaccurate, it is crossed out. Since it is necessary, it remains legible)" (xiv). For listeners, readers, and TV viewers of any text, an awareness of any segment of the text written, crossed out, but still visible is a relatively infrequent experience, and when we see or are made conscious of a revision retained in the text, we are likely to regard it as a typographical error or a kind of experimental or nonstandard strategy. In the main, we expect the text to be polished so that any editorial decisions regarding deletions are made invisible and have no vestigial effect on the interpretation. If we consider the existence of deletions, we assume they have been resolved before we have an opportunity to respond to the text. In cases of revised editions, we have been implicitly trained by the practice and efforts of the music, publishing, and television industries to regard each version as a replacement that negates the previous version. Even while we may be aware of a predecessor, we are encouraged to consign it to oblivion and look upon the successor as the only credible version upon which to formulate a response.

In leaving out "Housework" from the 1974 TV special, we have the appearance of a form of erasure, particularly when we consider the possible effects of the negative comments from Jowitt's review and the letters received by *Ms.* But, as with Spivak's definition, the responses undermine its status in the *Free to Be* agenda as potentially inaccurate or inappropriate. Its presence in the 1974 text renders it legible and valid, but whether it was validated as necessary, particularly given the textual changes, is unclear. Although not all content from the album was included in the TV special, we can construct a specific perspective for "Housework" being subjected to a standard different than other segments, as discussed earlier with "William's Doll."

Similarly to "William's Doll," "Parents Are People" met resistance from network representatives, particularly when they viewed the visual accompaniment to the song. The male portion of the song had already been recorded by Harry Belafonte, a musician of Caribbean descent who had had mainstream success since the early 1950s and had also been a political activist for a similar length of time. Part of the visuals for the song included Thomas and Belafonte pushing baby carriages through a city intersection, and as Carole Hart remembers the network response, "they were very disturbed by Marlo and Harry [. . .] because they might look like a married couple and the network executives said, 'We'll lose the South,'"[18] implying that TV audiences in the U.S. South would refuse to watch or worse, complain to sponsors and advertisers of the show and possibly others, boycotting or undermining the commercial position of the advertisers and network. Although the lyrics focused on the wide spectrum of professions and roles parents undertake, network uneasiness fixated on the possibility of misinterpretation. To some extent, we may regard that fear as a form of overinscription, or the opposite of erasure. On a visual level, we can see that the network anticipated that, in the eyes of some in their audience, the convention of same-race marriage could be seen to be violated, or to use another word, "denigrated," even when no such intention existed, and that they would be held accountable. As she writes in her memoir, Thomas not only insisted all aspects remain unaltered by the network, she was irritated by their position of pandering to racist proclivities (250–51). The broadcast aired with both "William's Doll" and "Parents Are People" intact as the *Free to Be* creators intended.

Carole Hart recalls that there was some backlash of the kind the network predicted,[19] but commercial worries were assuaged by the awards the show garnered: an Emmy and the prestigious Peabody.[20] For the segments that had been included in the TV special, the conferring of those honors would translate into an explicit critical seal of approval, one that did not fully include "Housework." Rotskoff and Lovett draw a clear line from reviews such as Jowitt's and letters that criticized "Housework" for denigrating domestic workers to the absence of the skit in the TV special. Since their book, *When We Were Free to Be*, includes essays from several key participants in the project, including Thomas, Steinem, Hart, and Pogrebin, we may assume their assessment of the fate of "Housework" is essentially validated.

To mark the publication of *When We Were Free to Be*, as well as the fortieth anniversary of the record's release, Carole Hart participated in several public appearances and interviews. To John Schaefer of WNYC's *Soundcheck*, she singled out "Housework" as a mistake, saying, "I think, in retrospect, we probably wouldn't have done it." Hart's hesitation in this statement is audibly discernible in the archived version of the interview, in contrast to her equally audible enthusiasm elsewhere in the interview,[21] suggesting regret, discomfort, or both. To assess the tempting interpretation that her voice also betrays regret over including "Housework" on the album or excluding it from the TV show, we must also consider other aspects of the skit in the *Free to Be* media.

Hart's comment to Schaefer in late 2012 of a revisionist view suggests that if she and Thomas could have anticipated the negative response to "Housework," they would not have included it on the 1972 album, but since the vinyl records had been pressed, they could not correct the issue retroactively. Their only option would seem to be not to include it in the TV special and hope that those who had criticized its inclusion would be mollified and those who did not have a strong opinion would not notice or care. Such a conjecture is in contrast to Thomas's statement regarding her team's objective in creating the TV special: "Yes, the visuals made our controversial material that much stronger and possibly more inflammatory. But we were not going to back down. And we didn't. And to its credit, ABC aired our complete version of *Free to Be . . . You and Me*—in prime time. And guess what. The sky did not fall down" (Rotskoff and Lovett, *When We Were Free to Be* 18). In this comment, Thomas does not specify segments that constituted the "controversial material," and the implication is that she and her team defied any and all critics and detractors, despite the impression engendered by Carole Hart's comment.

Ostensibly, their intent was not to specifically put "Housework" under erasure, but their decisions did make the skit and, by extension, the issue of sharing domestic responsibilities, as well as fostering media literacy, less visible. In the decades since *Free to Be* became a familiar cultural artifact for young children, "Housework" became among the less frequently cited segments by nostalgic commenters.[22] Many profess to have "memorized every word," although whether the reference is to the album or the book, or both, is unclear. But few, possibly none, including Waldman (who does not make reference to the TV special), have noticed the textual alteration of "Housework." Perhaps this status was also the culmination of other factors; the more popular and more visible segments addressed gender stereotypes, aspirations, and emotions. As the *Free to Be* creators have emphasized over the decades, children should be encouraged to explore possibilities; housework, in contrast, emphasizes responsibilities. And while "Housework" sought to position household responsibilities as a gender-neutral activity, as well as a necessary undertaking, the concept may have been both too abstract for young children and, because of the absence of discourse in the mainstream, too mundane for adults.

Moreover, the objective of encouraging children to become media critics, specifically to question television commercials at the same time as the *Free to Be* project was being developed as a television program on a network that depended on the very commercials the skit suggested questioning would seem to be an inescapable irony if it had been part of the television broadcast.

Perhaps this aspect is what Carole Hart is referring to when she states that "Housework" would have been a problem for the TV special.

Jowitt's review appeared at the end of 1972, and we can assume that during 1973, as Thomas and her team were working on the TV special and book, perhaps as *Ms.* was receiving letters regarding the album, came the decision to exclude "Housework." In Carole Hart's view, however, as noted earlier, the issue was less about exclusion and more about logistics. As well, including "Housework" in the book suggests at least a measure of support regardless of the negative criticism. On the album, "Housework" is nearly three minutes long, the length of a typical pop song on the radio in the same era, and in the book, it is given six out of 143 pages in the whole book, along with illustrations. In "Beyond the Fun and Song" from the anthology edited by Rotskoff and Lovett, Francine Klagsbrun, who edited the 1974 text, explicitly defends "Housework":

> Harnick [. . .] wanted to eliminate the imbalance [of the lot of too many wives who bore all of the household burdens alone] and prevent the bitterness by letting children know that as men and women, they would need to share the burdens. Some people criticized "Housework" back in the 1970s, arguing that by bashing housework it denigrated paid domestic workers, most of them women. But that missed the point. Harnick echoed [. . .] dozens of women [writers] who had come to realize that they had been boxed into roles they had not chosen and wanted to discard. (64)

Klagsbrun does not hesitate in articulating the reality of housework for children in the future when she states that "as men and women, they would need to share the burdens." And her reflection on *Ms.* writers, specifically Jane O'Reilly and Judy Syfers,[23] "who had come to realize that they had been boxed into roles they had not chosen and wanted to discard" recalls Friedan's conception of many women's experience documented in *The Feminine Mystique.* Her assertion that "by bashing housework it denigrated paid domestic workers missed the point" also provides some helpful points: the accusation of denigration was communicated widely enough to those with key roles that it is a remembered response to "Housework" after several decades. If such a response had been anticipated, it was met with disappointment or not fully understood by both the creators and the audience. Whether there was more than one letter with such a response, the frequency of "denigration" as the problematic assessment suggests the possibility that a single letter could have such an effect or that the word was cited often enough for conflation and concern. Perhaps under Klagsbrun's editorship, the appearance of "Housework," without the lines expressing a universal hatred of it, represents a kind of compromise, as it would seem the creators were giving readers ample opportunity to read the text and absorb its message as commensurate to other content in the book. The chief difference between the reading experience and listening to the album is hearing Carol Channing's voice.

Channing's voice, with its distinctly husky quality, her "three-pack-a-day rasp," as Waldman describes it (42), contrasts with the mellifluous timbres typically associated with voices featured in commercials. At the time *Free to Be* was recorded in 1972, Channing had been a successful and well-established Broadway performer, best known for launching the title role in the long-running production of *Hello, Dolly!* (1964). Her popularity and name recognition were comparable to many other performers on the *Free to Be* record. Channing's participation is also representative of the slightly subversive quality both Thomas and Hart favored for the project. Thomas was determined that *Free to Be* "couldn't be preachy. It would have to be entertaining and have some razzmatazz [. . .] these kids had rock concerts blaring from the TVs in their living rooms. And it would have to make the kids laugh. That's the only way they'd get it—and *remember* it" (*Growing Up Laughing* 247).[24]

But while Channing would seem to fulfill Thomas's objective, the effect, as with Jowitt's review, would seem to have been other than its intention. Despite her own affection for the skit, Waldman views the aim of Channing's "Housework," to share the chores among all family members, fell far short of its goal, seemingly right from the start. "[T]he mothers who bought us the *Free to Be* albums never really expected that their husbands would take on half the childcare and household responsibilities. But we, as their daughters, listened to the record and took for granted that our husbands would" (46). The implication of the generational divide is that the mothers can bequeath the promise of a brighter future for their daughters in the package of *Free to Be*, and Waldman assumes that in receiving the gift from their mothers, the daughters fully incorporated it into their lives and their domestic expectations. But Waldman reflects upon and feels compelled to advocate for many of her peers—virtually the same daughters who, like her, listened to the record and formulated their expectations—but are now "surprised and, frankly, pissed off to find themselves, like their mothers before them, shouldering the bulk of the domestic burden" (46). This disgruntled status is frequently discussed in mainstream and online media,[25] but where did this dissatisfaction come from?

To some extent, "Housework" is a departure from the core sensibility expressed in many other segments in the *Free to Be* media. As Rotskoff and Lovett note,

> From the first bright notes, [. . .] children entered an imaginary "land" that was freer and more equitable than the world they actually inhabited. This place was fantasy, of course. But it isn't that what many inspiring works of children's literature do? Invite children into a make-believe world where so much seems

possible? Where the narrative puts *them* at the center of the moral universe it constructs? (*When We Were Free to Be* 6)

But if children were being encouraged to critique media and question consumerist behavior on top of sharing housework, they were essentially being discouraged from entering an imaginary land that was freer and more equitable, as well as scrutinize the real world they already inhabited. Where "Housework" is concerned, the fantasy of some of the other segments was to be put aside for the tangible and not-always-exciting aspects of the kitchen and bathroom and whatever inescapable untidiness they saw or ignored every day. To make the issue even more tedious, these rooms are parts of the home that they would not likely think as central to their lives. Even when they were, such as helping to prepare a meal or taking a bath, the issue of cleaning up, particularly for the benefit of others, was not usually the compelling part of the narrative. If media literacy, especially media criticism, were seriously part of the *Free to Be* agenda, perhaps the bar had been set unrealistically high or expressed in a more complex way than a mainstream audience was really willing to accept and engage with. Although Carole Hart emphasized the importance of not talking down to children both during the development of *Free to Be* and in recent interviews, we must consider that "Housework" was not as positively conceived and accepted as other segments were.

With the status of "Housework" problematized, the issue and any substantive discussions have largely been marginalized or trivialized during the period that many women focused on or were pressured to pursue careers outside the home. As Waldman was memorizing much of *Free to Be*, her mother was actively hiring housecleaners even when finances were difficult (53). Waldman was well versed in the theory of doing housework as she watched her mother manage others who undertook housework. In *The Second Shift* (1989, 2012), Arlie Hochschild's observations of many couples suggest a similar bifurcation as well as an anxiety over sharing domestic responsibilities. Hochschild concludes that this anxiety essentially becomes folded into existing relationship issues and enlarges conflicts but often is not specifically identified. Of her research, Hochschild notes, "I came to realize that those husbands who helped very little at home were often indirectly just as deeply affected as their wives through the resentment their wives feel toward them and through their need to steel themselves against that resentment" (7–8). This circularity of resentment, Hochschild suggests, intensifies with each unverbalized sweep but remains visible only to the observer outside the relationship.

Like Friedan's observation of college undergraduates about three decades earlier, Hochschild notes a similar suppressed recognition among her female undergraduate students. Many told her they do not discuss sharing child care and housework with their boyfriends, even though they expressed interest in having children and working full time outside the home. "I don't believe these lively, inquiring eighteen- to twenty-two-year-old students haven't thought about the problem. I believe they are afraid of it. And since they think of it as a 'private' problem, each also feels alone" (xvii). It may be argued that Hochschild essentially takes up where *Free to Be* leaves off on the subject of housework, but as Hochschild's observations strongly suggest, her students convey no prior awareness of any discussions on housework, much less any memory of "Housework" from *Free to Be*. From Hochschild's perspective, the issue, and any attendant discussion, appears to have no personal, cultural, or family weight among her students.

This perspective also recalls Friedan's concern for women who lack a "private image" of themselves. Hochschild suggests that in the absence of a public discourse, women such as her undergraduate students are not sufficiently motivated to develop autonomous ideas on how to resolve these issues philosophically, and so view their futures with significant blank spots.

Hochschild began her research for *The Second Shift* in the late 1970s and updated the book for its 2012 reprint, so her arguments are drawn from observation in the periods, "at the height of the women's movement, [when] many [. . .] couples were earnestly and self-consciously struggling to modernize the ground rules of their marriages" (5), as well as the periods in which the core issues of the movement, including gender equity and reproductive rights, were contested and sometimes suppressed. If Hochschild's students meditate on their professional and domestic futures but feel, as Hochschild suspects, isolated in exploring how to achieve their goals with the person who may be sharing their lives, what holds them back? What has engendered the vacuum in the discourse? Would a cultural discussion initiated by Thomas and her team have facilitated broader and deeper thinking on housework?

Waldman recalls that although she treasures her husband's "domestic prowess" (45), at the beginning of her relationship, Chabon suggested that they "avoid any discord about who was going to do the really gross jobs by hiring a cleaning service" (54), and they continue to employ various domestic workers. For many, this option is the simple solution to any anxiety about sharing household responsibilities, and some point out that hiring a housecleaner is significantly less expensive than couples therapy or the legal (and other) costs of a divorce. While such an argument is irrefutable, the fact that a cleaning lady is cheaper than either a therapist or a lawyer points to entrenched socioeconomic and gender values. Far worse than any denigration that "Housework" may have engendered is the systemic classism routinely expressed through low pay and a reinforcement of hierarchy. Waldman herself notes, "[W]hile I am grateful to them beyond measure, I am never anything but uncomfortable with the idea of being a lady with, essentially, a maid" (54). Even when one's politics are firmly egalitarian, our cultural memory, propagated by fiction, movies, and TV, all too easily can summon up images of servants submissively taking orders and disappearing after the house is free of dust and clutter, well before the dinner guests arrive.

The reverse perspective of this class privilege, even when it is temporary, is infrequently documented, but in *Nickel and Dimed* (2001), Barbara Ehrenreich chronicles her experience of working as a housecleaner. Although she undertook the assignments as part of a journalistic assignment for *Harper's* that led to the book, Ehrenreich's firsthand view immediately gave her a thorough, if protected, understanding of the routine challenges many housecleaners endure. These challenges include prolonged inhalation of chemicals from cleaning products in rooms with improper ventilation, chronic physical pain and unattended injuries, little or no compensation for time missed to address injuries, inadequate breaks, threats of dismissal or wage penalties from clients or agencies, among other adversities. The image of the trap Friedan articulated, the unpleasantness of housework Channing enunciated, and the Sisyphean sensibility Waldman references are, as Ehrenreich vividly communicates, routine and exacerbated in the daily life of the domestic worker.

But if Ehrenreich complicates the straightforward argument for hiring housecleaners, her position is not to stop the practice, but rather, for all of us, to gain a better understanding of its implications. Perhaps to some extent, we can regard Ehrenreich as taking up the issue of housework that *Free to Be*'s creators retreated from. But while Ehrenreich's readership undoubtedly includes many who grew up listening to *Free to Be*, any connection between Channing's encouragement to share housework and Ehrenreich's reporting of the typically terrible working conditions for housecleaners is too diffuse to identify.

This diffusion is part of Hochschild's consideration in *The Second Shift*. Hochschild extensively explores the experience of women feeling trapped between generational shifts and gender expectations as she identifies couples separately and together as traditional, transitional, and egalitarian, according to their conception of gender ideology (15). She describes a "typical" transitional man as "all for his wife working, but expects her to do the lion's share at home too" (15), a corollary of the husbands of the mothers Waldman describes (46). Hochschild also notes that this category was the largest among her interview subjects. These interviews took place largely from 1975 to 1980, coinciding with the time Waldman dates her assessment of *Free to Be*'s reception by her peer group and their parents. But even if some or most of those fathers could fit Hochschild's definition of "transitional," many could also fall into Hochschild's category of "traditional," which she describes as a man who bases his identity on work and wants more power than his wife (15).

Hochschild also suggests that the frustration experienced by many women arises not just because they were not motivated by a manifesto, as many women regarded *The Feminine Mystique*, but that the women did not always stride confidently on the trail that the women's movement was blazing. Along with her definition of a "transitional" man is her definition of a "transitional" woman: she "wants to identify *both* with the care of the home and with helping her husband earn money, but wants her husband to focus on earning a living" (15). Although many couples Hochschild interviewed embodied contradictions and variations of these types, clearly several decades after Friedan's text was published and other influences of the women's movement followed, long-standing conventions were still intact and largely dominant. In a project such as *Free to Be*, we may regard it as a valiant attempt, scant as it may be, to address at least a small portion of these entrenched issues.

But, as the name suggests, the transitional group signaled the possibilities of change for the next generation. Clearly, Waldman suggests that she and her peers, and perhaps even their mothers, were not just sufficiently aware of this possibility but expected their future partners to be equally aware and expectant of progressive behavior in their adulthood. Hochschild notes, "The 'pure' egalitarian [woman] wants to identify with the same spheres as her husband does, and to have an equal amount of power in the marriage" (15). This description matches the message Waldman remembers receiving in her upbringing and apparently the state of her marriage to Chabon. By her account, such reality eludes many women she knows. So, despite everyone's awareness of what could be and should be, Waldman feels compelled to advocate "for the women who are surprised and, frankly, pissed off to find themselves, like their mothers before them, shouldering the bulk of the domestic burden" (46). According to Hochschild's categories, these women are egalitarian, at least philosophically, but are in domestic relationships where their partners would seem to be transitional and perhaps with latent traditional tendencies. While we cannot blame *Free to Be* for this asymmetry, these perspectives from Hochschild shed some light on the difficulties of resolving the idea of sharing housework both within individual households and as a philosophical concept.

As a disciplined student of her mother's lessons, Waldman reaches her expected standard of success after marrying Chabon who, without prompting, elects to be a stay-at-home father while she returns to work as a public defender after the birth of their first child. In her account, Waldman's narrative is in contrast with her mother's experience, characterized by the parent who sacrifices her own happiness because she is part of what we might consider an unenlightened generation, but endures so that the child can succeed and redeem that parent's suffering. Waldman is conscious of being designated to fulfill not only her mother's hopes but also of benefiting from the domestic grooming of her husband by her mother-in-law as she asserts, "It's Michael, and the mother who trained him, who are the engineers of our happiness" (57). The smugness of her statement also gestures to the difficulty of such achievement. Waldman positions her mother as Friedan's acolyte, implicitly a reminder for herself of those women she describes as presently "pissed off" as they live out their mothers' housework-filled lives (46). Through her portrayal, Waldman prompts such women to consider indoctrinating their children, whether through *Free to Be* or other relevant cultural instruments, as she and her husband were guided in their respective childhoods, to demand parity with their partners in parenthood. Embedded in this idea is the promise that the women who are presently pissed off can, in the future, experience satisfaction in their children's progressive families and can be as delighted as the mothers of Waldman and Chabon are now.

But what relevant cultural instruments other than *Free to Be* would encourage children to be entertained into the idea of sharing housework (and possibly developing media literacy) that would also satisfy their parents? One may argue that the vacuum of discourse regarding housework can be and has been assumed by *Sesame Street* (1969–), another pioneer of children's media.[26] While the long-running TV series has broadcast encouraging messages about all family members participating in housework, their demographic of preschool-aged children tends to be younger than the school-aged children who have been (and in many cases still comprise) the audience for *Free to Be*. Ideally, *Sesame Street* can function as a prelude to a child's engagement with *Free to Be*, but with the absence of "Housework" on the DVD and few to no other options to fill the gap after *Sesame Street*, one thread has been dropped and not really picked up again.

In her research at the *Ms.* archives, Lori Rotskoff remembers one particular letter that criticized "Housework." Reviewing her notes, she recalls this letter being generally positive, but the letter writer also considers "Housework" through the perspective of her housekeeper and asks *Ms.*: "Can't we do better?" In many ways, her question is both rhetorical and, then as now, expectant of an answer. As noted earlier, Rotskoff suggests the criticism of "Housework" provided an unexpected consciousness-raising opportunity for the creators of *Free to Be*. But if Thomas has revised her views, she has not commented publicly or visibly and has yet to stand behind "Housework" in a way similar to her advocacy of "William's Doll" or "Parents Are People." This reticence is similarly true of other participants on the project, with the possible exception of Gloria Steinem. Although she has never commented specifically on "Housework," Steinem has written and spoken about domestic labor issues on numerous occasions. Her advocacy of domestic workers' rights has no discernible connection to "Housework" or any negative responses to it, but her activism is visible, consistent, and widely acclaimed.[27] However, although her work often commands widespread attention among feminists and sometimes from a mainstream audience, it rarely penetrates children's media. Her sensibilities may influence readers and expand her audience when they become familiar with her public profile and writing, likely when they are adults, or teenagers at the earliest. If children are conscious of her and, in the unlikely instance, of her advocacy of domestic workers, it is an unrealistic hope to apply such awareness to the idea that they are part of the issue of sharing domestic responsibilities. This gap would seem to be ideally filled with Carol Channing's "Housework," or an updated version with a performer who would entertain a new generation as Marlo Thomas once envisioned in the early 1970s.

NOTES

1. "Housework" is written by Sheldon Harnick (b. 1924), best known as the lyricist of *Fiddler on the Roof* (1964); he also wrote the lyrics to "William's Doll," another featured segment on *Free to Be . . . You and Me*.

2. *Free to Be . . . You and Me* was published as a book in 1974 (and reprinted in 2008) by Running Press Book Publishers, Philadelphia; the record, originally released on Bell Records, was reissued as a compact disc by Arista Records beginning in 1983.

3. "The Politics of Housework" was published in *Sisterhood Is Powerful* (1970), edited by Robin Morgan, and the essay is available online at http://www.uic.edu/orgs/cwluherstory/CWLUArchive/polhousework.html.

4. In "How Do You Spell Ms.: An Oral History of 'Ms.' Magazine" by Abigail Pogrebin, Susan Brownmiller comments, "I'll say that for me, *Ms.* never had anything that was a revelation. We radical feminists, we were raising new issues first, and then they would get to *Ms.* eventually, but not initially."

5. Deborah Jowitt, "Free to Be . . . You and Me."

6. Interview with Anna Maria Tremonti, *The Current*, CBC Radio, 4 Dec. 2012.

7. Curiously, the next song on the album, "Helping," written by Shel Silverstein and sung by Tom Smothers, was renamed "Agatha Fry" on the DVD. "Agatha Fry" is the name of the first character identified in the song and the title appears on the DVD reissue of 2001. In the 2008 print edition, the song reverts back to its original name, "Helping."

8. In "How Do You Spell Ms." some of the magazine's cofounders discuss some of the business decisions in developing *Ms.* as an ongoing monthly. Brenda Feigen, who cofounded the Women's Action Alliance with Steinem, recalls the decision to release Betty Harris, *Ms.*'s first publisher: "It was extremely important to Gloria and Pat [Carbine, *Ms.*'s second publisher] that they resolve that internal dispute and not take the whole magazine down with it." After giving Harris all the income from the first issue, Carbine explains, "It was a way to let her know that feminists don't try to destroy each other." Although unconnected to the decision to exclude "Housework" from the TV special of *Free to Be*, this episode suggests the sensibility engendered by *Ms.* and presumably shared by Thomas and her team.

9. This situation is in significant contrast to "William's Doll," coincidentally also written by Sheldon Harnick. As Thomas writes in *When We Were Free to Be*, ABC tried to convince her to exclude the song and its visual accompaniment from the TV special. "You're going to turn boys into little sissies," Thomas recalls being told by a TV executive (18). As Carole Hart discusses the issue in a 2012 radio interview (*Cat Radio Café*), Thomas insisted on keeping "William's Doll," threatening to take the program to another network. ABC acquiesced and the broadcast was aired according to Thomas's wishes.

10. On August 20, 1970, members of NOW, including Betty Friedan and Gloria Steinem, marched down Fifth Avenue in New York City to commemorate the fiftieth anniversary of the passage of the Nineteenth Amendment to the U.S. Constitution, which guaranteed women the right to vote. Police attempted to keep the marchers to the sidewalk, but the estimated fifty

thousand participants made crowd control impossible. See Breasted, "Women on the March: 'We're a Movement Now!'" and Bazelon, "The Mother of Feminism."

11. Although the ERA was not passed, the efforts of many of its supporters served to illustrate its high priority and its potential to raise the national consciousness even if it could not be formally legislated. Because of its high-profile supporters, including Thomas, Steinem, and actor Alan Alda (who also participated in the *Free to Be* project), the ERA's liminal status still had a visibility and therefore a viability throughout most of the 1970s.

12. In "Death of a Revolutionary," Susan Faludi chronicles the life of Shulamith Firestone and the struggles she and many other "radical" feminists experienced in the late 1960s and later. Faludi discusses their challenges as both against external patriarchal conventions and amongst themselves as they attempted to define their principles and political positions. After Firestone's memorial, Faludi notes: "It was hard to say which moment the mourners were there to mark: the passing of Firestone or that of a whole generation of feminists who had been unable to thrive in the world they had done so much to create."

13. Interview with author, 9 May 2013; requested revision, 15 July 2013.

14. This assessment comes from an overview of comment boards discussing *Free to Be . . . You and Me*. A representative example would be the comments that follow "Free to Be" by Dan Kois, Slate.com, 22 Oct. 2012.

15. On the audio version, this line is spoken after "Your mommy hates housework, / Your daddy hates housework, / I hate housework, / And when you grow up, so will you," and so appears earlier in the text in the altered print edition.

16. On the audio version, this line is spoken just before "Your mommy hates housework" and remains in the 1974 print edition.

17. In *Growing Up Laughing*, Thomas recounts asking Edgar Scherick, head of programming for ABC, to read *The Feminine Mystique* as her TV show *That Girl* was being developed in the mid-1960s: "He called me after he finished the book and said, 'Is this going to happen to my wife? [. . .] Everybody thinks I'm crazy, but I'm going to go with you on this'" (305).

18. Carole Hart, interview by Janet Coleman, *Cat Radio Café*; Hart, interview by John Schaefer, *Soundcheck*.

19. Hart, *Soundcheck*.

20. First presented in 1941, the George Foster Peabody award recognizes distinguished achievement in electronic media, selected by a panel of academics, TV critics, and industry practitioners at the University of Georgia. Named for the financier and major university benefactor, the Peabody was awarded to *Free to Be . . . You and Me* in 1974 along with WGBH-TV's science program *Nova* and several other TV and radio documentaries (http://peabody awards.com/).

21. Hart, *Soundcheck*.

22. Frequently cited segments, including "William's Doll," "Atalanta" (by Betty Miles), and "Ladies First" (by Shel Silverstein, adapted by Mary Rodgers) appear on each format and have been included in each reissue.

23. Jane O'Reilly wrote "The Housewife's Moment of Truth," which was published in the *Ms.* preview edition of *New York* magazine, and Judy Syfers wrote "I Want a Wife," available online at http://www.columbia.edu/~sss31/rainbow/wife.html.

24. Channing, similarly to Thomas, has also not publicly discussed her work on *Free to Be*. She did not mention any aspect of her participation in her memoir *Just Lucky I Guess* or in the documentary *Carol Channing: Larger Than Life*, but we can assume any slight regarding "Housework" being excluded from the TV special is a smaller disappointment in comparison to Channing being passed over for the role of Dolly Levi in the film version of *Hello, Dolly!* in favor of Barbra Streisand. In both her memoir and documentary, Channing is restrained in conveying her disappointment and entirely silent about "Housework" and *Free to Be*, a project that surfaced just a few years after *Hello, Dolly!* was filmed.

25. Some typical articles and recent media coverage: "Chore Wars," *Time* (21 July 2011, http://newsfeed.time.com/2011/07/21/time-cover-story-why-men-and-women-should-end-the-chore-wars/); the Motherlode blog in the *New York Times* (see http://parenting.blogs.nytimes.com/2012/03/13/why-children-need-more-chores/; http://parenting.blogs .nytimes.com/2009/10/27/kids-picking-up-the-slack/), and *The Globe and Mail* series "Dirty

Work" (http://www.theglobeandmail.com/life/relationships/dirty-work-how-household-chores-push-families-to-the-brink/article12300024/?page=all).

26. Carole Hart, along with her husband Bruce Hart, was among the original writers of *Sesame Street* and they won an Emmy in 1970 for outstanding achievement in children's programming (see http://www.emmys.com/nominations/1970/OUTSTANDING%20 ACHIEVEMENT%20IN%20CHILDREN'S%20PROGRAMMING).

27. In a 2001 interview with Eleanor Wachtel, broadcast on CBC Radio, Steinem reflected on her grandmother, a notable feminist in early-twentieth-century Toledo, Ohio: "My grandmother, like many in her generation was a feminist in public life but not in private life. She didn't change the power structure of her household, and therefore came across to my mother as just someone who was superwoman, who could do it all. I think clearly we have that problem right now, that most women in the country have two jobs, one inside the home and one outside the home. We haven't yet gotten to the place where women, a critical mass of women anyway, feel they have a right to say, *Wait a minute, men have to be raising babies and little children as much as women do,* and to demand child care and other structural changes that we need if women are not to have an impossible double burden."

WORKS CITED

Bazelon, Emily. "The Mother of Feminism." 31 Dec. 2006. *New York Times*. Web. 10 May 2013.

Belafonte, Harry, and Marlo Thomas, perf. "Parents Are People." By Carol Hall. *Free to Be . . . You and Me*. 1974. Free to Be Foundation, 2001. DVD.

Breasted, Mary. "Women on the March: 'We're a Movement Now!'" 3 Sept. 1970. *Village Voice*. Web. 10 May 2013.

Carol Channing: Larger Than Life. Dir. Dori Berinstein. Dramatic Forces, 2011. iTunes.

Chabon, Michael. *Manhood for Amateurs: The Pleasures and Regrets of a Husband, Father, and Son*. 2009. Toronto: Harper Perennial, 2010. Print.

Channing, Carol, perf. "Housework." By Sheldon Harnick. *Free to Be . . . You and Me*. 1972. Arista, 1983. CD.

———. *Just Lucky I Guess*. New York: Simon & Schuster, 2002. Print.

Ehrenreich, Barbara. *Nickel and Dimed*. 2001. New York: Picador, 2011. Print.

Faludi, Susan. "Death of a Revolutionary." *New Yorker*. 15 April 2013. Web. 15 April 2013.

Friedan, Betty. *The Feminist Mystique*. 1963. New York: Norton, 2001. Print.

Harnick, Sheldon. "William's Doll." *Free to Be . . . You and Me*. 1972. Arista, 1983. CD.

Hart, Carole. Interview by Janet Coleman. *Cat Radio Café*. 17 Dec. 2012. Web. 21 April 2013.

———. Interview by John Schaefer. "When We Were 'Free to Be.'" *Soundcheck*. WNYC, New York. 13 Nov. 2012. Web. 24 April 2013.

Hochschild, Arlie, with Anne Machung. *The Second Shift: Working Families and the Revolution at Home*. Rev. ed. New York: Penguin, 2012. Print.

Jowitt, Deborah. "Free to Be . . . You and Me." *New York Times*. 24 Dec. 1972. Web. 31 Jan. 2013.

Kois, Dan. "Free to Be—Forty Years Ago, a Bunch of Feminists Made an Album. They Wanted to Change . . . Everything." Slate.com. 22 Oct. 2012. Web. 24 April 2013.

Mainardi, Pat. "The Politics of Housework." 1970. *CWLU Herstory Archive*. Web. 12 Jan. 2013.

O'Reilly, Jane. "The Housewife's Moment of Truth," *Ms*. preview edition, *New York* magazine. 20 Dec. 1971. Web.

Pogrebin, Abigail. "How Do You Spell Ms.: An Oral History of 'Ms.' Magazine." *New York*. 30 Oct. 2011. Web. 30 May 2013.

Rotskoff, Lori, and Laura L. Lovett. *When We Were Free to Be*. Chapel Hill: University of North Carolina Press, 2012. Print.

———. Interview by Anna Maria Tremonti. "The Free to Be You and Me Movement." *The Current*. CBC, Toronto. 4 Dec. 2012. Web. 4 Dec. 2012.

Spivak, Gayatri Chakravorty. "Translator's Preface." *Of Grammatology*. By Jacques Derrida. 1974. Baltimore: Johns Hopkins University Press, 1997. Print.

Steinem, Gloria. Interview by Eleanor Wachtel. "Gloria Steinem Encore." *Writers and Company*. CBC, Toronto. 7 July 2013. Web. 19 July 2013.

Syfers, Judy. "I Want a Wife." *Literature for Composition*. Third Edition. Eds. Sylvan Barnet, Morton Berman, William Burto, Marcia Stubbs. New York: HarperCollins, 1993. 775–76. Web.

Thomas, Marlo. *Growing Up Laughing: My Story and the Story of Funny*. New York: Hyperion, 2010. Print.

Thomas, Marlo and Friends. *Free to Be . . . You and Me*. 1972. Arista, 1983. CD.

———. *Free to Be . . . You and Me*. Philadelphia: Running Press, 1974; 2008. Print.

———. *Free to Be . . . You and Me*. 1974. Free to Be Foundation, 2001. DVD.

Waldman, Ayelet. *Bad Mother: A Chronicle of Maternal Crimes, Minor Calamities, and Occasional Moments of Grace*. New York: Doubleday, 2009. Print.

Chapter Eight

Spaces of Masculinity and Work

Bringing Men Back into the Domestic Sphere

Elizabeth Patton

Most scholarship on masculinity is a discourse of crisis, beginning in the nineteenth century with industrialization and the changing nature of work.[1] As John Beynon states, "[C]risis is constitutive of masculinity itself" (90), as definitions are always changing. One key aspect of this crisis is the work-life dilemma and changing definitions of fatherhood in relation to family and work after World War II. Whereas most middle-class women's lives revolved around family and home, men's lives were expected to occupy both work and home. As in the late nineteenth century, men in the postwar period were confronted with contradictions in popular culture. Men were encouraged to provide for families by participating in market work in the public sphere and consequently were absent from the home for the majority of the day, and simultaneously were expected to establish a palpable presence in the home by providing a masculine role model for children by embracing the ideology of togetherness.

POSTWAR MASCULINE DOMESTICITY

The origin of the notion of togetherness is attributed to *McCall's* magazine (1873–2002). In 1954, Otis Wiese, the editor of the popular American women's magazine, revamped the periodical as part of its "Togetherness" campaign to shift the readership to the entire family.[2] According to Jessica Weiss, the ideology of togetherness was an attempt to reconcile the divergent models for family life that emerged from the nineteenth century: the middle-class companionate marriage and separate spheres (118). Middle-class mar-

147

ried couples were expected to focus on parenthood in favor of the entire family in the pursuit of work-life balance championing the home over the office. However, the togetherness promoted by social critics, represented in magazines and on television, was not so easily achieved. As Weiss further articulates, some social critics at the time noted that the ideology of togetherness was contradictory (120). Togetherness was intended to allow couples to obtain fulfillment through the joining of the family, eliminating the strict separate spheres where women were expected to dedicate time and labor to their home and children and men worked outside the home. But in devoting all their time to parenting, little time was left for the couple. In addition, togetherness was supposed to restore men's presence in the home after a prolonged absence largely due to the wars.

The ideology of togetherness dictated that family work be shared equally among married couples, but that did not happen in reality. Togetherness failed to reconcile the dual expectations of success at work and maintaining the role of involved father at home. According to Weiss, social critics in popular magazines and newspapers argued that ideal family life was best achieved with the father regarding the home as a place of leisure, not a place of work (120). For men, supporting the family was a primary role and togetherness was a leisure-time pursuit in the 1950s. This chapter examines attempts to resolve these contradictions in the promotion of togetherness by finding a space for men bringing work into the home, in television, film, and surrounding discourse on shifts in the notion of family life, specifically ideas about fatherhood and work-life balance during the "turn toward home" (Coontz 92) in the postwar period and the 1980s and early 1990s. As historian Stephanie Coontz noted, during periods of rapid socioeconomic transformation in the United States, the focus turns toward home life, represented by the family (97). Coontz proposes that the attention to the private sphere in the 1950s and the 1980s is actually a symptom of, not a solution to, economic inequality and perceived ruptures in the moral fabric of society.

Popular postwar discourse implored men to become active fathers and take their rightful place as head of the family. At the same time, prominent social critics such as David Riesman expressed concern about the role of women in the feminization of men. Historian James Gilbert writes, "[B]y invoking a discourse that had come to identify mass consumer society with women, and by adding his own vivid terminology to explain this phenomenon, Riesman implicitly wrote the history of character as a story of the decline of masculinity," as Riesman linked the new mass society and culture of the 1950s with feminization (54). Fathers were getting mixed messages from television, film, and popular social critics—men were expected to play a vital role in the family and at the same time make a contribution to society and reclaim their individualism (manhood) in the public sphere. According to Weiss, the Great Depression was psychologically damaging to American men's sense of manhood and their ability to take care of their families. World War II restored their status as the household's main source of income as the economy, particularly in the United States, expanded. However, because so many men were absent from the home due to service during the war, child-rearing experts of the period such as Dr. Benjamin Spock and social critics writing for *Parents* magazine (1926–) started to question the social ramifications on society and the impact on children growing up without fathers present in the home (Weiss 92).

In the postwar period, masculinity was primarily defined by male employment outside of the home despite the consequences of inadequate interaction with one's children. Among other social observers, Spock noted that male role models were necessary for children to properly develop, and especially for boys, a male presence at home was important in developing masculinity.[3] The belief was also understood to be good for American society as a whole. Mainstream magazines such as *Life* (1936–1972)[4] and *Ladies' Home Journal* (1883–) published numerous articles on mass anxiety related to popular social topics in relation to the family.[5] For example, young parents were reportedly anxious about child rearing in relation to finances, juvenile delinquency, and sexual morality. By the late 1940s, families were thought to be in crisis because of the absence of fathers due to the increase in divorce rates since the beginning of the 1920s, problems with family readjustment after the mass return of men after World War II, and the changing nature of the U.S. economic system. Therefore, fathers had to take their place in the home. Jessica Weiss further explains that advice columnists and parenting experts through popular magazines, newspapers, and best-selling books such as *The Common Sense Book of Baby and Child Care* (1946), instructed men to spend more time at home participating in parenting, modernizing the concept of fatherhood. *Life* and *Parents* urged men and women to view parenting as a shared effort and to be flexible within the conventional gender roles (Weiss 122). Postwar television reflected this trend in shows such as *Father Knows Best* (1954–1960) that emphasized the role of men within the family. This emphasis did not change the belief in togetherness in that mothers still took primary responsibility in raising the children and men financially supporting the family, but that men could help out around the house and spend time with their children. Fatherhood could be about hobbies, do-it-yourself household projects, friendship, and having fun with children without jeopardizing their position outside the home and their masculinity.

For some postwar social critics and psychiatrists, masculine presence in the home was necessary but had gone too far as the boundary between mother and father was becoming too hazy. In a 1956 *Life* editorial, psychiatrist Dr. Ralph Greenson explains the danger of swapping traditional gender roles in the modern marriage: "[T]he [father] confuses being fair with submitting to her aggressiveness. Finally he begins to trade roles and to take on more and more of the maternal role with the children, protecting and nurturing and worrying about them."[6] Dr. Greenson prioritized the role that men played in the home over the amount of time they spent, resulting in the possibility that children would lose sight of their fathers as breadwinners and the head of the family. The unfortunate outcome, he indicated, was that children would perceive their father as another mother figure or that this perception would destabilize the father's masculinity in their acquiescence to the mother in the home. A subversive thread emerged in popular men's magazines about the role of the home in the feminization of American men, bolstering this perceived crisis of masculinity. By the late 1950s, the influence of *Playboy* magazine (1953–) is discernible, and prominent and influential writers such as Philip Wylie in his best-seller *A Generation of Vipers* (1942) railed against what they perceived as the takeover of the American home by women and consequently the domestication of America. Wylie, writing for *Playboy*, argued that women (with no consideration of the desires of men) had removed the spaces of masculinity within the home (e.g., the smoking room, the study) and all that remained as the center of the home was the kitchen, nursery, and the master bedroom, which he implied was the domain of mothers (52, 77).[7] The feminization of the home (encouraged by mass marketing and the emergence of consumer culture) was happening in the home despite what Wylie argued was the debt that women owed men in freeing women from traditional domestic labor by creating domestic technological advances such as the washing machine. Men needed a space to retreat and avoid the constant bombardment of feminine influences within the middle-class suburban home.

A look at postwar television and romanticized magazine depictions of life in the 1950s affirms that television producers characterized the suburban home as a space of feminine domesticity, separate from the sphere of work, a space of leisure. For example, in television shows such as *Leave It to Beaver* (1957–1963) and *The Donna Reed Show* (1958–1966), the spaces within the home were marked clearly as public (kitchen and living room) or private (bedrooms and bathrooms) compared to the hybridized public-private layout of current houses. The postwar suburban home was also depicted as a space of childhood and entertainment, especially for watching television (Spigel 45). However, in terms of actual use, the spaces within the postwar suburban home were not homogeneous. For middle-class men to take their place as head of household, be active fathers, and at the same time have successful careers without spending too much time away from home as men did in the past, a solution needed to be found in the suburban house. Consequently, extra bedrooms acting as multiuse rooms or the study/den served as hybrid public-private spaces within the home.

Even though the study (sometimes referred to as the den) was reintroduced into the middle-class home, this accommodation did not necessarily solve the problem. In popular magazines such as *Kiplinger's Personal Finance* (1947–) and *Life*, writers argued that builders failed to create spaces wholly dedicated to the father in the promotion of multipurpose rooms in the modern house. Instead, men had to share space with the family as the study often served as a study-guest-family-TV room due to the limited space in most middle-class homes. The standard houses built during the postwar middle-class housing boom lacked additional spaces like a study or play/nursery room that were associated with upper middle-class suburban homes. In actuality, the majority of homes built during the postwar period were not the typical upper-middle class suburban homes represented on popular postwar sitcoms such as *Leave It to Beaver* or *The Donna Reed Show*. The majority of the homes were modeled for economic reasons after the four-room layout popularized in Levittown, New York. A standard floor plan for a starter home often featured four rooms: a kitchen, living room, and two bedrooms within 900–1000 square feet, small enough to fit on a 50-ft. suburban lot and accommodate outdoor space for a front lawn and backyard. Although aspirational, writers in men's magazines such as *Kiplinger's* and *Playboy* complained that men didn't really want togetherness but aloneness, and advocated for dedicated masculine spaces in the home. As one male writer bemoaned, "[T]he beauty of a bona fide den is that a man can interrupt a complicated job of work [. . .] at his place and come back later expecting to find everything as he left it" (Lady Stay 'Way 45). With TV watching and the telephone migrating to other areas of the house besides the living room, and the changing need for flexible/multipurpose space in the modern household, a space exclusively for men was impossible for most of the middle class even though men argued in publications such as *Kiplinger's* that the den should not be shared as a family room.

Television reinforced the practice of "togetherness" and the ideal of father as sole breadwinner as both natural and the normative American middle-class suburban experience. The message was widely disseminated, as 65 percent of U.S. households owned at least one television by 1955 (*TV Basics*). Popular family domestic comedies made very clear the importance of the father in relation to the family, the significance of fatherhood, and the need to obtain work-life balance. Consider the following titles that highlight the cultural importance of fatherhood: *Father Knows Best* (1954–1960), *My Three Sons* (1960–1972), *Make Room for Daddy* (1953–1965), and *The Bachelor Father* (1957–1962). All of these shows focused on fatherhood and, considering the popularity and high ratings of *Father Knows Best* and *My Three Sons*, one could say that postwar television was obsessed with masculine domesticity in finding a space for men in the suburban middle-class home. Television dads were mostly upper-middle class by occupation, were the sole providers for their family, were able to buy the latest consumer products and owned large houses in established upper-middle class neighborhoods. Like their counterparts in reality, television fathers had a den that served as a study or home office. In some shows, the den actually doubled as a TV room (for the Nelsons on the *Adventures of Ozzie and Harriet*, 1952–1966) or as a bedroom (for the grandfather on *My Three Sons*). In the case of *My Three Sons*, Steve Douglas used his bedroom as an office and Ozzie Nelson on the *Adventures of Ozzie and Harriet* did not have a den for his exclusive use, as his occupation was never defined as a 9-to-5 white-collar professional. In fact, in real life Ozzie was a band leader, an artistic profession that is typically not associated with an office.

However, in a typical depiction of the den, the room represents a space of masculinity and is exclusively the domain of the father. For example, on *Leave It to Beaver* (1957–1963), Ward's den is equipped with a telephone, library area, and two leather chairs facing the desk, evoking the layout of what we might suppose is his office at the job he goes to during the day. There is also a globe and wood paneling to code the room as masculine compared to the other rooms of the house. The den is a space where Ward conducts family business and disciplines or lectures the boys for many of their misguided adventures. Ward does not take long business trips or work long hours at the office. He is home before dinner to spend time with the boys. Although Ward does not actively talk about his job often or seems to have any problem balancing work and home, the den does appear to be a space for Ward to work at home. He is depicted working in his den, mostly reading reports on the weekend. In one episode, Beaver spills ink on his father's work report, getting into serious trouble as Ward made it very clear that his desk was off limits to the boys. On television the den is designated as the territory of the father and a space to establish and assert masculine authority within the perceived feminine domesticity of the suburban home.

Although all of the television fathers are portrayed as professionals—a manager (Ward Cleaver on *Leave It to Beaver*), engineer (Steve Douglas on *My Three Sons*), lawyer (George Baxter on *Hazel*, 1961–1966), or doctor (Alex Stone on *The Donna Reed Show*), professions that normally would demand long hours at work—their jobs rarely interfere with their ability to be physically present in the home. The details of their occupations are glossed over in most cases, and very few depictions of the workplace were aired on television compared to their life at home, driving home the point that the happiness and well-being of the middle-class family was dependent on the physical presence of the father. To maximize the presence of the television father, storylines had to minimize the father's occupation or incorporate a space for work in the home.

The most explicit examples were Dr. Alex Stone on *The Donna Reed Show* and Steve Douglas on *My Three Sons*. Dr. Stone worked as a pediatrician but also had a home-based practice. With the benefit of the telephone, Dr. Stone could work from the home and be accessible to his patients in case of emergencies. One of the themes of the show is Alex's struggle to be present to his family despite his medical practice being located in the den. When patients called for medical advice or called Alex away from the home on weekends and in the evening, Donna and the children were expected to tolerate the many interruptions. Steve Douglas, a widowed aeronautical engineering consultant, used his bedroom, outfitted with a drafting table, to complete projects at home but maximized his ability to be present to his sons during the evening and weekends. Although he did occasionally go on long work trips, for the most part his hours seemed to be flexible and not the typical 9-to-5 work schedule.

In both cases the fathers are characterized as hardworking and busy professionals and, despite the demands of their jobs, in the end are able to be present for their families. They are not condemned by other characters (and, by extension, some aspects of society) for bringing work into the home, compared to the fathers of their children's friends, other men in the neighborhood, or from the father's workplace who are collectively depicted as workaholics. In the case of the other fathers, such men are portrayed as failing to balance home and work life by their continued absence from the home. Failing to be present in the home is a failure of fatherhood and neglecting the central role of fathers in the middle-class family. This message is driven home when Ward acts as a surrogate father and has to discipline Beaver's friend Larry as his mother struggles to raise him because his father is often out of town on business (see, for example, "School Bus," 1959). In the discourse of 1950s television, working at home is acceptable for noble professions such as doctors, but working many hours at home to get ahead or satisfy a materialistic boss is also a failure of fatherhood. Missing a son's baseball game on a Saturday is portrayed as a serious threat to the father's work-life life balance and ultimately the well-being of the family.

In *Living Room Lectures* (1995), Nina Leibman notes that advertisers and the networks' marketing departments heavily influenced television narratives during the 1950s. Because many television fathers were employed as executives or managers, advertising and corporate culture in general could not be portrayed as a source of social problems. However, the ideology of family togetherness was central to the middle-class value system at the time. Therefore, on shows such as *Leave It to Beaver* and *The Donna Reed Show* the neighborhood fathers who spent too much time at work were criticized. Also, postwar family sitcoms often featured narratives that portrayed employers and clients negatively. Even on shows such as *Hazel*, outwardly successful fathers such as Mr. B., a partner at a law firm, somehow reached the pinnacle of their profession without compromising their responsibilities as family men.[8] They make just enough money to be comfortably upper-middle class and avoid the negative associations of materialism and greed associated with the wealthy. Mr. B. is often depicted working in his study, but not to an extent that he is unable to attend to the family. In contrast, his business partners and clients are characterized as greedy workaholics who do not understand the importance of slowing down and enjoying life with family and friends. For example, on *Hazel*, a wealthy client is depicted as difficult because he insists that Mr. B. work on Sunday ("Hazel's Day Off," 1963). The show constructs clients and bosses who demand unreasonable workloads and take televised fathers away from their homes outside of normal business hours as threats to the primacy of the nuclear family and the practice of togetherness. Ironically, only Hazel the housekeeper, whose relationship to the family is defined by housework, is able to teach the client to relax, allowing Mr. B to spend time with his family.

In each of the above examples, work is represented on postwar television as a necessary and natural aspect of men's role in society reflecting cultural norms of the period. However, to also reflect the postwar emphasis of togetherness in popular culture, television fathers maintained a continued presence in the home, and this sustained presence had the appearance of domesticating men and associating masculinity with what was traditionally characterized as the feminine sphere. Nevertheless, I argue that incorporating a space for work in the home and emphasizing the fathers' professional occupations (situated in the public sphere traditionally associated with masculinity) mitigated any threat of the feminization of fathers within the middle-class home as lamented by influential writers such as Philip Wylie.

My Three Sons went so far as to even remove all possibility of feminine influence in the home by representing a new family type, the single-parent household. Steve Douglas is a widower raising three boys with the help of his father-in-law, Bub, who acts as the "mother" in the household.[9] Steve spends most of the first few seasons entrenching himself in bachelorhood by avoiding any woman who appears to have marriage in mind, or he pursues women with no desire to drop their careers to settle down. As Steve is a busy professional and wants to be available emotionally and present as a role model for the boys, Bub handles most of the domestic labor. Interestingly, Bub is depicted laboring around the house, cleaning and cooking in soiled and tattered work clothes compared to his meticulously dressed female television counterparts on other popular shows (see figure 8.1).

Instead, female neighbors and guest stars are depicted as neurotic and anxiety-driven compared to the Douglas men, who run an efficient household and balance work and home life on a daily basis. The show clearly implies that men are not incompetent in domestic matters as portrayed on programs such as *The Donna Reed Show*, and goes so far as to claim that men are actually superior to women as they do not let "emotional" decisions guide household management. Steve runs the house like a business, making home and work life seamless, and Bub, a tough and assertive character, takes on housework as if it was his professional occupation.[10] Masculinity does not

Figure 8.1.   William Frawley ironing on *My Three Sons*. Source: ©CBS/Photofest
1965–1972

preclude the practice of domesticity. Images of male domesticity on *My Three Sons* reintegrated domesticity into the definition of masculinity.

THE NEW MAN AND DOMESTICITY

One influential social change that helped reintroduce men into the domestic sphere was the emergence of the men's movement in the early 1970s and 1980s and the ideology of the "New Man," or sometimes referred to by scholars as the "New Father," in the 1990s. In the early 1970s, major newspapers such the *New York Times* and *Washington Post* published editorials on the fledgling men's liberation movement.[11] As Lisa Hammel, a journalist for the *New York Times* argued, the movement was "unorganized but significant" as the ideals were starting to emerge across the nation during the 1970s (46). More men were publicly expressing their frustration with society's demands on them because of the need to "conform to a standard male image that prevents them from having or displaying emotions, being vulnerable human beings, and demands instead that they be strong, responsible, dominating, competitive, aggressive, successful breadwinners" (Shirley, "Men's Lib").[12] According to Jessica Weiss, one of the central themes of the men's movement was the proximity of the father to the family (113).

Scholars such as Andrew Singleton and JaneMaree Maher argue that the emergence of the "New Father" was in response to late-1960s second-wave feminist critiques of the role of gender within the institution of the family (236). In 1976, author and psychologist Herb Goldberg wrote *The Hazards of Being Male*. Authors like Dr. Goldberg and the emerging men's movement criticized the feminist movement for "stopping too soon" and not doing anything to help men dismantle masculine stereotypes.[13] Although these representations were not typical, the feminist critique, women's increased labor-force participation, and changing roles of fathers within the domestic sphere are evident in depictions of fatherhood in popular culture. Examples of this perspective include Dustin Hoffman's portrayal of a single father in the critically acclaimed *Kramer vs. Kramer* (1979) and Michael Keaton's role as a stay-at-home dad after losing his job in the popular film *Mr. Mom* (1983). Along with the attention paid to masculinity and fatherhood in the mass media, academia also focused scholarly attention to the issue. In fact, in 1984 the University of Southern California established the first professorship in men's studies, expanding its Program for the Study of Women and Men in Society. The development of men's studies as a new discipline was not without controversy, but supporters such as Dr. Judith Stiehm, one of the program founders, argued that the study of masculinity was a natural step from the men who accepted feminist philosophy.[14]

The discourse on fatherhood in mass media during the 1980s followed two contrasting themes: 1) the absent "deadbeat dad" typified by black fathers and divorced fathers; and, 2) the nurturing "Mr. Mom" or the nice guy (typically white, married, and middle class) that internalized second-wave feminism.[15] Both representations undermined the traditional "good provider" role of men as head of the household. The growing percentage of children living in homes without fathers characterized the 1980s and early 1990s as "the age of the vanishing father" in popular discourse on the family (Gardner 13).[16] Between three of the highest circulating newspapers in the United States (*Los Angeles Times*, *New York Times*, and *Washington Post*), there were over 1,100 articles published on the problem of absent fathers. Simultaneously, to counter negative images and to encourage fathers to embrace child rearing and the role of provider, popular publications such as *Time* (1923–) and *Esquire* (1933–) published editorials and cover stories on the importance of fatherhood.[17] Bill Cosby capitalized on the success of *The Cosby Show* and the new focus on fatherhood with his 1986 book, *Fatherhood*, which reached number one on the *New York Times* best-seller list on May 25, 1986, selling 2.5 million hardcover copies. *Esquire* diverged from its traditional focus on men's fashion, health, politics, and popular culture in publishing the cover story "Father Love" in November 1982, promoting the joys of fatherhood. The publication bookended the decade with a cover story titled "How to Raise a Perfect Kid: A Fearless Handbook for Fathers and Fathers to Be" in November 1989.

Mary Douglas Vavrus mentions the influential role of the protagonist in *Mr. Mom* (1983) in her research, but primarily situates the emergence of the "Mr. Mom identity" as a reaction to "significant societal shifts vis-à-vis gender and domesticity occurring during the 1990s" (355). I argue that these societal shifts and the possibility of Mr. Mom as a masculine identity are rooted in the postwar period's emphasis on involved and present fathers in popular culture. Mr. Mom is plausible only as a stay-at-home father and participates in the reproductive sphere without contributing income after representations of the work-at-home father materialized in popular culture. Therefore, these emergent social changes can be understood by examining the ideological messages of fictionalized representations of the work-at-home father, as well as news accounts in mass media. The television shows *Growing Pains* (1985–1992) and *The Cosby Show* (1984–1992) are particularly significant in examining the reinsertion of men as the central role in family sitcoms during the 1980s and early 1990s, through the depiction of the home office and work-at-home fathers. As Andrew Gorman-Murray writes, "[T]he private space of the home enabled men to negotiate alternative masculinities, where they could be expressive, emotive, and engage in domestic labour and child care" (369).

The political climate of the 1980s has been described in the mass media as a culture war between conservative and progressive visions of the future of America. According to sociologist James Davison Hunter, the Reagan administration legitimized the "conservative cultural revolution" (299). Hunter argues that under President Reagan politics and public policy moved to the right, but American culture moved to a more secular and pluralistic cultural order (299). Since the 1960s, the United States experienced significant social changes in rising divorce rates, the legalization of abortion, increased use of birth control and subsequent decline in birth rates, rise in unwed mothers, greater participation of women in the workforce, single-parent families, and increased visibility of homosexuality. One of the central values of the conservative movement was a "call to revive commitment and responsibility through a 'rediscovery' of family values" (Coontz 94). The political validation of the heterosexual nuclear family as a social force was an attempt to reverse the liberalization of American culture.

Growing Pains, a family sitcom, featured the typical TV upper-middle class suburban family with a twist that reflected the rise in professional working mothers of the period. After staying home for fifteen years, Maggie Seaver decided to return to work as a reporter. Jason, a psychiatrist, supported her decision by working at home to take care of their three children.[18] The show featured story lines that addressed the family's difficulty in adjusting to the new family arrangement. The fictional family experienced "growing pains," but more significantly, the show reflects the perceived growing pains of society at large. Preserving the nuclear heterosexual middle-class family, *Growing Pains* legitimized the mother's decision to work outside the home by allowing the father to both financially support and adopt a central role in the domestic sphere.

The fictional fathers on mainstream shows such as *Growing Pains, The Cosby Show, Family Ties* (1982–1989), *Blossom* (1990–1995), and *Full House* (1987–1995) represented "the phenomenon of the 'New Man' whose loyalties and energies are centered on the home" (Tosh 86). According to Gorman-Murray, and Singleton and Maher, the "New Man" emerged as a reaction to women's increased presence in the workforce. The ideal partner for the New Working Woman, the New Man participates in domestic activities by doing his fair share of housework and parenting. For example in *Growing Pains*, Dr. Jason Seaver was portrayed as a well-meaning father who had to prove that he could see patients and take care of the kids and the home without Maggie's help during the day. Therefore, many story lines featured Jason trying to balance being a cool father and disciplinarian, and learning to cook and do laundry while struggling with his wife's new role as busy professional. As Gorman-Murray claims, "The New Man is, thus, a new model of hetero-masculinity moulded through perceived greater participation in domestic activities and labour. As a result of his domestic masculinity, the home is also expected to be de-feminised, and housework de-gendered" (371). Dr. Seaver appears to be a successful media representation of Gorman-Murray's New Man.

In an episode titled "Superdad!" (1985) the Seaver's daughter Carol tried to reach her mom at work, but Maggie was busy. Jason offered to talk with Carol about her boy problems. Maggie tells Jason that he is a great psychiatrist "but not a mom." Maggie still tried to maintain her role as the emotional center of the family. Jason is offended by her desire to remain the emotional center, questioning Maggie, "you don't think I can handle my end of the bargain?" Jason argued that he could take care of the kids both emotionally and physically—he *is* a psychiatrist. The show established Jason's identity as a professional and an expert and reminded the audience of his masculinity, despite his character's location in the home. In redefining images of masculinity, it is not enough for a father to participate solely in child rearing. As a point of crisis, re-constructed notions of masculinity must retain links to the public sphere. Jason did participate in the new model of masculinity as proposed by Gorman-Murray; however, in TV discourse, fictional fathers must retain some semblance of the traditional androcentric order.

Therefore, to emphasize Jason's status as a doctor and establish his masculinity, the narrative included a productive space within the home. Jason's practice was conducted in a study by the front of the house. Jason's study was decorated in dark masculine colors: an abundance of wood shelving and books, a telephone and globe are prominently displayed on his large desk, echoing earlier postwar images of television fathers' domestic space. Within his study, Jason used his professional experience/knowledge to counsel his children (just like Ward Cleaver) and discuss important topics with his wife. Jason's professional experience extended to his management of the domestic sphere—a refashioned image of the postwar father. Although experts at work, television husbands in the past often left home management to their wives as revealed in close readings of postwar family sitcoms. Jason represented the new model of fatherhood, fully capable and competent in both domains because of his professional status.

Struggling with her role as a professional outside of the home, Maggie was jealous of Jason's relationship with the kids and wanted to be better at "mothering." A central theme of the show, as Maggie claims, as a mother and professional, is "want[ing] to have it all, but you can't" ("Superdad!" 1985). Jason's main role as the "New Man" was to be emotionally available and supervise the children. Jason and Maggie eventually figured it out in each episode and learned to adjust to their unconventional family arrangement depicting a father working at home. By portraying a successful and loving upper-middle-class family that challenged the gendered roles of the typical nuclear family, the Seavers simultaneously represented "the vanguard of contemporary domestic relations" by normalizing masculine domesticity and "reinscribe[d] significant aspects of patriarchal privilege within domestic space" (Vavrus 353).

In addition to addressing new forms of masculinity, sitcoms that foreground the father's role in the family also disguise race and opportunities of class. *The Cosby Show* debuted September 20, 1984, on NBC and aired for eight seasons. It had the highest Nielsen ratings for five consecutive seasons from 1985–1986 through 1989–1990 despite low expectations from NBC and prior rejections from the other major networks, according to Cosby (Gold 42). The sitcom featured a black affluent two-income couple and their five children living in Brooklyn, New York. Bill Cosby played Dr. Heathcliff "Cliff" Huxtable, married to a lawyer, Clair Huxtable (Phylicia Rashād). Watched by 30 million households during its peak, *The Cosby Show* was a mass-media success that crossed race and class.

Despite *The Cosby Show*'s commercial success, the show was criticized widely by African-American critics as a "sanitized '50s-style white show in blackface" (Christon, "the Cos"). Bill Cosby widely admitted that the show deliberately avoided overtly talking about issues of race and the problems associated with being a black family in America: "My first defense is that the show is about Americans [. . .] I won't deal with the foolishness of racial overtones on the show. I base an awful lot of what I've done simply on what people will enjoy. I want to show a family that has a good life, not people to be jealous of" (Christon, "the Cos"). *The Cosby Show* displaced real-life resistance to social, political, and economic domination into fictional "celebrations of black middle class visibility and achievement" (Gray, *Television, Black Americans* 378). This unwillingness to engage in racial issues seemed to drive the popularity of the show across racial and socioeconomic demographics. Therefore, Cosby's decision contributed to the aspirational sociocultural atmosphere in popular culture of the 1980s and the political validation of the upper-middle class professional family.

The television networks initially rejected Bill Cosby's idea for a family sitcom until he convinced NBC to produce a pilot. As Cosby states, "[S]o here I come, with all these marketing negatives: a black family that is not going to be of the street-level humor; a wife who's a professional person; five children; and a show that deals with the human behavior of the people in the series" (Gold 42). Cosby defended his decision to feature an affluent black family as a more difficult marketing choice in not depicting conventional representations of a black family as a working-class maternal household. For Bill Cosby, family, not race, was the primary focus of the show. In many ways the show reflected his life. Bill Cosby, although not a medical doctor in real life, did earn a doctorate in education from the University of Massachusetts at Amherst in 1976, arguing that television has the ability to educate people (Gold 42). Bill Cosby, like his counterpart Cliff Huxtable, had five children, four girls and one boy.[19] His wife, Dr. Camille Olivia Cosby, is also a professional like his fictional wife, Clair.

The merits of hard work and education were a consistent theme on *The Cosby Show*. The children were depicted doing chores in the home to learn lessons about responsibility. There were signs of the importance of work and education throughout the house. Like the bedrooms of their sitcom counterparts in the 1950s, the children's bedrooms were equipped with bookshelves and desks for studying. However, *The Cosby Show* departed from typical postwar depictions of master bedrooms on television with the inclusion of a small writing desk as well as an office-sized desk with an electric typewriter and telephone. The living room also had a desk for working in the corner, in addition to Cliff's study and medical practice in the English basement[20] of their brownstone. Finally, Cliff was always on call for work, as he carried a pager on his person and was available to his patients through the many telephones located throughout the house.

Story lines involving Theo, the Huxtables' only son, often depicted Cliff's struggle to impart guidance on the importance of education and hard work. For example, Bill Cosby's decision to push Theo toward success is in response to negative images of black young men on television. As Cosby stated in 1989, "Run down what you saw of black people on TV before the Huxtables. You had *Amos 'n' Andy*, one of the funniest shows ever, people say. But whoever went to college? Who tried for better things? In *Good Times*, J. J. Walker played a definite underachiever" (Christon, "the Cos"). Although his characterization of these representations is valid, *The Cosby Show* also omitted the realities that young black men faced. In Cosby's narrative Theo's problem is framed as laziness, a lack of trying. Consequently, "such ideological representations appear natural and universal rather than as the result of social and political struggles over power" (Gray, *Television, Black Americans* 377). However, considering Cosby's comments and the dominance of this narrative on the show, the decision to focus on hard work and academic achievement seems to be Cosby's response to what he perceived to be at the root of black issues and reflected his approach to engaging racial socioeconomic inequality. If African Americans were poor in the 1980s, it was not because of structural forces and the history of racism, it was their own fault. Although Cosby discerned early on the increasing significance of education in American socioeconomic mobility, *The Cosby Show*'s representation of the black family, as Henry Louis Gates Jr. argues, suggested that "blacks are solely responsible for their social conditions, with no acknowledgement of the severely constricted life opportunities that most black people face" ("TV's Black World Turns").

In the discourse of television sitcoms, success is found in professional, knowledge-based professions, not the service-class or blue-collar jobs. This point is further underscored by Cliff and Clair's disappointment with their oldest daughter, Sandra, and her husband in their decision to disregard their educational training in law and medicine, respectively, to run a camping store. For Cosby, being a professional is tantamount to the good life. I argue that Bill Cosby's decision to make Cliff's character an obstetrician whose practice is located in the home allows Cliff to integrate his professional and private life as an ideal representation of the good life. Cliff Huxtable could not be a present father, actively involved in parenting, and filling in the maternal space vacated by Clair's status as a working mother and lawyer without his ability to be at home for most of the day. Similarly to *Growing Pains*, *The Cosby Show* was a departure from earlier representations of the New Father in the crisis of masculinity. In notable examples, such as *Kramer vs. Kramer* and *Mr. Mom*, both fathers occupy the domestic sphere *temporarily* due to family crisis—the mother abandoning the family to pursue her career and the mother returning to work out of necessity because of the father's job loss, respectively. Although Cosby's representation also moves away from normative representations of masculinity, this new model of fatherhood, again like Dr. Seaver on *Growing Pains*, avoids feminine associations through the justification of Cliff's position as a family "expert"; who is better to model new forms of masculine domesticity than a man who brings babies into the world? Consequently, this representation of the New Father may have undermined the expanding professionalism working mothers were seeking by reestablishing paternal hegemony in the domestic sphere.

The Cosby Show became the dominant representation of the black family on television. Bill Cosby's decision to create a television show that featured an upper-middle-class black family also recoded popular significations of race. In eliding race, *The Cosby Show*, says John D. H. Downing, "operate[d] as a reinstatement of black dignity and culture in a racist society where television culture has generally failed to communicate these realities, and has often flatly negated them" (67). Cosby himself alluded to this perspective when he stated, "I have a saying, 'African Americans are the only people who do not have any good ol' days,'" in response to criticisms of the show's explicit celebration of black success (Christon, "the Cos"). It is significant that Bill Cosby situated his character, a black father, within an idealized upper-middle-class home. Not only was Dr. Huxtable present and head of the family, his practice was located on the garden level of the family's brownstone in Brooklyn Heights. Furthermore, the Huxtables lived in the city (although a tree-lined, family neighborhood), not the suburbs of the typical televised family narrative, but in a gentrified area. Cosby's large home in a brownstone Brooklyn neighborhood seems to represent a liminal space compared to the typical televised locations of the African American domesticity in the gritty, inner city or in upscale high rises (e.g., *The Jeffersons*, 1975–85). Families of color were confined to the apartment in the city as the suburbs signified the space of heterosexual white families in television and film. In addition, as noted by many historians and media critics such as Stephanie Coontz, Nina Leibman, and Lynn Spigel, the single-family home in the suburbs was depicted, particularly on television, as the space of the white middle class. American cities were steadily becoming associated with African Americans, crime, and poverty because of public policy and historical developments. Prior to *The Cosby Show*, popular shows featuring African

American families such as *Good Times* (1974–1979) and *What's Happening!* (1976–1979) situated black domesticity in the working-class inner city. These representations "'racialized' the image of the city and the social problems it came to represent" (Fraterrigo 95). Cosby's decision to locate an African American, two-parent, upper-middle-class household in the city is a political choice to counter racialized representations of the black father and the black city.

This representation of an affluent black family is the opposite of the fictional families preceding *The Cosby Show* in the 1970s. For example, *Good Times*, *That's My Mama* (1974–1975), and *What's Happening!* featured working-class single-mother households, though *Good Times* started off as a nuclear family, but the father, James Evans Sr. (John Amos), was killed at the end of the third season, leaving the family to struggle even more without the benefit of his income. Unlike typical media representations of the black male—i.e., unemployed or working class, irresponsible or absent—Dr. Huxtable was a professional working family man, actively participating in the domestic sphere by sharing household and parenting responsibilities with his wife (see figure 8.2). In season one, the episode "How Ugly is He?" illustrates the point. Cosby wears an apron (just like Bub in *My Three Sons*) with the phrase "I'm Trying." This term may refer to cooking but also refers to Cosby's image as the New Man within the domestic sphere. Bill Cosby's character conflated the New Black Father with the New Man that emerged in popular culture during the 1980s. He is both a role model for black males in his presence in the black family and a model of the new middle-class father that actively participates in the domestic sphere. Ultimately, *The Cosby Show* signifies the domestication of the black father—absent from fictional representations, news accounts, and sociological analysis such as the influential 1965 Moynihan Report on the black family and Bill Moyers's 1986 CBS documentary, "The Vanishing Black Family: Crisis in Black America." Reading *The Cosby Show* against the prior decade's programs and discourses of race and the black family in which those shows were embedded, as Herman Gray (1991) puts it, "helps account for its middle class focus and more importantly for its consistent reappropriation of the stable black middle class family" (*Recodings* 121).

Counter to Gorman-Murray's argument that the New Man emerged on the threshold of the work-home boundary (371), the New Man emerged fully within the boundaries of the domestic sphere as a consequence of productive labor associated with masculinity entering the home. These types of shows further erased the boundaries between work and leisure, public and private life. *Growing Pains* and *The Cosby Show* make visible the possibility of productive work within the home for middle-class men. These shows also normalized greater participation by males in managing the household. However, in placing fathers as the focus of the home, shows like *Growing Pains*

Figure 8.2.   Bill Cosby in an apron on *The Cosby Show*: **"How Ugly Is He?"**
Source: *The Cosby Show* ©Carsey-Werner Productions 1984–1992

and *The Cosby Show* reinforced "paternal dominance within," or what Vavrus calls the "domestication of patriarchy" (353). Watching the shows, Dr. Cliff Huxtable and Dr. Jason Seaver still appear as heads of household, albeit domesticated and progressive.

NOTES

1. See, for example, Michael Kimmel's *Manhood in America* (2012), Roger Horrocks's *Masculinities in Crisis* (1994), and Sally Robinson's *Marked Men* (2000).
2. See Otis Wiese, "Live the Life of McCall's."
3. See Benjamin Spock, *The Common Sense Book of Baby and Child Care.*
4. These publication dates refer to the weekly version.
5. See for example Robert Coughlan, "How to Survive Parenthood," *Life*, June 26, 1950; "The American Family in Trouble," *Life*, July 26, 1948.
6. Quoted in Robert Coughlan, "Changing Roles in Modern Marriage." *Life*, 24 Dec. 1956, 115.
7. Philip Wylie, "The Womanization of America."
8. In the groundbreaking book *The Organization Man* (1956), William Whyte describes the working experience of executives and white-collar professionals at various career levels and the impact that work had on life at home. Men reported working on average fifty to sixty hours per week, with an average day at work accounting for 9.5 hours of the day. In almost all

of the companies he surveyed, a five-day work week did not exist and most men reported that their employers expected them to work on the weekend and the evening.

9. To maintain the family dynamics on the show, Bub's character was replaced in 1965 by Uncle Charlie when William Frawley (who played Bub) became too ill to work.

10. This pattern is continued by Uncle Charlie.

11. See, for example, Lisa Hammel, "Men's Lib: An Unorganized but Significant Movement"; Don Shirley, "Men's Lib? 'It's about Time.'"

12. Ibid, "Men's Lib."

13. See, for example, Janet Wiener, "Private Lives: The Ungentle Sex's Quiet Revolution."

14. See, for example, Pauline Yoshihashi, "New Boy on Campus: Men's Studies."

15. See, for example, Paul Taylor, "Two Faces of Fatherhood: Dads Become More Domesticated, More Distant."

16. See, for example, Marilyn Gardner, "Good Dad/Bad Dad: Modern-Day Images of Fatherhood."

17. See, for example, *Time* magazine's June 28, 1993, cover story titled "Fatherhood."

18. A fourth child was introduced in 1988, keeping with the traditional image of the large nuclear family as opposed to the reality of smaller families in the 1980s. In fact, the opening credits featured historical images of families from ancient times to the postwar period creating a sense of assured continuity and permanence of the nuclear family.

19. Bill Cosby's son was murdered in 1997.

20. An English basement is a separate apartment which has its own entrance on the lowest floor of townhouse or brownstone. The apartment is partially below and partially above ground level.

WORKS CITED

Beynon, John. *Masculinities and Culture*. Buckingham: Open University, 2002. Print.

Christon, Lawrence. "The World According to the Cos." *Los Angeles Times Calendar* 10 Dec. 1989. Web.

Coontz, Stephanie. *The Way We Never Were: American Families and the Nostalgia Trap*. New York: Basic, 2000. Print.

Downing, John D. H. "*The Cosby Show* and American Racial Discourse." In *Discourse and Discrimination*. Ed. Geneva Smitherman-Donaldson and Teun A. Van Dijk. Detroit: Wayne State University Press, 1988. 46–73. Print.

Fraterrigo, Elizabeth. Playboy *and the Making of the Good Life in Modern America*. Oxford: Oxford University Press, 2009. Print.

Gardner, Marilyn. "Good Dad/Bad Dad: Modern-Day Images of Fatherhood." *The Christian Science Monitor*. 16 June 1994: 13. Print.

Gilbert, James. *Men in the Middle: Searching for Masculinity in the 1950s*. Chicago: University of Chicago Press, 2005. Print.

Gold, Todd. "Bill Cosby: The Doctor Is In." *The Saturday Evening Post*. April 1985: 42. Print.

Goldberg, Herb. *The Hazards of Being Male: Surviving the Myth of Masculine Privilege*. New York: Nash Publications, 1976. Print.

Gorman-Murray, Andrew. "Masculinity and the Home: A Critical Review and Conceptual Framework." *Australian Geographer* 39.3 (2008): 367–79. Print.

Gray, Herman. "Recodings: Possibilities and Limitations in Commercial Television Representations of African American Culture." *Quarterly Review of Film and Video* 13 (1991): 117–30. Print.

———. "Television, Black Americans, and the American Dream." *Critical Studies in Mass Communication* 6 (1989): 376–86. Print.

Hammel, Lisa. "Men's Lib: An Unorganized but Significant Movement." *New York Times* 11 June 1974: 46. Print.

Horrocks, Roger. *Masculinity in Crisis: Myths, Fantasies and Realities*. New York: St. Martin's Press, 1994. Print.

Hunter, James D. *Culture Wars: The Struggle to Control the Family, Art, Education, Law, and Politics in America*. New York: Basic, 1992. Print.

Kimmel, Michael S. *Manhood in America: A Cultural History*. New York: Oxford University Press, 2012. Print.

"Lady Stay 'Way from That Den." *The Kiplinger Magazine* Sept. 1956: 45. Print.

Leibman, Nina. *Living Room Lectures: The Fifties Family in Film and Television*. Austin: University of Texas Press, 1995. Print.

Robinson, Sally. *Marked Men: White Masculinity in Crisis*. New York: Columbia University Press, 2000. Print.

Shirley, Don. "Men's Lib? 'It's about Time.'" *Washington Post*, 16 June 1974. *ProQuest*. Web. 8 June 2013.

Singleton, Andrew, and JaneMaree Maher. "The 'New Man' Is in the House: Young Men, Social Change, and Housework." *The Journal of Men's Studies*. 12.3 (2004): 227–40. Print.

Spigel, Lynn. *Make Room for TV: Television and the Family Ideal in Postwar America*. Chicago: University of Chicago Press, 1992. Print.

Spock, Benjamin. *The Common Sense Book of Baby and Child Care with Illustrations by Dorothea Fox*. New York: Duell, Sloan and Pearce, 1946. Print.

Taylor, Paul. "Two Faces of Fatherhood: Dads Become More Domesticated, More Distant." *The Washington Post* 16 June 1991: A01. Print.

Tosh, John. *A Man's Place: Masculinity and the Middle-Class Home in Victorian England*. New Haven, CT: Yale University Press, 2007. Print.

TV Basics: A Report on the Growth and Scope of Television. Television Bureau of Advertising, Inc., 2010. Tvb.org. Web.

Vavrus, Mary Douglas. "Domesticating Patriarchy: Hegemonic Masculinity and Television's 'Mr. Mom'." *Critical Studies in Media Communication* 19.3 (2002): 352. Print.

Weiss, Jessica. *To Have and To Hold: Marriage, the Baby Boom, and Social Change*. Chicago: University of Chicago Press, 2000. Print.

Whyte, William H. *The Organization Man*. New York: Simon & Schuster, 1956. Print.

Wiener, Janet. "Private Lives: The Ungentle Sex's Quiet Revolution." *Washington Post* 18 Feb. 1980. B5. Print.

Wiese, Otis. "Live the Life of McCall's." *McCall's* May 1954: 27. Print.

Wylie, Philip. "The Womanization of America." *Playboy* Sept. 1958. Print.

Yoshihashi, Pauline. "New Boy on Campus: Men's Studies." *New York Times* 15 Apr. 1984: ES16. Print.

Chapter Nine

Kuaering "Home" in Ang Lee's *The Wedding Banquet*

Gust A. Yep and Ryan Lescure

Characterized by its spatialization (i.e., a place, a location), fluidity (i.e., elastic boundaries, variability across time, space, and culture), affective valences and intensities (i.e., positive and negative feelings, degrees of attachment), and relational patterns (i.e., types of social roles, gender performances, and relationships), a home is a complex and culturally specific mixture of structure (e.g., physical space) and texture (e.g., ideological frames of culture and gender), which Jeffrey McCune calls "architexture" (311). For individuals moving across cultural borders and contexts, meanings of home become more complex. Since "culture makes itself at home in motion," for transnational subjects, Victoria Chen reminds us that "home is never a place where one 'just lives'" (491). For non-normative intercultural social arrangements, such as intimate same-sex coupling and interethnic family relationships, home becomes a unique invention that involves identity, community, power, and politics. Put differently, the meanings of home for transnational non-normative subjects involve different architextures. Focusing on the film *The Wedding Banquet* (1993), we examine such meanings and architextures in this chapter. To accomplish this, our essay is divided into four sections. The first provides an overview of *The Wedding Banquet*. The second identifies different cultural discourses for understanding the sexuality of its main protagonist, Wai Tung, a transnational subject inhabiting multiple cultural worlds, and introduces kuaer theory as a framework to further this understanding. Asserting that the protagonist's sexuality creates multiple meanings of home, the next section provides three readings of "home" in the film. In addition to providing a summary, the final section discusses some of the implications of kuaer theory for the study of home in a transnational world.

THE WEDDING BANQUET: AN OVERVIEW

At the time of its release in 1993, *The Wedding Banquet* was the "highest grossing film in Taiwan, with great success in the United States and other international markets" (Chiang 374). It was released to great critical acclaim, winning best picture at the Berlin International Film Festival and a Palme d'Or at Cannes (Ma 200). The film also propelled director Ang Lee to international prominence. *The Wedding Banquet* is considered to be both a Taiwanese and U.S. film production, with a predominantly Asian cast, but a largely white U.S. American production staff (Chua 103). Lee himself is a Taiwanese American who has since gone on to direct several diverse, popular, and critically acclaimed films such as *Crouching Tiger, Hidden Dragon* (2000), *Brokeback Mountain* (2005), and *Life of Pi* (2012).[1] *The Wedding Banquet* and *Brokeback Mountain* both prominently feature multiculturalism and intragender sexuality in a way that is still rare in popular Western film, though the representations are considered by some to be problematic (Leung 23; Yang 41).

The Wedding Banquet was released at a cultural moment when Western independent films were increasingly featuring the topics of intragender sexuality, queer theory, culture, and identity (Chua 101; Leung 23). According to William Leung, *The Wedding Banquet* was released as the New Queer Cinema movement was occurring in film, a movement that is characterized by films that prominently feature these topics (23). In an interview with director Todd Haynes, Justin Wyatt characterizes Jennie Livingston's *Paris Is Burning* (1990), Gus Van Sant's *My Own Private Idaho* (1991), and Gregg Araki's *The Living End* (1992) as examples of films in the New Queer Cinema movement (2). Despite the increasing number of films exploring intragender sexuality, queer theory, culture, and identity in the early 1990s, homosexuality was—and is—still largely portrayed in Western film as being a distinctively white phenomenon (Chua 105). In this sense, *The Wedding Banquet* serves as an important exception to the infrequency of Asian intragender sexuality being represented in popular Western film. As such, it remains a cultural artifact worthy of discussion and analysis. The film's prominent themes, such as culture, sexuality, domesticity, and individualism provide a historical understanding for us to engage with, as these themes have evolved but are still prominent in U.S. cultural narratives and discourses.

The Wedding Banquet continues to have significant relevance at this historical juncture for at least two additional reasons. First, the film offers a historical perspective on how ideas and attitudes about sexuality and intragender relations have changed through time, both locally and transnationally. As neoliberal ideologies take hold locally and globally, the development of non-normative sexual cultures has been both enabled and limited (Kong 202). Such cultures are enabled through greater visibility of gay and lesbian identities as depoliticized consumer citizens in the global marketplace, which simultaneously function to limit other expressions and articulations of these identities. Second, the film provides a representational field to view multiple discourses of sexuality in a transnational world. As such, it offers Western perspectives of sexuality and intragender relations as well as more culturally specific views that are informed by an Asian sensibility and governed by what Travis Kong calls "family biopolitics," which refers to normative practices that regulate functional and productive bodies within Chinese families for economic well-being and success (97). Although these practices are certainly not exclusive to or inherent in Chinese culture, they do have culturally specific manifestations in Chinese refugee, immigrant, and diasporic communities. In sum, *The Wedding Banquet* is a cultural artifact that provides the opportunity to see historical changes regarding sexuality in a transnational world as well as to understand the interplay of multiple sexual discourses informed by Western views and Chinese sensibilities.

Featured as a comedy about identity, *The Wedding Banquet* focuses on a triadic intercultural domestic arrangement between Wai Tung (a successful Taiwanese American businessman living in New York City), Simon (Wai Tung's white American life partner), and Wei Wei (a poor Chinese woman artist who is having trouble with the U.S. Immigration and Naturalization Service). The film focuses on Wai Tung, who works as a landlord and is in a romantic relationship with Simon. This fact is unbeknownst to his parents, Mr. and Mrs. Gao, who live in Taiwan and are constantly pressuring Wai Tung to marry a Chinese woman and start a family. One of Wai Tung's tenants, Wei Wei, has a difficult time paying rent and is facing deportation to China. Simon suggests that Wai Tung and Wei Wei get married, a plan that would solve Wai Tung's ongoing issues with his parents and Wei Wei's immigration problems. This marriage would be for the sake of appearances only. Somewhat unexpectedly, the Gaos announce that they will be coming to New York City to meet Wei Wei and attend the wedding ceremony. In order for their plan to work, Simon, who is previously represented as being skilled at performing a heteropatriarchal "wife" role in the home, must teach Wei Wei how to perform this role in a manner that impresses the Gaos, showing them that she is a suitable match for their son. This scheme requires Simon to teach Wei Wei, who was previously represented as a messy and disorganized person (as well as an inept cook), how to perform his former domestic roles, which include activities such as cooking, cleaning, and doting on Wai Tung.

Their plan becomes complicated by the fact that the Gaos are very disappointed with their son's minimal civil wedding ceremony and ultimately plan a more lavish wedding banquet. In order to appease his parents and continue concealing his romantic relationship with Simon, Wai Tung reluctantly agrees. Much to his chagrin, the wedding banquet turns out to be a very well-attended drunken night of debauchery. The night culminates in Wei Wei, who was already attracted to Wai Tung, seducing him and the two of them having sex. Wei Wei ultimately becomes pregnant with Wai Tung's child, which causes a massive argument between Wai Tung and Simon in front of the Gaos, who presumably do not speak English. The pregnancy introduces a new tension in Wai Tung and Simon's relationship, but one that is put on hold when Wai Tung discovers that his ailing father is hospitalized due to a stroke. At the hospital, Mrs. Gao alludes to Wei Wei's pregnancy, but Wai Tung thinks she is talking about knowing about his relationship with Simon. He tells his mother about his romantic relationship with Simon and is overheard by Simon and Wei Wei. Their plan is unraveling, but Mrs. Gao tells Wai Tung that Mr. Gao is not to know.

Mr. Gao returns to Wai Tung's home after being released from the hospital. While out with Simon, Mr. Gao confesses that he knows about Wai Tung's romantic relationship with Simon. Unbeknownst to the other characters, Mr. Gao has a rudimentary knowledge of English and could tell what Wai Tung and Simon's fight was about. Mr. Gao symbolically accepts Simon into the family, but tells him not to let Mrs. Gao know about the relationship.

Ultimately, Wai Tung, Simon, and Wei Wei reconcile and agree to share the responsibility of raising the child between the three of them. The ending of the film is very bittersweet, with Wai Tung, Simon, Wei Wei, and the Gaos waiting at the airport looking at photos taken at the wedding banquet and reminiscing about the events that transpired. The Gaos walk toward their gate happy with the news that they will have a grandchild, but disappointed about the events that transpired during their visit. In an emotionally meaningful scene, Wai Tung, Wei Wei, and Simon watch the Gaos walk away as they prepare to embark on their new life together, a new life that will involve alternative meanings of love, family, and home.

While this ending scene suggests that the characters accept (and therefore, the film endorses) transformed meanings of love, family, and home, we argue that there are multiple readings of this scene. In addition, we argue that there are also multiple readings of other aspects of the film, including the ways that domesticity and housework are represented.

KUAER THEORY AND WAI TUNG'S SEXUALITY

As a transnational subject, Wai Tung's sexuality can be read and understood through multiple cultural discourses. As a Taiwanese American intragender loving person, his sexuality can be rendered meaningful in at least two different ways—the ubiquitous Western closet paradigm and a culturally specific "open secret" system of understanding sexuality (Ross 180, 183).

Perhaps the most common reading of Wai Tung's sexuality is through the dominant Western closet paradigm. Through this lens, Wai Tung is simply a closeted man, who is deeply ashamed—and perhaps even self-hating—about his own sexuality, which drives him to conceal it from his parents. This reading of Wai Tung's sexuality is based on the ubiquity and pervasiveness of the Western closet paradigm in current understandings of sexuality in a global world (Ross 169; Sedgwick 68). "The closet," according to Steven Seidman, is a "'life-shaping' social pattern" of concealment about one's sexuality that virtually all lesbian and gay individuals have experienced in recent decades (8). It is produced by heterosexual domination of the social world and perpetuated by its normalized form, heteronormativity. It is so powerful and pervasive that Eve Kosofsky Sedgwick, in her influential volume *Epistemology of the Closet*, calls the closet "*the* defining structure of gay oppression [of the twentieth] century" (71, emphasis added). In so doing, the closet became the universal paradigm for intragender attraction, identification, sexuality, and politics. To put it differently, the closet is the master narrative of modern sexuality (Ross 161).

What are the effects and consequences of the closet as a universal and master paradigm of modern sexuality in a global world? An obvious effect is the creation of a powerful hierarchy between "modern" and "pre-modern" sexualities in which "coming out," or living openly as a sexual minority person complete with sexual identity and personal pride, is a sign of positive evolution and cultural progress. Marlon Ross further explains:

> The "coming out" or closet paradigm has been such a compelling way of fixing homosexual identification exactly because it enables this powerful narrative of progress, not only in terms of the psychosexual development of an individual and the sociopolitical birth and growth of a legitimate sexual minority group, but also more fundamentally as a doorway marking the threshold between up-to-date fashions of sexuality and all the outmoded, anachronistic others. (163)

This narrative continues to re-center whiteness through "evolutionary notions of the uneven development of the races [and cultures] from primitive darkness to civilized enlightenment" (Ross 163). Further, the closet paradigm—and its imperative to "come out"—also re-centers Western middle-class values of individualism, economic independence, and personal visibility afforded to individuals who have the symbolic and material resources to leave their families and communities if their sexual identities are not accepted when they come out.[2] In short, the closet paradigm with its assumptions of unequal sexual development among cultures, races, and social classes reproduces the ideology of Western superiority of visible and explicit articulations and expressions of sexual desire, identity, practices, and politics in a global world.

Another reading of Wai Tung's sexuality is through a more culturally specific mode of articulation, perhaps one with an Asian sensibility. His sexuality could be viewed as an "open secret," which Ross defines as "a strong sense that it is impossible *not* to know something so obvious among those who know [Wai Tung] well enough [e.g., his parents]" (180, emphasis in the original). This reading suggests a tacit acknowledgment—and silent acceptance—of non-normative modes of sexual expression without overt verbal articulation and explicit discussion. Unlike the closet paradigm that underscores its vital and critical role, this culturally specific mode of articulation of sexuality downplays and diminishes the importance of coming out. Indeed, it might even downright discourage coming out, as Wai Tung's sexuality is already known. In this case, coming out is deemed unnecessary and irrelevant (Ross 179).

The interplay between these competing cultural discourses is compellingly illustrated in two moments in the film—Wai Tung's disclosure of his sexuality to his mother and Mr. Gao's acknowledgment of his son's homosexuality to Simon. In such moments, we see different transnational subjects—Wai Tung, Mrs. Gao, Simon, and Mr. Gao—embodying and articulating competing cultural discourses of sexuality.

The first moment is about Wai Tung's disclosure of his sexuality to his mother. After Mr. Gao has a mild stroke, Wai Tung rushes to San Sebastian Hospital to find his mother alone in the lobby. In a highly emotional exchange, Wai Tung tells his mother, "My marriage is a fraud. Simon is my real friend" before declaring, "Ma, I'm gay. Simon is my lover. We've been living together for five years." His disclosure suggests a transnational subject's embodiment of the ideology of sexual visibility in Western cultures. Such visibility is accomplished through a coming-out narrative in which Wai Tung unapologetically announces his sexual identity to his mother. Mrs. Gao responds by asking, "Simon led you astray?" Her reaction to the revelation reproduces the discourse of homosexuality as a Western disease. She concludes by telling Wai Tung, "[Y]our father must not know. It would kill him." Mrs. Gao's request reproduces popular views of homosexuality as an abject, stigmatizing, and horrific condition that must be kept hidden from significant others.

The second moment involves a scene when Mr. Gao gives Simon a birthday gift, suggesting that Gao speaks—and understands—English. Such an event leads Simon to figure out that Mr. Gao has known about his son's homosexuality all along and the following exchange occurs:

Simon: Then you know?

Mr. Gao: I watch, I hear, I learn. Wai Tung is my son so you're my son also.

When Simon brings up the possibility of telling the family about Mr. Gao's knowledge, the conversation continues:

Mr. Gao: Not Wai Tung, not mother, not Wei Wei shall know. This is our secret.

Simon: But why?

Mr. Gao: For the family. [switching to Chinese] If I didn't let them lie, I would have never gotten my grandchild.

Simon's comments suggest an adherence to the Western ideology of sexual visibility while Mr. Gao's tacit acceptance of his son's homosexuality reproduces the discourse of silence commonly associated with Asian cultures. Such discourse, as Eric Reyes and Gust Yep note, is based on heterosexist presumptions of interpersonal relationships and characterized by a lack of explicit discussion of sexual desires, particularly non-normative ones, which create and perpetuate lesbian and gay invisibility in Asian cultures (94). Mr. Gao's last comment also suggests that the maintenance of heteropatriarchy through a grandson is more important than sexual non-normativity.

Together, the two scenes show the interplay between two different and competing modes of articulation—one that expects explicit verbalization of sexual difference and another that requires tacit knowing—about Wai Tung's sexuality. The two episodes suggest, in our view, that the revelation of Wai Tung's sexuality—his disclosure to his mother and his father's knowledge of his sexuality—does not necessarily suggest a progress narrative from closeted to liberated sexual subject, as his father had accepted his sexuality all along. If Wai Tung were to come out to his father, "it can be judged a superfluous or perhaps even a distracting act, one subsidiary to the more important identifications of family, community, and race within which [his] sexual attractions are already interwoven and understood" (Ross 180).

To move away from the narrative of unequal sexual development between cultural groups with all its racist, classist, and Eurocentric assumptions that perpetuate views of more evolved and modern sexuality in the West and marginalize other experiences and representations of intragender relations, Ross suggests that "[Western scholarship] must be able to articulate the cultural differences in modes of sexual expression represented in various populations without falling—as a reflex reaction—into the closet paradigm as an easy common denominator for same-sexual identity" (181). Kuaer theory can provide us with such possible articulations.

Introduced in 2003 by communication scholar Wenshu Lee, kuaer theory is a critique and extension of what Gust Yep, Miranda Olzman, and Allen Conkle call "first-generation" queer theory (125). In particular, it critiques queer theory's tendency toward omission of race and class and extends the analysis to include them in a transnational context (Lee 160). As such, our analysis of the film uses a transnational lens that incorporates Western and Asian sensibilities and their ongoing tensions. Kuaer theory offers four important features for the analysis of social relations and cultural products. First, it focuses on "awakenings" (Lee 151) and "takes" (155), which generally refer to multiple layers of meaning in a particular social relation (e.g., how transnational subjects negotiate the multiple meanings of home). Second, it highlights the interlocking dynamics of nation, gender, sexuality, class, and race in a globalized world characterized by uneven flow of symbolic and material resources (e.g., how intersecting modes of difference, such as identities, produce specific forms of intelligibility and visibility for transnational sexual minority subjects in the West). Third, it stresses the importance of geographic and historical specificity for the understanding of social relations (e.g., how intragender relations are understood by a particular culture at a specific moment in time). Finally, it focuses on the interplay between the local and the global in the production specific forms of social relations (e.g., how regional understandings of sexuality interact with local and culturally specific conceptions to produce particular types of subjectivities). Together, the four features of kuaer theory offer the promise of producing a layered, nuanced, and complex analysis of social relations in a global world.

Wai Tung's sexuality is central to the plot in *The Wedding Banquet*. Kuaer theory directs our attention to the competing cultural discourses of sexuality that create all the complications in Wai Tung and Simon's home. In our view, Wai Tung's sexuality produces a home for "multi-racial, multi-sexual, multi-gendered, and multi-class" (Lee 162) subjects—Wai Tung, Simon, Wei Wei, and the Gaos—who engage in both reification and contestation of the (trans)national meanings of domesticity, family, and heteropatriarchy.

KUAERING "HOME"

Using kuaer theory to engage in multiple readings of *The Wedding Banquet* with a focus on the architexture of home that Wai Tung's sexuality creates, we provide three "takes" on the meaning of home (Lee 155). They are: heteropatriarchal, queer, and hybrid.

Our first "take" on the meaning of home offered by *The Wedding Banquet* is a heteropatriarchal take. As we have previously discussed, *home* is a multifaceted concept. Andrew Gorman-Murray argues that while having the potential appearance of being free from political meaning and hierarchical structures of power, home serves as a space where heteropatriarchy is maintained and contested ("This Is Disco-Wonderland!" 437). Heteropatriarchy, according to Yep, "is an overarching system of male dominance through the institution of compulsory heterosexuality" (31). In a heteropatriarchal society, the normative conception of home is one that is structured according to a specific set of requirements. Heteropatriarchy creates a hierarchical binary between the public sphere (e.g., commerce, industry, government) and the domestic sphere (e.g., the home, the family). The domestic sphere is then coded as being feminine, subordinated, trivial, and, perhaps paradoxically, sacred (Nilliasca 393). The public sphere, in contrast, is coded as being masculine, dominant, and consequential. In heteropatriarchal notions of "home," a male patriarch, who supports the home financially by working in the public sphere, is at the top of the home and family hierarchy. The home itself would be the realm of his dutiful wife, who is expected (because of heteropatriarchal structures) to maintain the domestic space through domestic work and to take care of the patriarch and his demands. These expectations mirror larger society and reinforce the meanings associated with gender identity (Bowlby, Gregory, and McKie 345).

Heteropatriarchy influences the structure of the home and the appropriate roles that the characters are expected to play in *The Wedding Banquet*. Wei Wei is expected to impress the Gaos with her performance of the "dutiful wife" as required by heteropatriarchy. The ultimate success of Simon, Wai Tung, and Wei Wei's plan in front of the Gaos depends completely on their replication of the appearance of a heteropatriarchal home. To accomplish this, Wei Wei must be socialized into the role of "dutiful wife" in relation to Wai Tung, who is the home's patriarch.

Simon, who himself fulfills the heteropatriarchal role of "dutiful wife," essentially gives Wei Wei a crash course in heteropatriarchal socialization by showing her how to take care of Wai Tung and how to perform the home's domestic work. He walks briskly through the house, giving Wei Wei instructions about the intricacies of taking care of Wai Tung as Wei Wei follows, carefully taking notes. Simon shows Wei Wei where everything in the house is located, tidying up as he goes along. Simon even delves into the minutiae of Wai Tung's life, including his dietary habits and which pair of underwear he wears on each day of the week. This is done in the name of performing the dutiful wife as defined by heteropatriarchy in front of Mr. and Mrs. Gao.

After the Gaos arrive, Wei Wei must appear to perform the role of dutiful wife correctly in front of them. This performance serves as a major source of comedy in the film, as Wei Wei was earlier shown to be quite messy and disorganized. Wei Wei is characterized in the beginning of the film to be an independent, Westernized, avant-garde artist. Wei Wei will have to mute these elements in her performance of identity, as it is implied that Simon and Wai Tung do not believe that the Gaos would accept the components of her identity that appear to contradict her ability and proclivity to clean, cook, and take care of Wai Tung. In a particularly meaningful scene, Wei Wei is shown cooking dinner for Wai Tung and the Gaos, though it is actually Simon doing the bulk of the cooking. When Mrs. Gao enters the kitchen, Simon feigns noninvolvement, but still carefully observes Wei Wei. When Mrs. Gao asks where the dishes are, Wei Wei gestures using her cooking spoon, flinging food all over the kitchen. While humorous, this scene also reinforces the notion that Simon's performance of domesticity is non-normative, but Wei Wei's is encouraged and expected. It also shows that Wei Wei does not quite fit the role that heteropatriarchy requires and that she constantly requires Simon's assistance and careful observation. Mrs. Gao does not realize this and compliments Wei Wei on her cooking ability, stating, "Wai Tung is lucky. He found a girl who can cook. Today that's rare." This statement exemplifies the value that Mrs. Gao places on the performance of normative gender roles in the home according to the structures of heteropatriarchy.

Wai Tung also acts as the patriarch in the home. Wai Tung is the home's breadwinner, participating in the public sphere in order to support Simon and the home. Additionally, he is shown to take great pride in his dedication to his work, which further develops his character as being kind, but stoic and serious. At the beginning of the film, heteropatriarchal tensions are shown affecting Wai Tung and Simon's relationship. Wai Tung spends a great deal of time working in the public sphere, which Simon perceives as being a detriment to their relationship. Ultimately, Wai Tung does not consent to Simon's wishes, choosing to attend an important business meeting instead of going on vacation with Simon. Wai Tung's choice reflects his reification of the public sphere above the domestic sphere and of business above personal relationships, which further develops his character as being a patriarch. Finally, and very meaningfully, Wai Tung only agrees to Simon's plan when Simon mentions the "big tax break" that he will receive if he marries Wei Wei. This further develops Wai Tung as the patriarch of the home as his motivation occurs as a result of Simon framing his persuasive appeal in the language of business and finance. In addition, Simon is deferential to Wai Tung in this scene, reaffirming his subordination to the patriarch of the home.

Our second "take" on the meaning of home in *The Wedding Banquet* is a queer take. Though the term "queer" is often applied to sexual non-normativity, we use the term in a much broader manner in this discussion. We use it as a signifier of non-normativity in general, as a term that describes what is typically labeled "deviant" and allows for the identification of the role of power in constructing what does and does not constitute "the normal" (Yep 36). David Halperin (1995) expands upon this notion, arguing that "queer is by definition *whatever* is at odds with the normal, the legitimate, the dominant" (62). A queer take on the meaning of home in *The Wedding Banquet* would look at the ways in which heteropatriarchal normativities are disrupted in the domestic sphere. We argue that Simon being the home's master domestic worker and his overall presence in the home constitutes a queer take on the meaning of home.

Simon is shown to be the character that most completely fulfills the role of "dutiful wife" as required in the heteropatriarchal home. As Simon is a white, male, middle-class American, we argue that his fulfillment of this role constitutes a non-normative, queer performance. Simon is shown to know the intricacies of taking care of Wai Tung and a great deal about Wai Tung's family, including his father's health problems. Simon is also shown frequently cooking and cleaning. Simon's representation as the primary and the most skilled homemaker problematizes notions of the home as a heterosexual, feminized realm. Simon is so good at domestic work that it can be argued that he fulfills the heteropatriarchal dutiful wife role much more completely than Wei Wei does. In fact, Simon is often working behind the scenes to help Wei Wei come across as a skilled domestic worker in front of the Gaos in order to gain their acceptance. Simon also seeks the same kind of validation, however, and inquires as to how the Gaos like the meal that they think Wei Wei cooked (though Simon did most of the work). Mr. Gao compliments Wei Wei on Simon's meal by saying, "[V]ery good. Right amount of soda, perfect soaking time, just the right tenderness. Wei Wei, what an effort." Simon is thrilled that the Gaos like his cooking, even though they are unaware that he was the one who did most of it. Also, when Wai Tung expresses frustration with Simon's presence in the home and the complications that his presence creates in front of his parents, he turns to Simon and frustratingly says, "[W]e should have moved you out." Simon responds by saying, "[N]ot if Wei Wei keeps cooking." This statement covertly demonstrates the necessity of his presence and domestic skill in the overall success of their plan.

Simon's presence in the home also serves to queer the normative heteropatriarchal meanings associated with home. Simon is introduced to the Gaos as Wai Tung's landlord and roommate, which satisfies their curiosity as to his presence in the home. The Gaos accept the fact that Simon, who they think is the landlord, lives with Wai Tung and Wei Wei and is intimately involved in many aspects of their lives. Simon takes a very proactive role in being involved with the functions of the home, spending so much time with the Gaos that they are ultimately surprised that he has friends and a social life. Simon's hands-on presence in the house challenges dominant readings of home as a heterosexualized family space as described by Gorman-Murray ("Queering Home" 233), therefore constituting a queer take.

Our third "take" on the meaning of home in *The Wedding Banquet* is a hybrid take. We argue that a hybrid take is a distinct third reading that recognizes that the meaning of home does not necessarily have to be either heteropatriarchal or queer, but can incorporate elements of both. There are several moments in the film where non-normative subjects are operating within the structural boundaries and requirements of heteropatriarchy, therefore reproducing normative constructions of home while changing its superficial appearance. In his analysis of two Australian television shows that prominently feature gay domesticity, Gorman-Murray's observations resemble our arguments about *The Wedding Banquet*. He argues that "the image of the 'domestic' gay man presents a *paradox* . . . the image of the domestic gay man both *queers* ideas of home and *domesticates* a 'deviant' sexuality" ("Queering Home" 233). We argue that *The Wedding Banquet* presents a queer home, but one that has been made palatable through the domestication of deviant or non-normative performances of identity. We argue that the concept of home is *allowed* to be queered as long as it meets the structural requirements of heteropatriarchy, which take precedence.

At the end of the film, Simon, Wai Tung, and Wei Wei decide to create a new home, one with a non-normative, queer, and seemingly non-heteropatriarchal structure. Their new home is a place of belonging and collective invention, with two gay men and a heterosexual woman raising a child together. This arrangement challenges normative heteropatriarchal conceptions of love, family, and parenting. Considering the dominant conceptualization of home as a space that is influenced by and reflective of heteropatriarchal power structures, a conceptualization that still persists despite discursive changes over time, this certainly constitutes a queer alternative.

Despite the fact that their new home will be a decidedly queer, non-normative space, the structural requirements of heteropatriarchy are still maintained. Wai Tung is still unequivocally positioned as being the patriarch of the home. He is dedicated to his job and he serves as the breadwinner and primary decision maker of the home and family. Wei Wei and Simon have certain deficiencies in regard to home and family when viewed from a heteropatriarchal perspective. Wei Wei is shown to never have mastered the domestic responsibilities as required by heteropatriarchy, and Simon and his relationship with Wai Tung do not fit in with the normative heteropatriarchal mother and father model of parenting. The inclusion of both Wei Wei and Simon in the home makes up for their collective deficiencies. Wei Wei will be present in the home, which satisfies heteropatriarchal demands for a child to be raised by a mother and a father. Simon will be present in the home, which satisfies heteropatriarchal demands for domestic work to exist outside of the patriarch's realm. Through being domesticized, Wei Wei and Simon are transformed into feminine subjects that are considered more appropriate and legible in heteropatriarchal conceptions of home and family. This ultimately maintains the underlying structure of heteropatriarchy and shifts its dynamic to accommodate queer or otherwise non-normative subjects.

Finally, Wai Tung and Simon queer the racial order in interracial coupling, with Wai Tung, who is Taiwanese American, performing the role of the symbolic "man" and Simon, who is a white American, performing the role of the symbolic "woman." In heteropatriarchal societies, individuals belonging to non-white races tend to be feminized and granted less access to participation in the public sphere (Espiritu 18). This is not necessarily the case with Wai Tung and Simon, who appear to queer racial hierarchies while maintaining heteropatriarchy at the same time. Despite being a white, male American, Simon is clearly represented as subordinated and feminized in his relationship with Wai Tung, which serves to reaffirm dominant heterosexual relationship structures and gender hierarchies while also inverting racial hierarchies and what Yen Le Espiritu refers to as "the exclusion of Asian men from Eurocentric notions of the masculine" (17).

SUMMARY AND IMPLICATIONS

In this chapter, we discussed home as a social construction with multiple dimensions and meanings. *The Wedding Banquet* serves as an illustration both of the complex meanings associated with home in a transnational context and in an increasingly globalized world. Focusing on Wai Tung's sexuality, we discussed competing cultural discourses of sexuality—the universal Western closet paradigm and a culturally specific "open secret" system of understanding sexuality. In the process, we identified the major problems produced by the closet paradigm and the need to understand transnational systems of sexuality within their own culturally specific modes of articulation. Since much of queer theory is based on the assumption of the closet, we introduced Lee's kuaer theory (147) to provide more layered and nuanced readings of the meaning of home created by Wai Tung's sexuality. We went on to discuss three readings of the architexture of home—heteropatriarchal, queer, and hybrid—in the film.

   The Wedding Banquet, as noted earlier, presents multiple competing discourses of sexuality in a transnational world through Wai Tung. He navigates between the Western closet paradigm and a more culturally specific articulation, governed by Chinese family biopolitics. Based on individualism, the closet paradigm originates from a confessional model that requires a person to come out as an expression of authenticity and self-development (Boellstorff 209). Based on collectivism, the Chinese family biopolitics system emphasizes economic success and harmonious family relationships in which sexual silences may not be necessarily restrictive or oppressive. Kong elaborates,

> [Such silences] should not be seen as merely negative and repressive, . . . [or] as preserving the power of heterosexism by fashioning a self-loathing homosexual. Rather, [these silences] might also be seen as productive, as they not only avoid the risks of unintended exposure, but also create a protected social

space that permits individuals to fashion gay selves and to navigate paths
between straight and gay worlds. (107)

Living in a transnational world, Wai Tung's tensions—and the source of
much of the comedy in the film—could be viewed as the embodiment of the
demands of closet paradigm and its homosexual-heterosexual binary, and
family biopolitics and its heteropatriarchal gender roles. In the end, he simultaneously reinforces and challenges both systems. More recent research with
Chinese intragender loving people (Chou, *Tongzhi*; Kong, *Chinese Male
Homosexualities*) and Korean gays and lesbians (Cho, "Wedding Banquet
Revisited") confirm these patterns.

One of the implications of applying kuaer theory to the analysis of home
and domesticity is that it encourages different "takes" for multiple readings,
which also allows for a more nuanced understanding of a phenomenon. This
is a postmodern method to approaching textual analysis that emphasizes the
existence of multiple subjective "truths." Lee's notion of takes (155) in kuaer
theory account for a both/and approach, rather than forcing an either/or approach, which further dismantles the notion of normativity as perpetuated by
dominant readings of a text. This allows for greater nuance in the interpretation of an artifact. Instead of passively accepting the dominant reading of a
text, the recognition of multiple takes allows for a greater understanding into
the ways that power influences which readings are "correct" and which readings are not. Contradictory readings of a text also demonstrate the very real
notion that texts are unstable and that meaning is not inherent in a text, but is
instead created when individuals interact with it.

Mark Chiang argues that *The Wedding Banquet* "certainly offers a useful
test case for investigating how patriarchies respond to the pressures and
tensions of postmodernity and globalization" (374). We argue that a hybrid
take on the meaning of home in *The Wedding Banquet* demonstrates that a
queering of home is acceptable as long as the structure of heteropatriarchy is
ultimately maintained. This demonstrates the elasticity of power structures in
adapting to re-exert social control, even in the face of changing conditions
and tensions. Kuaer theory—with its emphasis on multiple readings; the
interlocking dynamics of nation, gender, sexuality, class, and race; the importance of cultural and geographic specificities; and the interplay between
the local and the global—is an effective approach for analyzing how heteropatriarchy—and its corollary conceptions of home and domesticity—reacts
to an increasingly postmodern and transnational world.

Finally, kuaer theory aids in the analysis of competing discourses between modernity and postmodernity through concepts of nation, home, and
sexuality. It also provides a lens to understanding sexuality in a transnational
world by highlighting culturally specific modes of articulation existing with
and against universal and modernist conceptions of progress associated with

the Western closet paradigm. Through multiple "takes," we can see the integral role that culture and nation have in the construction of the meanings of home and sexuality, as well as the potential deconstruction of the meaningfulness of home and sexuality in a transnational context.

NOTES

1. *The Wedding Banquet* was nominated for an Oscar in the Best Foreign Language category in 1993, as was *Eat Drink Man Woman* in 1994; Lee won the category in 2000 for *Crouching Tiger, Hidden Dragon*, and later won Best Director for *Brokeback Mountain* (2005) and *Life of Pi* (2012).

2. We are certainly not denying the potential pain and suffering experienced by individuals who encounter rejection because of their sexual difference. In the film, for example, Wai Tung's white neighbors seemingly disapprove of his relationship with Simon. Our point, however, is that people with sufficient material resources (e.g., middle-class individuals) have the option to leave such communities while people with fewer resources (e.g., working-class individuals) may not. In the process, a class hierarchy is erected with middle-class individuals perceived to be more accepting, less homophobic, and possibly more evolved.

WORKS CITED

Boellstorff, Tom. *The Gay Archipelago: Sexuality and Nation in Indonesia*. Princeton, NJ: Princeton University Press, 2005. Print.

Bowlby, Sophie, Susan Gregory, and Linda McKie. "'Doing Home': Patriarchy, Caring, and Space." *Women's Studies International Forum* 20.3 (1997): 343–50. Print.

Chen, Victoria. "Authenticity and Identity in the Portable Homeland." *The Handbook of Critical Intercultural Communication*. Ed. Thomas K. Nakayama and Rona Tamiko Halualani. Malden: Blackwell, 2010. 483–94. Print.

Chiang, Mark. "Coming Out into the Global System: Postmodern Patriarchies and Transnational Sexualities in *The Wedding Banquet*." *Q & A: Queer in Asian America*. Ed. David L. Eng and Alice Y. Hom. Philadelphia: Temple University Press, 1998. 374–95. Print.

Cho, John Song Pae. "*The Wedding Banquet* Revisited: 'Contract Marriages' Between Korean Gays and Lesbians." *Anthropological Quarterly* 82.2 (2009): 401–22. Print.

Chou, Wah-shan. (2000). *Tongzhi: Politics of Same-Sex Eroticism in Chinese Societies*. New York: Haworth Press, 2000. Print.

Chua, Ling-Yen. "The Cinematic Representation of Asian Homosexuality in *The Wedding Banquet*." *Journal of Homosexuality* 36.3/4 (1999): 99–112. Print.

Espiritu, Yen Le. "All Men Are *Not* Created Equal." *Men's Lives*. Ed. Michael S. Kimmel and Michael A. Messner. Boston: Pearson, 2013. 17–25. Print.

Gorman-Murray, Andrew. "Queering Home or Domesticating Deviance? Interrogating Gay Domesticity through Lifestyle Television." *International Journal of Cultural Studies* 9.2 (2006): 227–47. Print.

———. "'This Is Disco-Wonderland!' Gender, Sexuality and the Limits of Gay Domesticity on *The Block*." *Social & Cultural Geography* 12.5 (2011): 435–53. Print.

Halperin, David M. *Saint Foucault: Towards a Gay Hagiography*. New York: Oxford University Press, 1995. Print.

Kong, Travis S. K. *Chinese Male Homosexualities: Memba, Tongzhi, and Golden Boy*. London: Routledge, 2011. Print.

Lee, Ang, dir. *The Wedding Banquet*. MGM Home Entertainment, 1993. Film.

Lee, Wenshu. "*Kuaering* Queer Theory: My Autocritography and a Race-Conscious, Womanist, Transnational Turn." *Queer Theory and Communication: From Disciplining Queers to*

Queering the Discipline(s). Ed. Gust A. Yep, Karen E. Lovaas, and John P. Elia. Bingham-
ton, NY: Harrington Park Press, 2003. 147–70. Print.
Leung, William. "So Queer Yet So Straight: Ang Lee's *The Wedding Banquet* and *Brokeback
Mountain*." *Journal of Film and Video* 60.1 (2008): 23–42. Print.
Ma, Shen-mei. "Ang Lee's Domestic Tragicomedy: Immigrant Nostalgia, Exotic/Ethnic Tour,
Global Market." *Journal of Popular Culture* 30.1 (1996): 191–201. Print.
McCune, Jeffrey Q. "'Out' in the Club: The Down Low, Hip-Hop, and the Architexture of
Black Masculinity." *Text and Performance Quarterly* 28.3 (2008): 298–314. Print.
Nilliasca, Terri. "Some Women's Work: Domestic Work, Class, Race, Patriarchy, and the
Limits of Legal Reform." *Michigan Journal of Race & Law* 16.2 (2011): 377–410. Print.
Reyes, Eric E., and Gust A. Yep. "Challenging Complexities: Strategizing with Asian
Americans in Southern California Against (Heterosex)isms." *Overcoming Heterosexism and
Homophobia: Strategies That Work*. Ed. James T. Sears and Walter L. Williams. New York:
Columbia University Press, 1997. 91–103. Print.
Ross, Marlon B. "Beyond the Closet as Raceless Paradigm." *Black Queer Studies: A Critical
Anthology*. Ed. E. Patrick Johnson and Mae G. Henderson. Durham, NC: Duke University
Press, 2005. 161–89. Print.
Sedgwick, Eve K. *Epistemology of the Closet*. Berkeley: University of California Press, 1990.
Print.
Seidman, Steven. *Beyond the Closet: The Transformation of Gay and Lesbian Life*. New York:
Routledge, 2002. Print.
Wyatt, Justin. "Cinematic/Sexual Transgression: An Interview with Todd Haynes." *Film Quar-
terly* 46.3 (1993): 2–8. Print.
Yang, Che-ming. "The Paradox of Transgressing Sexual Identities: Mapping the Micropolitics
of Sexuality/Subjectivity in Ang Lee's Films." *Asian Culture and History* 2.1 (2010):
41–47. Print.
Yep, Gust A. "The Violence of Heteronormativity in Communication Studies: Notes on Injury,
Healing, and Queer World-Making." *Queer Theory and Communication: From Disciplining
Queers to Queering the Discipline(s)*. Ed. Gust A. Yep, Karen E. Lovaas, and John P. Elia.
Binghamton, NY: Harrington Park Press, 2003. 11–59. Print.
Yep, Gust A., Miranda Olzman, and Allen Conkle (2012). "Seven Stories from the 'It Gets
Better' Project: Progress Narratives, Politics of Affect, and the Question of Queer World-
Making." *Producing Theory in a Digital World: The Intersection of Audiences and Produc-
tion in Contemporary Theory*. Ed. Rebecca A. Lind. New York: Peter Lang, 2012. 123–41.
Print.

Chapter Ten

Good Luck Raising the Modern Family

*Analyzing Portrayals of Sexual Division of Labor and
Socioeconomic Class on Family Sitcoms*

Nancy Bressler

In 1963, Betty Friedan introduced the term "housewives' syndrome" or "housewives' fatigue" in her book *The Feminine Mystique* (16). Women all over the country, she argued, were facing a persistent depression even though they were living the quintessential American Dream. These women stayed at home to care for the children, while their husbands went to work. They had a beautiful home to care for, loving children to raise, and disposable income. What could possibly be the problem? Friedan paints the ideal picture: "The suburban housewife—she was the dream image of the young American women and the envy, it was said, of women all over the world" (13). Friedan concludes that the "problem" was that educated women lacked a desire to simply be housewives and mothers. Friedan notes that a 1960s housewife observed how "a century earlier, women had fought for higher education; now girls went to college to get a husband" (12). The viewpoint that women could only be wives and mothers was an indication of a deeper problem ingrained in American society. Friedan argues that young women "were taught to pity the neurotic, unfeminine, unhappy women who wanted to be poets or physicists, or presidents. They learned that truly feminine women do not want careers, higher education, political rights—the independence and the opportunities that the old-fashioned feminists fought for" (11). Clearly, there was an ingrained interpretation of gender roles in American families. Men went to work and women worked at home. Sociologists David Croteau and William Hoynes note in their 2003 book:

It's easy to see from today's perspective that the traditional family structure
was an attractive one for some people. It enabled them to fit neatly into clearly
defined roles that brought them significant rewards. Husbands and children
were nurtured and cared for. Wives were spared the pressure of holding down
a job outside the home, while often enjoying autonomy in the home. (21)

Betty Friedan's *The Feminine Mystique* examined white, college-educated, middle-class women who were suffering from a form of depression called
"housewives' syndrome." These women could not understand the source of
their depression, since they were living the quintessential American
Dream—their husbands had high-paying jobs, while they cared for the house
and the children.

Perhaps a key explanation was the media images presented to housewives, just a decade before (Mann 57). In order for women to continue to
want to do housework, an idealized form was presented to them. Alongside
this industrialization of women's work a new discourse emerged, which romanticized women's roles as housewives, homemakers, and mothers—often
referred to as the "cult of domesticity" or the "cult of true womanhood." This
discourse entailed a "doctrine of separate spheres," which deemed the private
realm of the household as women's sphere and the public realm outside of
the home as men's sphere (Mann 39).

By the 1950s, the traditional idea of domestic housewife was diminishing
because of technological advances that made housework increasingly easier
to complete. As a result, media images began altering their depictions of
women and housework to show women that their presence was needed in the
home. Images of the happy, white, middle-class housewife began to appear
on television and implied that domesticity was the goal of all housewives.

Mann observes that "powerful images of the postwar, intact nuclear family with stay-at-home moms and breadwinner dads continue to beam into our
living rooms in countless reruns of 1950s television sitcoms" (57). While
these images appear in today's television reruns, even family sitcoms in 2012
tend to follow the pattern of the happy nuclear family. These new sitcoms,
such as *Modern Family* (2009–) and *Raising Hope* (2010–), may send the
same powerful message that the 1950s sitcoms showed: traditional gender
norms, such as separate tasks for men and women. Or perhaps there is a new
and distorted version of the "cult of domesticity" being presented to housewives today. Consequently, this chapter will investigate the television portrayals of division of labor between mothers and fathers on family sitcoms
that aired in 2012.

Friedan's *The Feminine Mystique* urged women to question the deeply
ingrained ideologies about gender roles that had always been taken for
granted. This study addresses that call to action because the prevalent conventional gender roles perpetuated in the media serve to maintain those deep-

ly fixed ideologies. While media's portrayals of society do not often reflect reality, "the fear is that media images normalize specific social relations, making certain ways of behaving seem unacceptable. If media texts can normalize behaviors, they can also set limits on the range of acceptable ideas. The ideological work lies in the patterns within media texts" (Croteau and Hoynes 163). While grounded in ideas from *The Feminine Mystique*, this analysis will also build upon Friedan's observations. Friedan examined white middle-class women who had access to higher education, but failed to investigate the intersections of gender and class. How does the socioeconomic status of the family play a role in women's "housewife syndrome"? Therefore, this project will also focus on the intersections of class status within the television families. It will also address to what extent class status plays any role in the division of labor found in 2012 media depictions. In what ways has the "cult of domesticity" become a shifting, changeable, and less concrete concept than ever before?

SEXUAL DIVISION OF LABOR

The sexual division of labor refers to the idea that each gender has its own specific role. For example, males may be the breadwinners and females could be the caregivers for the house and children. After industrialization in the West, the sexual division of labor was especially prominent; a clear distinction between workplace and home emerged. Because women manufactured the products for their families, even housework in the colonial era was vastly different than today (Davis 225). Housewives in the eighteenth and early-nineteenth centuries made bread, butter, clothing, soap, and other commodities the family needed to survive (Ehrenreich and English 156).

As capitalism advanced, men necessarily became the breadwinners and women became dependent on their financial success. According to Friedrich Engels, the problem remains that housework is unpaid for women and therefore assigns a sexual division of labor within capitalism (Ferguson and Hennessy, *Feminist Perspectives*). In the nineteenth century, Engels commented, "In the great majority of cases today, at least in the possessing classes, the husband is obliged to earn a living and support his family, and that in itself gives him a position of supremacy, without any need for special legal titles and privileges" (Engels 486–87). Because housework remains unpaid labor, it also became the marginalized form of labor in the household. Thus, a theoretical framework of the family as an economic system is needed because familial labor is intertwined with profitability and ultimately diminished (McKie, Bowlby, and Gregory 4). Political activist and author Angela Davis adds that housewives could rarely provide proof of their work. She argues, "Housework, after all, is virtually invisible: No one notices it until it isn't done—we notice the unmade bed, not the scrubbed and polished floor" (222). Mann observes that "what was once homemade could now be purchased so that women no longer had to produce such items as bread, butter, cheese, soap, candles, or clothing" (39). While colonial women played a vital role in the manufacturing of the goods needed by their families, today's housewives can rely on more modern conveniences.

Bernardes further argues that the family is depicted as a safe place that automatically provides appropriate roles for each of its members: father, mother, husband, and wife (qtd. in Gregory 61). Each of these roles also comes with its previously conceived behavioral roles and until those roles are challenged by family members, they will remain the norm: "The family and the roles assumed by its members are demonstrated and reinforced through day-to-day activities. Within the private world of the family, it is in what women do, and to an extent in what men do not do, that these gender roles are evident" (Gregory 61). Susan Gregory states that while other household tasks are often divided, cooking and tasks based around food remain primarily the responsibility of women (61).

While these authors discuss various historical viewpoints on the sexual division of labor, an updated conversation about their theoretical beliefs is needed. Both within society and in mediated images, the conceptualizations about family and the sexual division of labor are in flux. Will a more recent examination find similar themes surrounding the "cult of domesticity"? Moreover, none of these authors considered the socioeconomic status of the family as a whole. Thus, the inclusion of economic class in analyzing the sexual division of labor remains a flaw in these discussions.

Consequently, while fixed gender roles were present in previous decades, how are they displayed in society today? Leslie Stratton (2003) analyzed real-life married couples and coded her respondents' answers for various forms of housework. Stratton observes that married women spent nearly double the amount of time on housework as married men, but also acknowledged that the men in her sample worked twice as much as women at their full-time employment. Stratton concludes, "The key difference appears to be in who specializes in what" (73–74). She found that 60 percent of households reported extreme specialization when it came to household chores. Women primarily prepared meals, washed the dishes, cleaned, and did the family laundry. Men, on the other hand, did more outdoor and maintenance work on the house or car. Shopping, driving the children, and paying bills were all found to be neutral activities (77). Stratton further observes that the higher the income of the husband, the less he contributed to work at home. This led Stratton to question whether these conclusions were based on deeply held gender roles, or economic imbalances based on gender. Yet, once again, the socioeconomic background of the family was ignored. Bianchi, Milkie, Sayer, and Robinson also found similar conclusions in their study in 1995 in which married men, and men who earned significantly more than their wives, did less housework (215). They also investigated employment hours and found smaller gender gaps in housework when the wife had a college degree and worked; the wife's housework hours decreased, while the husband's hours increased (215). Additionally, the greater the wife's income, the smaller the gender gap (217). Because these conclusions were based on real-life examples, they emphasize the need for updated research on mediated examples of the sexual division of labor, specifically analyzing how female working characters portray sexual divisions of labor. As more women enter the workplace, what impact does that have on the sexual division of labor within mediated samples?

HEGEMONIC MEDIA IMAGES OF GENDER

Because the findings of these previous studies demonstrate that a sexual division of labor still exists in the twenty-first century, what forces contribute to its seemingly natural continuation in society? Through the use of Gramsci's concept of hegemony, this chapter argues that media representations are a significant contributor to the continuation of the sexual division of labor in households. Hegemony provides a "tool of analysis for understanding the sites of gendered oppression in society" (Ledwith 687). By questioning the natural assumptions within society, this chapter contributes to feminist critique through its analysis of mediated texts.

Karl Marx argues that through the use of ideology and hegemony, the ruling class could conceal the differences between the social classes and maintain an inequality that gives the ruling class an advantage. By perpetuating their own societal views, the capitalist class can dominate the classes beneath them (Williams 153). Thus, hegemony acts as a large, overarching mechanism that creates common-sense ideas from social inequalities:

> Hegemony operates at the level of common sense in the assumptions we make about social life and on the terrain of things that we accept as "natural" or "the way things are." After all, what is common sense except for those things we think are so obvious that we need not critically evaluate them? Common sense is the way we describe things that "everybody knows," or at least should know, because such knowledge represents deeply held cultural beliefs. (Croteau and Hoynes 166)

Consent, therefore, is an understated process that occurs at a common sense level. The concepts become "natural" and the resulting inequalities are ignored (150).

While Marx references the differences in class issues, his argument also relates to conventional gender roles and the sexual division of labor. Marx argues that the ruling class, or bourgeois, could hide any social differences in an effort to maintain their established order. Once the lower (proletariat) class believes that the ideologies of the bourgeois represent their own interests and what is best for them, they have reached a state of false consciousness because they no longer embrace the fact that the two classes have distinct interests. The same can be true for gender inequalities that are hidden away within society in order to allow the male-dominated class to implement policies that facilitate their goals because women believe it will serve their interests as well (Williams 147–48). Therefore, this chapter will investigate to what extent television content also further conceals the continuation of sexual division of labor, but presents it as equal in the twenty-first century.

DOMESTIC TELEVISION SITCOMS

Beginning in the 1950s and 1960s, domestic sitcoms became a popular type of situation comedy. While they still feature a recurring cast and a situation that needs to be resolved, domestic sitcoms tend to focus only on the family. Judy Kutulas observes that "family is the one experience to which virtually all viewers can relate. It evokes symbols and images advertisers like. And its plot possibilities are endless" (49). Perhaps the family sitcom is beloved by so many because of the idealistic images it conveys. Family sitcoms are often fantasies in which the real world problems do not permeate. Kutulas further adds, "Objectively we know that the Cleavers represent an ideal rather than a norm, and one that confines and constricts individuality. Emotionally though, we cannot escape the sense that life would be so much better if our lives were just like the Cleavers" (49). Rather than concentrating on broader social problems that need to be addressed, the focus of the plot of family sitcoms is on developing the characters as part of the family. In other words, a family problem is more likely to be the main plot of the episode and contain a simplistic situation (Campbell, Martin, and Fabos 2010 228). The problems and conflicts presented emphasize the family unit. Yet, the solutions presented only solve that episode's individual problems. It provides minimal closure to an immediate problem, rather than addressing any fundamental concerns about society. Therefore, a domestic comedy will solve the family's immediate problems in that episode, without continuing to address broader issues over several episodes. However, the majority of sitcoms of the 1950s typically conformed to traditional gender roles and sexual divisions of labor. Dad went off to work, while mom cared for the home and children. Because 1950s sitcoms served as cultural educators, their images contributed to reinforcing traditional gender roles. Superficially, sitcoms and the representation of family on them have differed over the past fifty years, but what about the underlying ideologies of the sexual division of labor? Consequently, it is vital to investigate to what extent contemporary domestic sitcoms are presenting a varied adaptation of the "cult of domesticity" today. Richard Campbell, Christopher Martin, and Bettina Fabos noted that "generally, viewers identify more closely with the major characters in domestic comedies than with those in a sitcom" (2010 228). Thus, no matter the time period, the representation of family on television emphasizes some small aspect of recognizability for its audience members.

The family sitcoms included in this discussion are *Modern Family* (2010–), *Good Luck Charlie* (2010–), *The Middle* (2009–), and *Raising Hope* (2010–). ABC's *Modern Family* tells the story of three very different families that are all related to one another. Two of these families, the Pritchetts and the Pritchett-Tuckers, are upper-middle-class or wealthy. Jay Pritchett is a successful business owner and is married to Gloria. Mitchell Pritchett is a lawyer and is in a committed relationship with his boyfriend, Cameron Tucker. Both the Pritchetts and the Pritchett-Tuckers not only have prestigious careers but also lavish homes and spending habits. Therefore, they are designated as upper-middle-class or wealthy. The third family from *Modern Family*, the Dunphys, are classified as middle class. Phil Dunphy is a real estate agent, but he and his wife, Claire, have relatively conservative spending habits. Disney Channel's *Good Luck Charlie* features a middle-class family, the Duncans, in which both parents, Bob and Amy, work to support their five children. *The Middle* airs on ABC and depicts the Hecks, a working-class family. Frankie and Mike both work and struggle to pay their bills. Finally, Fox's *Raising Hope* features the Chances, another working-class family. Virginia and Burt Chance also both work to financially support their family.

SUPERFICIAL CHORES VERSUS SPECIALIZATION

To discover the overall trends and patterns, this discussion will now focus on how the individual examples presented contribute to the broader implications of the findings. Upon first observation, the visual examples of housework on family sitcoms appear mainly equivalent. Men completed 40.5 percent of the household chores, while women completed 45.1 percent (table 10.1). Tasks were even completed by couples together 14.4 percent of the time. To the casual viewer of these family sitcoms, it appears as though men and women perform a nearly equal amount of the housework; these findings reinforce that general observation.

However, while the overall examples of housework suggested a diminished sexual division of labor, by further dividing the examples into specializations, a broader picture emerges. The sexual division of labor became more evident when housework was divided by certain household chores. For example, shopping for household goods, laundry, and outdoor/general main-

Table 10.1.   Household Chores Performed, by Gender and Socioeconomic Class

	Lower-Class	Middle-Class	Upper-Middle-Class / Wealthy	Total
Men	22	15	8	45
Women	30	18	2	50
Both	11	3	2	16
Total	63	36	12	111

tenance did result in obvious gender roles. Female characters shopped for groceries and other household goods 66.67 percent of the time (table 10.2). Women also completed 71.4 percent of the laundry tasks, including washing and folding. In contrast, men completed 76.47 percent of the outdoor/general maintenance tasks either alone or with a female character. Moreover, lower-class men completed 90 percent of the outdoor/general maintenance tasks. This category alone contributed to 22.22 percent of the household chores men did overall. Therefore, women were responsible for the family's laundry and shopping, while men were obviously responsible for fixing areas of the house and general maintenance. Consequently, there were clear gender roles portrayed in the categories of shopping, laundry, and outdoor/general maintenance. Through the division of household chores by specialization, women are still depicted as responsible for work inside the home, while men are in charge of work outside the home. In this respect, these images show little change in the idea that women's work—and by extension, place—is in the home.

While analyzing child care chores, a prevailing pattern of gender roles became even more apparent. With the exception of driving the children, the mothers clearly are responsible for the child care chores. For example, Claire, the mother on *Modern Family*, provides emotional support to her children and comforts Haley, her oldest child, when she is rejected from colleges ("Election Day"). She also puts the children to bed in one scene; her husband, Phil, is also clearly visible in the scene but is too preoccupied with work to tend to the children ("Tableau Vivant"). In a somewhat contradictory example, Jay babysits for his granddaugher, Lily, and enlists the help of his stepson, Manny ("Baby on Board"). However, the choice to babysit Lily is not theirs, since Gloria, Jay's wife, was supposed to watch Lily but was called away unexpectedly. Therefore the men are obligated to watch Lily, as opposed to choosing the responsibility. These scenes clearly depict that child care is a woman's task. Even when men are in the room and visible in the same scene, the women are responsible for caring for the children. In these scenes, men are portrayed as caring for the children only when an emergency arises that prevents the women from doing it.

Table 10.2.   Specific Chores Performed, by Gender and Socioeconomic Class

	Lower-Class	Middle-Class	Upper-Middle-Class / Wealthy	Total
Meals: Men	2	4	4	10
Meals: Women	12	3	1	16
Meals: Both	0	1	0	1
Meals Total	14	8	5	27
Dishes: Men	0	0	0	0
Dishes: Women	0	2	0	2
Dishes: Both	1	1	1	3
Dishes Total	1	3	1	5
Cleaning: Men	3	0	1	4
Cleaning: Women	4	0	0	4
Cleaning: Both	2	0	0	2
Cleaning Total	9	0	1	10
Laundry: Men	1	1	0	2
Laundry: Women	2	2	1	5
Laundry: Both	0	0	0	0
Laundry Total	3	3	1	7
Outdoor/General Maintenance: Men	9	0	1	10
Outdoor/General Maintenance: Women	4	0	0	4
Outdoor/General Maintenance: Both	3	0	0	3
Outdoor/General Maintenance Total	16	0	1	17
Auto Repair	0	0	0	0
Shopping: Men	0	2	0	2
Shopping: Women	3	3	0	6
Shopping: Both	1	0	0	1
Shopping Total	4	5	0	9
Driving Others: Men	2	4	0	6

Driving Others: Women	1	2	0	3
Driving Others: Both	1	0	0	1
Driving Others Total	4	6	0	10
Bills: Men	0	1	0	1
Bills: Women	0	0	0	0
Bills: Both	1	0	0	1
Bills Total	1	1	0	2
Child Care: Men	5	3	2	10
Child Care: Women	4	6	0	10
Child Care: Both	2	1	1	4
Child Care Total	11	10	3	24

On *Good Luck Charlie*, Amy, the mother, is primarily responsible for caring for the children. In flashbacks, she is seen rocking her son, Gabe, to sleep and feeding her daughter, Charlie, a bottle ("Make Room for Baby"). Amy has just brought a new baby home and is feeding him as well ("Welcome Home"). In order to punish Bob on multiple occasions, Amy tells him that he must change the new baby's diapers and clean his spit-up. First, caring for the children was seen as an obligation (*Modern Family*) and now caring for the baby is seen as a punishment (*Good Luck Charlie*), as opposed to a rewarding experience of spending time with the new baby. In both situations, men caring for a child is portrayed in a negative light. Consequently, the only time that men are depicted caring for a child, they are unenthusiastic and essentially coerced by a woman. The implication within these images is that men would not voluntarily care for children, since these images have strong pessimistic undertones. Within the *Raising Hope* episodes, Virginia and her son, Jimmy, are the ones who frequently take care of his baby, Hope. Since Jimmy is a single father, Virginia is clearly the female presence in the baby's life. In this scenario, there are equal divisions of labor between Virginia and Jimmy. However, Burt, Jimmy's father, spends significantly less time with Hope, perhaps indicating a more equal division of labor between Virginia and Jimmy. This scenario is somewhat suspect, since it implies that Jimmy cannot care for the child himself as a single father; instead a woman is also needed to care for the child.

THE IMPACT OF CHARACTERS' SOCIOECONOMIC STATUS

This study also sought to analyze whether class status played a role in the sexual division of labor. Even though both wealthy/upper-middle-class families feature wives who are stay-at-home mothers, there is very little evidence of them performing domestic labor. Instead, there are mentions of "housekeepers" who complete many household chores. This observation supports Stratton's real-life finding that the higher the income of the husband, the less he contributes at home. With these mediated representations, however, it appears as though both parents contribute very little to the household. The middle-class characters performed three times as much housework and the lower-class characters did five times as many household chores as the upper-middle-class/wealthy characters (see table 10.1). The majority of housework that upper-middle-class characters did was either meal preparation (41.67 percent) or child care (25 percent; see table 10.2); in fact, these are also the only categories in which upper-middle-class or wealthy characters performed work more than once.

Specifically, socioeconomic status influenced two categories of housework: meal preparation and outdoor/general maintenance. These categories also produced the most (meal preparation) and third greatest (outdoor/general maintenance) number of examples (see table 10.2). Overall, meal preparation resulted in twenty-seven visual examples, with men preparing 37.04 percent of the meals and women preparing 59.26 percent of them. Thus, the kitchen is no longer solely the symbol of women's domesticity. Yet, in families that were lower class, there were only two examples of men preparing meals; this resulted in 14.29 percent of the time. In comparison, women in lower-class families were responsible for meal preparation an enormous 85.71 percent of the time (see table 10.2). In particular, on *The Middle* the mother, Frankie, is the only one preparing meals; however, each example only shows her carrying in take-out containers or unwrapping store-bought sandwiches. The implication here is that any family member could pick up take-out for dinner, yet it is Frankie seen doing it. She is also shown in one scene barbecuing at work, where she is the only female employee ("The Telling"). In both examples, men could easily be viewed unloading take-out containers and grilling, yet the mother is seen as the only one who can do it. *Raising Hope* also appeared to provide a greater reinforcement that cooking was a female task in the household. The mother, Virginia, is the main cook in the family. When her son Jimmy attempts to cook in one episode, it results in a disastrous dinner ("Poking Holes in the Story"). These results imply that when it comes to the cooking and preparing of meals on family sitcoms, there is less of a gender divide in middle-class and wealthy families.

In addition, working-class families also saw an abundance of outdoor/general maintenance. Working-class characters were responsible for 94.12

percent of the outdoor/general maintenance, while men did 56.25 percent alone and 18.75% with a female character (see table 10.2). Mike, the father on *The Middle*, typically performed general maintenance around the house. He builds a shelf in the garage ("Leap Year"), unsuccessfully builds a bed ("The Guidance Counselor"), helps his father transport a dishwasher from Mike's house to his father's ("The Clover"), and skims the pool of dead squirrels ("The Wedding"). While he is not the only family member who works around the house, the two eldest children, Axl and Sue, must paint the garage as punishment for bad behavior ("The Telling"). Sue also replaces the light bulb on the back porch, and Sue and Brick, the youngest child, strip the living room wallpaper for their mother ("The Wedding"). Therefore, when maintenance is done by the children, it appears to be a form of penalty for disobedience. There was only one example where a working-class woman does outdoor/general maintenance: Frankie, the mother, covers cracks in the house and staples new wallpaper in the living room ("The Wedding"). On *Raising Hope,* Burt, the father, was typically seen landscaping and gardening outside. This is unsurprising since he owns an outdoor landscaping business, in which he does the majority of the work. Once again, there was a clear division of class, as well as gender. While *The Middle* portrayed somewhat of a blend in the division of labor, *Raising Hope* depicted the husband in charge of outdoor chores and general maintenance. The male members of the family were obviously responsible for building or fixing areas of the house.

Consequently, working-class families have a clear gender divide in that women prepare the meals and men work around the house or outside of it. These conclusions are not evident in middle-class and upper-middle-class/ wealthy families. This is particularly noted with Jay on *Modern Family* because he is considered the wealthiest character, yet does not contribute to daily household chores in any of the episodes; he watched his grandchildren once, but only because his wife had an emergency. Therefore, working-class status directly affects the conclusions. Even though the working-class women all have their own incomes and jobs outside the home, they still contributed significantly more domestic labor than stay-at-home women. While Bianchi, Milkie, Sayer, and Robinson observe that the greater the wife's income, the smaller the gender gap in real life (217), family sitcoms tend to portray the opposite. In fact, none of the wealthy or upper-middle-class women work; moreover, only one of the two middle-class women has an occupation: nursing. As a result, there must be a deeper, underlying cause to these images, since previous theoretical frameworks proposed that because the family is an economic system, familial labor is intertwined with profitability and ultimately diminished. The findings within these episodes suggest the opposite. Working-class women work all day and then still contribute significantly more work to the household. These images may not be the "idealized form" of domesticity that "romanticized" women in the 1950s (Mann 39).

Figure 10.1.   Martha Plimpton and Garret Dillahunt in *Raising Hope*, "Burt's Parents." ©Fox Network/Photofest Season 2, 2011–2012

Rather they imply that women can have jobs and contribute to the family income, as long as the housework is still completed and a sexual division of labor remains. Stratton questions whether deeply held gender roles or economic imbalances based on gender were the cause of the sexual division of labor in households and urges future research to propose which reasons explain the continuing inequality in regards to the sexual division of labor (81). These conclusions can eliminate economic imbalances as an explanation for sexual division of labor, at least within mediated examples. Thus, the socioeconomic status of the television families definitely affects the conclusions of this study.

DISCUSSIONS OF HOUSEWORK

While examining the discussions about housework on domestic sitcoms, the most significant pattern observed is that working-class families talk about domestic labor, while middle-class and upper-middle-class/wealthy characters readily ignore it. Working-class characters discussed housework twenty-three times; in comparison, there were only three examples of middle-class families and three examples of upper-middle-class/wealthy families who discussed it (table 10.3). Moreover, one of those three upper-middle-class/

wealthy examples resulted from Jay, the father on *Modern Family,* complaining that the housekeeper turned his sheets pink. Thus, when he mentions housework, it is only to complain that his staff did not do it correctly.

In contrast, *Raising Hope*, which features a working-class family, devoted an entire episode to determining which parent should do which household chore ("Spanks Butt, No Spanks"). The two parents, Virginia and Burt, discuss the chores that must be done around the house. They decide that each one will do the chores that the other hates to do. For instance, Burt will not crawl under the house to eliminate the animals that hide underneath it and refuses to clean up dog poop "if and when we get a dog." Virginia, on the other hand, does not want to discipline or spank their son. By the end of the episode, the parents discover that if they work together, as opposed to segregating the household chores, neither of them has to do all the "crappy jobs." The underlying message of the episode, as seen through the eyes of these characters, is that chores are better when there is not a division of labor and when partners complete the chores together. This is a particularly noteworthy episode as it is uncharacteristic to see two characters conversing about sharing housework. It also further demonstrates that only the working-class characters discuss housework. Moreover, the conversation occurs between two spouses who both work full-time. This implies that working-class women who have a job also discuss housework more than wealthy/upper-middle-class mothers who stay at home.

Another notable observation is that parents never encouraged their daughters to conform to or challenge traditional gender roles. This implies that the status quo is acceptable for female characters. In contrast, both fathers and mothers encouraged their sons to defy conventional gender roles. For example, on *The Middle*, Mike, the father, sarcastically suggested his son use a

Table 10.3.   Discussions of Housework, by Gender and Socioeconomic Class

	Lower-class	Middle-Class	Upper-Middle-Class / Wealthy	Total
Men	5	0	1	6
Women	6	0	1	7
Both	2	1	0	3
Father/Son	1	1	0	2
Father/ Daughter	0	0	0	0
Mother/Son	4	1	1	6
Mother/ Daughter	5	0	0	5
Total	23	3	3	29

chainsaw and blowtorch, since Mike's father would have encouraged the use of "manly tools" to solve problems. Frankie, the mother, also encouraged her son to vacuum on *The Middle*. On *Good Luck Charlie*, Bob, the father, sent his son to the store to buy a doll for his sister. Finally, on *Modern Family*, Gloria, the mother, suggested her son help her with the laundry. Therefore, while Lynn White and David Brinkerhoff argue that real-life parents differentiate household chores to their children based on the children's gender (171), there were no examples of their real-life observations presented in this mediated sample. In fact, when the situation could have clearly dictated a traditional gender chore, the show actually challenged a hegemonic portrayal in favor of the male children breaking traditional gender roles. On one hand, this is progress because the male children were encouraged to challenge preconceived gender roles and may contribute more to their own households in the future. However, the question remains: Why are the female children not afforded the same opportunity to defy traditional gender roles? This trend appeared across all the shows in the mediated sample, and economic class was not a factor in these findings. Interestingly, daughters and housework are not afforded any images that challenge conventional gender roles. The fact that it is completely absent from this sample suggests that while younger male characters can adopt alternative ideas about housework, younger female characters are still confined to traditional ones. The male characters are shown as evolving beyond conventional ideas of hegemonic masculinity, with the encouragement of their parents. In contrast, the female characters continue to be restricted to fixed gender roles, where they are told to shop for groceries, make dinner, and clean up around the house. These observations suggest that when housework is discussed with younger characters, the boys are allowed to challenge traditional ideas about the sexual division, but the girls are not.

CONCLUSIONS

While one might surmise that early twenty-first century family sitcoms portray more conventional sexual divisions of labor, the findings in this study are certainly more complex. The demographics of family configuration may have changed, since *Modern Family* features a gay couple raising a daughter and *Raising Hope* portrays a single dad raising a daughter. However, traditional gender roles still underlie these examples. These domestic sitcoms present housework examples that seem equal, but when the household chores are specialized, a traditional division of labor becomes evident. For example, women's responsibilities include shopping for household goods and doing the laundry, while men do outdoor/general maintenance. However, while a sexual division of labor is present, the results challenge Stratton's conclusions where women prepare the food, clean the house, and do the laundry; only one of those chores appears to be women's responsibility on family sitcoms. Meal preparation only finds a sexual division of labor in working-class families. There is no difference among middle-class and upper-middle-class/wealthy families. Therefore the sexual division of labor is more obvious when housework is separated into categories. This suggests that family sitcoms are depicting a more subtle, underlying version of the "cult of domesticity" in that gender equality seems prevalent on the surface. However, a more in-depth analysis reveals the contrary. In the 1950s, housewives were romanticized by popular images into interpreting that their roles were as housewives and mothers. Today's media images idealize gender equality when it comes to housework, rather than the underlying sexual division of labor that still persists.

A primary goal of this analysis was to determine to what extent the socioeconomic status of the family influences the sexual division of labor in the household. One significant conclusion can be observed: the higher the class status, the less family members do housework. The families with upper-middle-class/wealthy characters are not seen doing household work; they also discuss housework on only three occasions. In contrast, working-class families display and discuss the greatest number of household chores. Husbands and wives rarely work together to do household chores, particularly as their economic status increases. These observations are significant because they emphasize Marx's concerns about capitalism and working-class interests. In wealthy/upper-middle-class households, the sexual division of labor has not been disrupted. The wives stay at home to care for the house and children, and the husbands financially support the family. However, in contemporary working-class families, both parents work. Because both parents financially contribute to the household, a new conceptualization of gender roles needs to be created in TV sitcoms. Therefore, the increased devotion to household chores in working-class families indicates the media's perpetuation of an ideology that serves to facilitate male-dominated and upper-middle-class goals. As more women enter the workplace than ever before, media images in the early twenty-first century depict working-class women as not only capable of having a job that contributes to the household income, but also adept at still doing the majority of the housework as well.

Consequently, while the overall mediated examples do not display an obvious sexual division of labor, the separation of these examples by socioeconomic class and specialization of household labor confirm different results: Gender roles are still prevalent just as they were in 1950s sitcoms, but are even more deeply concealed in these media images in the early twenty-first century. Marx argues that through our common-sense assumptions and the naturalization of societal ideas, the bourgeois could continue to conceal the differences and inequalities in society (Croteau and Hoynes 158). These mediated representations demonstrate that Marx's notion of false consciousness continues today. Audiences see a greater number of men contributing to the household chores on television; however, the results of this paper reveal, through specialization of chores and socioeconomic class analysis, how little housework men actually do in mediated representations. Consequently, these hegemonic images of an underlying, yet recurring, pattern of the sexual division of labor continue to appear on family sitcoms, just at a more implicit level. Notably, one of the family sitcoms even has the name "modern" in its title. Yet the producers of these shows are really just presenting a varied depiction of the "cult of domesticity." Even though they may not "romance" real-life housewives in the same way that 1950s sitcoms such as *Father Knows Best* and *Leave It to Beaver* may have done, these sitcoms still seek to present the idea that greater equality in the sexual division of labor exists. By analyzing the sexual division of labor and its intersections with socioeconomic class, this chapter illuminates the persistent sexual division of labor that is embedded in twenty-first century family sitcoms. These seemingly natural images must be challenged to encourage ongoing discourse of what constitutes household labor on family sitcoms. There is still an underlying sexual division of labor present in these fictional households on television, but it is depicted as equal, natural, and a positive aspect of society.

WORKS CITED

Baby on Board." *Modern Family*. ABC. 23 May 2012. Television.
Bianchi, Suzanne M., Melissa A. Milkie, Liana C. Sayer, and John P. Robinson. "Is Anyone Doing the Housework? Trends in the Gender Division of Household Labor." *Social Forces* 79.1 (2000): 191–228. Print.
"Burt's Parents." *Raising Hope*. FOX. 15 November 2011. Television.
Campbell, Richard, Chris Martin, and Bettina G. Fabos. *Media and Culture: An Introduction to Mass Communication*. Boston: Bedford/St. Martin's, 2003. Print.
———. *Media Essentials: A Brief Introduction*. Boston: Bedford/St. Martin's, 2010. Print.
"The Clover." *The Middle*. ABC. 9 May 2012. Television.
Croteau, David. R., and William Hoynes. *Media/Society: Industries, Images, and Audiences*. Thousand Oaks: Pine Forge Press, 2003. Print.
Davis, Angela. *Women, Race and Class*. New York: Vintage, 1983. Print.
Ehrenreich, Barbara, and Deirdre English. *For Her Own Good*. New York: Anchor, 2005. Print.
"Election Day." *Modern Family*. ABC. 11 April 2012. Television.
Engels, Friedrich. "The Origin of the Family." *The Feminist Papers*. Ed. Alice S. Rossi. Boston: Northeastern University Press, 1988. 480–95. Print.
Ferguson, Ann, and Rosemary Hennessy. *Feminist Perspectives on Class and Work*. The Stanford Encyclopedia of Philosophy, 12 Oct. 2010. Web. 15 June 2012.
Friedan, Betty. *The Feminine Mystique*. 1963. New York and London: Norton, 1997. Print.
Gregory, Susan. "Gender Roles and Food in Families." *Gender, Power and the Household*. Ed. Linda McKie, Sophia Bowlby, and Susan Gregory. New York: St. Martin's, 1999. 60–75. Print.
Kutulas, Judy. "Who Rules the Roost? Sitcom Family Dynamics from the Cleavers to the Osbournes." *The Sitcom Reader: America Viewed and Skewed*. Ed. Mary M. Dalton and Laura R. Linder. Albany: SUNY Press, 2005. 49–60. Print.

"Leap Year." *The Middle.* ABC. 29 Feb. 2012. Television.

Ledwith, Margaret. "Antonio Gramsci and Feminism: The Elusive Nature of Power." *Educational Philosophy & Theory* 41.6 (2009): 684–97. Print.

"Make Room for Baby." *Good Luck Charlie.* Disney Channel. 6 May 2012. Television.

Mann, Susan A. *Doing Feminist Theory: From Modernity to Postmodernity.* New York: Oxford University Press, 2012. Print.

McKie, Linda, Sophia Bowlby, and Susan Gregory. "Connecting Gender, Power and the Household." *Gender, Power and the Household.* Ed. Linda McKie, Sophia Bowlby, and Susan Gregory. New York: St. Martin's, 1999. 3–13. Print.

"Poking Holes in the Story." *Raising Hope.* FOX. 20 March 2012. Television.

"Spanks Butt, No Spanks." *Raising Hope.* FOX. 13 March 2012. Television.

Stratton, Leslie S. "Gains from Trade and Specialization: The Division of Work in Married Couple Households." *Women, Family, and Work.* Ed. Karine Moe. Malden: Blackwell, 2003. 65–82. Print.

"Tableau Vivant." *Modern Family.* ABC. 16 May 2012. Television.

White, Lynn K., and David B. Brinkerhoff. "The Sexual Division of Labor: Evidence from Childhood." *Social Forces* 60.1 (1981): 170–81. Print.

Williams, Kevin. *Understanding Media Theory.* New York: Oxford University Press, 2003. Print.

Chapter Eleven

No Longer Whistling While You Work?

Reanimating the Cult of Domesticity in The Incredibles

Christopher Holliday

The fact that the 1950s family was not "traditional" but a new phenomenon, the product of new post-war conditions, however, does not make it any less valid or valuable as a benchmark or model. What it underscores is that our notions of the "traditional" and the "new" are not absolutes, but are revised and reimagined over time.
—Peter Winn, "Back to the Future: A GI Bill for the Twenty-First Century"

I never look back, darling. It distracts from the now.
—Edna Mode, *The Incredibles*

Housework and the portrayal of domestic chores across a multitude of animated films and cartoons have been traditionally exploited for their performative value. Chorally presented musical numbers in the style of Busby Berkeley, including "Whistle While You Work" from Walt Disney's *Snow White and the Seven Dwarfs* (1937) and "The Work Song" from *Cinderella* (1950), are choreographed to theatrically (re)present the pleasures of household labor. The hardship and drudgery of housework is self-reflexively re-inscribed as an engaging event that foregrounds the expressive majesty of everyday errands. Housework therefore becomes closely tied to the magic of animation as a highly creative medium. In the early Betty Boop short *House Cleaning Blues* (1937), fantastical inventions are conjured to craft housework as a more playful and alluring enterprise. Feature-length animated films like *Fantasia* (1940), *The Brave Little Toaster* (1987), and *Beauty and the Beast* (1991) coerce household appliances into agency to perform domestic tasks independent of their owners. Physical acts of household management in animation have ultimately become the locus for spectacular performance and the drama of visual display, drawing the spectator in through arresting images that testify to the inventiveness of these animated screen worlds.

What follows seeks to outline animation's particular traditions of housework, and to situate within its representational norms *The Incredibles* (2004), the sixth computer-animated film produced by the Pixar Animation Studio. Critical responses to the film have ranged from a Nietzschean critique of egalitarianism (Anton 209–30) to its parallels with the Bush administration and 9/11 atrocities (Dunn 559–62). But minimal focus has been afforded to *The Incredibles* as an animated text steeped in the 1950s cult of domesticity. Reinforced throughout by a striking Modernist domestic design influenced by Charles Eames, *The Incredibles* conveys a 1950s influence in conjunction with the mechanisms of the superhero genre to map out the retreat into domesticity experienced by women during the middle of the twentieth century. Jettisoning the musicality and spectacle of many of its cel-animated predecessors, the re-integration of superhero Helen Parr (a.k.a. Elastigirl) back into suburban life—in a narrative that imposes her refrain from superheroic deeds—bears out the dominant domestic ideology of the postwar period identified by Betty Friedan. Despite Elastigirl's contentment at conforming to her assigned role, the (super)naturally flexible protagonist lies at the forefront of what Friedan calls the woman's "search for identity" beyond the housewife image. The film offers a complex discourse on the achievability of domestic harmony within suburban mediocrity, suggesting that it is not Elastigirl's *secret* identity but her *super* powers that breed female empowerment. To avoid the trappings of the *feminine mystique*, Elastigirl must herself snap back into superheroism: rupturing the confines of an idealized domestic life to no longer melt into the anonymity of the normal. By drawing out the film's negotiation of its 1950s aesthetic, its visions of the good wife and happy homemaker, and by placing Elastigirl's powers within a resurgent feminist movement that was gaining increasing momentum, this essay argues that *The Incredibles* provides a compelling challenge to the ways in which popular animation has conventionally treated the spectacle of household management.

THE INCREDIBLE 1950S

Within the popular imagination, the 1950s are commonly earmarked as an era of American prosperity, one whose images and icons have evolved into symbols of affluence, optimism, and confirmation of the country's position of world leadership. The immediate postwar era "provided a chance for a second start; with the economic challenges of the Great Depression and the horrors of World War II now past" (Young xii). Major discoveries in the field of science and technology, from the invention of video tape recorders and the transistor radio to developments in space exploration and the hydrogen bomb, were matched by economic expansion, mass marketing, and consumer consumption. But such American splendor was not without its contradictions. With a new war commencing in Korea, the emergence of pop psychology, the effects of the Kinsey Report that opened up private sexual behavior (*Playboy* also arrived in 1953), the aggressive McCarthyist accusations of Communist sympathy, and the outrage against the rise of juvenile delinquency, America was in the grip of social conservatism. If there was a national priority for fifties America, it was to foster an altogether more safe and secure community across a country reeling from Cold War paranoia, the threat of nuclear attack, and the totalitarian Communist Soviet Union.

Given the rich sociopolitical currency of the 1950s and its popular conflation with the optimistic pursuit of the American Dream, it perhaps comes as little surprise that this same period of U.S. history has been the locus for a remarkable historical revisionism currently taking place across contemporary media culture. The nascent feminism (and virulent sexism), fashions, and fantasies of the decade have emerged as particularly conducive to mass media treatment. Feature films including, but certainly not limited to, *Quiz Show* (1994), *L.A. Confidential* (1997), *Pleasantville* (1998), *Catch Me If You Can* (2002), *Far from Heaven* (2002), *De-Lovely* (2004), *The Stepford Wives* (2004), *Good Night, and Good Luck* (2005), *Capote* (2005), and *Revolutionary Road* (2008) have drawn their formal and thematic inspiration from the societal insecurities that punctuated mid-century America, from the hysteria of televised McCarthy hearings to closeted sexual orientation (including the fear of homosexual deviancy). The retroactive resurgence of popular interest around the 1950s has continued to coalesce around the medium of television. The prosperity of the decade has inaugurated a new type of contemporary costume or period drama that has *adopted* a striking 1950s texture, rather than simply *adapting* a high-profile literary work as its source material. Recent high-quality, multi-camera U.S. series such as *The Company* (2007), *The Playboy Club* (2011), *Pan Am* (2011–2012), and *Magic City* (2012–) each sing from the same fifties hymn sheet as that of *Mad Men* (2007–). But AMC's critically successful period series about a New York advertising agency is not without its small-screen antecedents. A glimpse at the history of American television programming, whether *Happy Days* (1974–1984), *Brooklyn Bridge* (1991–1993), or *I'll Fly Away* (1991–1993), reveals the protracted magnetism of the fifties to episodic television serials.

The decade (including the early 1960s) continues to provide a cohesive and comforting teleological paradigm for the nostalgic, romanticized vision of mid-century events and icons across multiple media forms. The seductiveness of this era of American history lies, as journalist Natalie Haynes acknowledges, in its escapism from "our real lives [that] are full of austerity, of stagnant wages and rising prices" ("All These TV Series").[1] But beyond

alleviating any contemporary cultural malaise, one underdeveloped area regarding the resurgence of the 1950s cultural climate is its intersection(s) with
the emerging digital landscapes of mainstream computer-animated filmmaking. Written and directed by Brad Bird—the first time the Pixar studio had
sought external inspiration rather than drawing from its in-house personnel—
The Incredibles was the first computer-animated film period piece, a rare
retro-text that avoided the familiarity of a contemporary milieu or the uncer-
tainty of a dystopic future (epitomized by *Final Fantasy: The Spirits Within*,
2001).[2] *The Incredibles* tells the story of a family of gifted superheroes
forced into unexpected hibernation by the Superhero Relocation Program, a
government initiative requiring "Supers" to denounce their powers following
growing public dissent over their life-saving hero work. Provided with am-
nesty for their past actions but with their superheroic acts now extinguished
by this new legislation, Bob Parr (formerly Mr. Incredible), his wife Helen
(Elastigirl), and their three young children Violet, Dash, and Jack-Jack,
struggle with their enforced anonymity and domestic normalcy prompted by
their abrupt retirement from active duty. The comic mechanisms of familial
dysfunction certainly nudge *The Incredibles* into the narrative orbit of *The
Simpsons* (1989–) and *King of the Hill* (1997–2010), television programs on
which Bird had previously honed his craft as a writer.[3] But the film's striking
design policy and formal stylings ultimately situate *The Incredibles* adjacent
to another of the director's screen credits. Just as Bird's earlier feature-length
animated cartoon *The Iron Giant* (1999) staged the action of Ted Hughes's
original 1968 novel against the backdrop of a 1950s Cold War imaginary, the
director returned to plunder mid-century America for his Pixar debut. The
studio has flirted with the decade's icons and images elsewhere, from its
popular toys, drag-racing automobiles, and even the postwar graphic designs
of Paul Rand and Alvin Lustig (in *Toy Story 2* [1999], *Cars* [2006], and *Up*
[2009], respectively) (Geraghty 259). But the 1950s reached its nostalgic
maturity in *The Incredibles*. Much of the film's visual richness and formal
intrigue comes from its widespread and entirely deliberate 1950s texture,
which colors its content and shapes much of its subject matter.

Alongside the chief creative officer at Pixar, John Lasseter, Bird himself
was born in 1957 (in Kalispell, Montana; Lasseter in Los Angeles), and the
two shared classes in character animation at the California Institute of the
Arts during the 1970s with future animators John Musker, Henry Selick, and
Tim Burton. Describing his creative vision for his first computer-animated
effort, *The Incredibles*, Bird reveals that he saw the world of the film "as
looking sort of like what we thought the future would turn out like in the
1960s" (qtd. in *"Incredibles* Production Notes"). *The Incredibles* opens immediately on a series of intimate talking-head interviews with Mr. Incredible,
Elastigirl, and their superhero affiliate Frozone: each one of these personal
portraits instantly serving to date the film. J. P. Telotte points to these unex-

pectedly grainy and flat images "offered in Academy aspect ratio" which begin *The Incredibles* as locating the opening scenes of the film, and ultimately the now-forgotten prime of its superhero protagonists, "sometime in the 1950s" (213). From this pre-title preamble, the narrative forwards fifteen years to join the superheroes in their domestic exile, but maintains the residual presence of the preceding decade. Set in a deco-cityscape marked by the interwar skyscraper, Stuart Croft argues that "Mr. Incredible's great superhero acts are carried out in a set that looks very much like 1950s; the miserable present being represented as the 1960s (of course the beginning of the culture wars)" (20). The meticulous production design of *The Incredibles* was based on a distinctive branch of 1950s space-age futurism known as Googie, a modern architectural style commonly seen in coffee shops, motels, gas stations, and bowling alleys of the era. Art director Ralph Eggleston tenders his own description of the film's design: "I call the look suburban-mid-century-Tiki by way of Lou Romano," he explains, making reference to both another 1950s pop style and the influence of its production designer (qtd. in Bell, *The Incredibles*).

The Incredibles is composed of clean, Modernist lines not only in its portrayal of the architectural splendor of a 1950s milieu, but equally in the formal design and visual style of the digital animation itself. Teddy Newton and Tony Fucile's caricatured character design in *The Incredibles* is historically contiguous with the proliferation of "limited" animation pioneered by United Productions of America (UPA) during the 1950s.[4] In their book *Minding Movies* (2011), David Bordwell and Kristin Thompson further contend that *The Incredibles* "was deliberately cartoony looking, evoking the streamlined Populuxe look of 1950s cartoons" (230). A neologism of the terms *popular* and *luxury*, the ideological roots of Populuxe was, as Thomas Hine argues, "a way of referring to the moment when America found a way of turning out fantasy on an assembly line" (5). Innocently hedonistic, ebullient, and vibrant, Populuxe was a futuristic style marked by the frivolity and fun of the garish. With its 1950s setting and unique character design, then, *The Incredibles* expresses something of the postwar joy of Populuxe. The disproportionate anatomical design of Mr. Incredible's hulking upper body and the elongated jawline of antagonist Syndrome also resembles the attractive curved shapes of the jet fighter airplane that during the 1950s was "the new symbol of American power" (Banner 239).

Another contributing factor to the striking fifties aesthetic of *The Incredibles* is its connection to certain genres. The villainous plan concocted by antagonist Syndrome to eliminate every superhero is given the name Operation Kronos: a thinly veiled allusion to the science-fiction disaster movie *Kronos* released in 1957. *The Incredibles* is equally self-conscious about its status as the first computer-animated superhero film. The film's primary setting, Metroville, combines the two fictional cities in which Superman was raised (Smallville) and where he later settled (Metropolis). M. Keith Booker has further clarified how "the Incredibles themselves tend to seem more like 1950s or early 1960s superheroes than contemporary ones" (92). The attributes held by each member of the Parr family bear the traces of Marvel's Fantastic Four series that debuted in 1961. "Like Spiderman," as Audrey Anton adds, the Parr family remains entirely mortal despite their "freak genetic code" (220). The design of Mr. Incredible with his broad shoulders, enlarged torso, wavy blond hair, and muscular physique also bears striking resemblance to DC Comics' Aquaman, as well as cartoonist Martin Nodell's interpretation of the superhero Green Lantern produced in 1940. Indeed, it is only when the film forwards fifteen years to the drudgery of his enforced retirement that the Parr family patriarch sheds his typical superhero appearance. And yet it is precisely this narrative of superannuation in *The Incredibles* and its treatment of "Supers" that most prominently embeds the film within the superhero genre.

The 1950s was a pivotal era of adjustment for the superhero comic book across popular media, one in which it began to dramatically recede from mainstream view. German American psychiatrist Dr. Frederic Wertham's *Seduction of the Innocent* (1954) helped launch a congressional inquiry that censored the majority of comic book content upon its initial publication. Wertham's findings prompted the origination of the Comics Code Authority, retired the E. C. Horror Comics catalog, and led to sanitized versions of familiar comic book narratives. Marvel Comics parodied the new legislation with its inclusion of the Keene Act that outlawed costumed adventuring, while the DC Comics superhero group Justice Society of America (JSA) also fictionalized the measures through a miniseries explaining the demise of the Justice Society over their supposed disloyalty. By tapping into what Scott Bukatman has called the "'banned superhero' narrative," and by pairing the Super Relocation Act with its 1950s surroundings, *The Incredibles* not only gestures toward a comic book visual style, but also scores the ideological climate which engulfed the superhero genre in the fifties (116). Legislated into anonymity, the Parr family progressively return as covert and clandestine forces, thus adhering to many of the narrative conventions recycled in other "banned" superhero stories such as the graphic novels *Watchmen* (1986–1997) and *The Dark Knight Returns* (1986). Bob Parr in particular fits with Aeon J. Skoble's assertion that superheroes generically function as "unauthorized police auxiliary units" (30). *The Incredibles* stages both Bob's inability to abandon superheroic deeds and the seduction of this lifestyle through his nightly listening to the police radio frequencies in search of crimes to satisfy his irrepressible superheroic tendencies. Bob's superheroism and that of his family is finally reconfirmed, however, through their elevation and acceptance as public heroes now worthy of society's adulation (a society that had initially precipitated their outlawing). The Parr family's return within the public consciousness during the climax of *The Incredibles* therefore tallies chronologically with the reinvention of superheroes following the maelstrom of hysteria that surrounded comic books in the postwar period (Lopes 61). Just as editors and artists began to shape their superheroes to be "socially relevant," the homecoming of the aging Mr. Incredible and Elastigirl reflects the cultural maturation of a comic book industry that had suffered due to various distribution and licensing issues (61–62).

The Incredibles certainly operates within an ever-expanding constellation of film and television texts that approximate a mid-century milieu. The engagement with popular culture and iconography drawn from the 1950s provides strong points of identification for the viewing public across contemporary America. The references to fifties technology and architecture, its Populuxe animated style, the influence of the superhero and comic book formats, and the "banned superhero" narrative arc are the focal points for the playful contradiction inherent in *The Incredibles* between a 1950s aesthetic and a contemporary digital animation. But one particular connection to the 1950s, and a critical reading that the film's narrative robustly invites, is that of its gendered relationship to the cult of domesticity and its portrayal of housework. Nowhere was the second start and impetus of change perpetuated in the 1950s more than in the complex position of women and the increased centrality of the home space. Despite animation historian Michael Barrier claiming Elastigirl to be "the most real character in the film," particularly as a "thwarted career woman who tries to make the best of her diminished circumstances," little scholarly attention has been paid to her screen presence (Barrier, "The Juggler"). Critical emphasis among popular reviews has tended to fall upon Mr. Incredible's mid-life frustration and identity crisis (Scott, "Being Super in Suburbia"; Bradshaw, "The Incredibles"), rather than overstating the compromises and hushed desperation of his restless wife (Papamichael, "The Incredibles"). The argument pursued across the remainder of this essay, then, is one that attempts to chip away at Elastigirl to redress such critical (im)balance. It contends that *The Incredibles* calls upon the Parr family matriarch to both consolidate and pursue further the imprint of its signature fifties style, with the character featuring the most prominent, but as yet mostly encrypted, of the film's multiple fifties codes.

SUPERHERO IDENTITY AND DOMESTIC CONTAINMENT

Elastigirl was a character conceived by Bird as a tribute to modern-day mother figures who, as the director himself admitted, must "stretch in hundreds of different ways in each day" (qtd. in "Production Notes"). Her biological excessiveness physicalizes several of her demands as a matriarch: her (flex)ability to multitask, but also to stretch to keep her family under control.

She is lithe, but no less resilient for it. Elastigirl is particularly adept at assuming more functional alterations, especially when the narrative places her under villainous duress. She hurriedly reshapes her body to resemble a parachute-like canopy, catching her children as they fall through the sky following a plane crash. Recoiling immediately back into recognizable human form, she next contorts her middle-aged physique into a life raft as Violet and Dash finally fall into the water. If Bob's recklessness at work ultimately costs the Parr family his job at the Insuricare company (his relocated employment), then it is these moments that charge Helen with supporting her young family and (literally) keeping them afloat. But Helen's unique physical properties extend beyond the mechanisms of the superhero narrative that contains her, and she operates with a greater ideological significance on account of the sociohistorical climate that *The Incredibles* seeks to invoke. Managed by an absorbing mobility and without any overt physical limitations (there are few after-effects from her rapid reformations), Elastigirl's biological energies are nonetheless framed by a certain cultural conception of containment. It is these constrictive and restrictive states that have their roots in precisely the 1960s milieu in which the contorting character now finds herself.

The publication of Betty Friedan's influential *The Feminine Mystique* in 1963 had cast the spotlight upon the unsettled and unfulfilled sociocultural position of women during the 1950s as they acclimated to their new private sphere. Evoking a superhero's secret identity that must be preserved from public knowledge, Friedan famously described the postwar loneliness and boredom of women as the "problem that has no name." Forcibly displaced from prior duties in factories and among land armies to accommodate returning male veterans, postwar women in the United States now adopted more traditional pursuits. Friedan wrote of a "nameless aching dissatisfaction" experienced by these seemingly "happy housewife heroines" (30). She concluded that feelings of discontent among these women were therefore the fault of society, one which had collectively enforced onto them a cult of domesticity that perpetuated an idealized myth of a perfect (nuclear) family life. Stephanie Coontz has subsequently examined these social structures of the fifties as "part of a repressive post-war campaign to wipe out the memory of past feminist activism and to drive women back into the home" (xxi). But *The Feminine Mystique* brought into question the 1950s consensus that the home was the true place for women and queried the validity of stay-at-home motherhood, igniting a change in the decade's social fabric by challenging head-on the established traditions of white middle-class American women.

Subsequent commentators during the 1980s and 1990s have critiqued Friedan's conclusions on the basis of thier selective, one-dimensional perspective on the postwar female plight, and how they oversimplify and misrepresent the passivity of women (Coontz xix; Horowitz, "Rethinking Betty

Friedan" 1–42; hooks 3). Friedan's omission of the African American wom-
en who led civil rights demonstrations in the United States, and her own
Stalinist Marxist views and radical political activism, have equally been subjected to strong criticism (Coontz xix; Horowitz, *Betty Friedan*, 147; Tong
26–28). But despite vehement reaction(s) regarding its cultural relevancy and
anthropological credibility even today, Friedan's identification of the cult of
domesticity nonetheless spotlighted the disorientation that often confronted
postwar women. Such social paralysis is manifest in the specific portrayal of
housework in *The Incredibles*, emerging as a key element of its retro 1950s
style that is seldom analyzed. No longer valued by the society, Elastigirl's
retreat into a new kind of domesticity is marked by a shift from career (super)
woman to homemaker, and from its start the film draws out the character's
sudden shift into suburban stupor.

Elastigirl's superheroic 1950s prime that unfolds in the film's first scenes
finds an analogue in the "confidence-boosting years [spent] in factories and
fields" that Thomas Elsaesser attributes to postwar women (424). Before she
is forcefully sapped of her social function by the Super Relocation Program,
Elastigirl exuded self-assurance and even verbalized her fervent resistance to
cultural expectations during the opening fifties prologue:

> Settle down? Are you kidding? I'm at the top of my game. I'm right up there
> with the big dogs. Girls, come on. Leave the saving of the world to the men? I
> don't think so.

Her confidence in this period firmly embodies the female triumphalism of
women, captured across the United States in the icon of Rosie the Riveter,
and in J. Howard Miller's famous 1943 advertisement for Westinghouse
Electric accompanied by the slogan "We Can Do It!" The poster depicted a
female laborer with a fist raised not only in defiance, but in a drive for the
recruitment of women and charged with a sense of empowerment (the image
was rediscovered in the 1980s and co-opted by the feminist movement). As a
superhero, Elastigirl is certainly coded to be Mr. Incredible's equal. During
her entrance on the city rooftops, Elastigirl saves his life with one punch of
her empowered fist ("A simple thank you will suffice"), and then indulges in
provocative behavior with overtones of sexual intimidation. Following their
bout of verbal sparring, she teases Mr. Incredible that he should be "more
flexible," a line that is delivered as the supple female suggestively contorts
her body around her future husband's hulking physique.

Despite Elastigirl's initial protestations and reluctance to leave the saving
of the world "to the men," she must assume anonymity even in the face of
her prime. But the Super Relocation Program is not the first institutional
constraint placed upon the character. The enforcement of the legislation is
immediately preceded by a sequence showing the marriage of Mr. Incredible

to Elastigirl, and it is from the church that Bird cuts to a newsreel proclaiming the superheroes' public ban. Vicki Howard has identified how during the postwar period, the efforts of the wedding industry cemented the traditional white wedding ceremony, and the new cultural ideal of marriage emerged as a "validation of the American way of life" (4). The outcome, as Peter Winn recognizes, was that "an incredible 97 percent of Americans of marriageable age had taken the vows" (177). Instead of the city rooftops that she commanded and across which she expressively stretched, Elastigirl's new residence and latest roles are far more traditionalist. The first images of her post-super existence depict her fully ingrained in domestic duties. Freed from her superheroic identity, Helen stands hunched and contained at the kitchen sink washing her infant son Jack-Jack, her body squeezed up and visually enclosed by the vertical lines of the surrounding work units. With the telephone receiver clenched between her ear and shoulder, she visually rhymes with her husband's similarly oppressed body shape contained inside his work cubicle at Insuricare. Elastigirl's fluid freedoms and fun as a superhero are permitted to return only sporadically, the first instance of which occurs during an early dinnertime sequence. As the children frantically argue, with Bob distant and failing to "intervene," both parents explode as the valve on their latent superheroism is pried open. Helen impossibly flexes her arms to contain her rampant children, while Bob raises the entire dinner table high in frustration. The perilous instability and fractured qualities of the family are literally suspended in full view, their position and spacing momentarily held. Beyond the scene's familial tensions, this scene bears out for the first time the individual family roles. Bob might support and sustain the family (through both his superhuman strength and economic security), but it is Helen whose physical flexibility and elasticity is ultimately holding the Parr family together.

The kitchen, motor vehicle, dining room: these are the new spaces that *The Incredibles* allocates Elastigirl following her adoption of domestic duties. Art director Bryn Imagire adds that the animators worked hard to express how "everything that is in the house was probably put together by Helen" (qtd. in "Production Notes"). This suggests a particular relationship between the homey environment and the Parr family matriarch, one that marks the decor with an intrinsic feminine touch and corroborates her status as home*maker*. In fact, during the telephone call over the kitchen sink, Elastigirl excitedly reveals to her husband the most momentous of occasions, that of the final box finally being unpacked at their new suburban abode. ("We're officially moved in!") During the 1950s, the suburbs became the dominant method of social organization. Levittown, Long Island, represented the mass production of inexpensive, affordable tract housing geared toward the creation of communities. Eighty-five percent of the thirteen million new homes built in the 1950s were located in the suburbs, and thus the Parr family's geographical relocation is typical of rapid U.S. suburbanization. Furthermore, the anonymity available within these tract homes—a symbol of congenial postwar suburbia and a style of housing development rooted in similarity, repetition, and homogeneity—is implied within the film's wider narrative structure. The thematic balance that *The Incredibles* strikes between mediocrity and superiority is fuelled by the 1950s setting in which its events take place. The chains of tract housing, mirroring the rows of tight cubicles that gridlock Bob at Insuricare, become an ideal location for the enforced secrecy of the superheroes to be preserved. As Dash Parr himself clarifies, if everyone's special that means "no one is."

Immediately defined by her interiority and by her connections to suburban household duties, Helen is continually associated throughout *The Incredibles* with images and icons of domestic drudgery. This is particularly intensified during one short montage sequence. Bob has been fired from his mundane job at Insuricare and, unbeknownst to his wife, has been lured back to superheroic action by Mirage, a mysterious femme-fatale figure and ally of Syndrome, whose motives are as opaque as her name implies. Shots of Bob's intense training regimen (undertaken under the guise of his defunct Insuricare role) are intercut with Helen performing simple household activities. The sequence marks the return of the sexual chemistry that had previously been a staple of Bob and Helen's public (and private) relationship, but which suburban life, domestic duties, and growing marital conflict had otherwise buried. Family stability is also consolidated through Bob's playful involvement with his children. He kisses Violet, plays sports with Dash, and takes pleasure in feeding Jack-Jack—activities that previously held less attraction than the police radio scanner. But the sequence is supported by two alternating versions of household activities that parallel each other. The first is Bob's superheroic routine (lifting trucks, pulling freight trains), impossible exer-

Figure 11.1. No longer incredible, household duties constrict Helen in *The Incredibles*. Source: *The Incredibles* ©Disney Pixar 2004

tions that the film has already equated with the drudgery of more domestic chores during Mr. Incredible's opening talking-head interview:

> No matter how many times you save the world, it always manages to get back in jeopardy again. Sometimes I just want it to stay saved! You know, for a little bit? I feel like the maid. I just cleaned up this mess! Can we keep it clean for . . . for ten minutes!

The second incarnation of housework that plays out in this sequence is those acts undertaken by Helen, such as watering plants, collecting washing, and even waving Bob off to "work." A jump cut immediately illustrates the monotony of Helen's daily routine: she resumes the same spot in the garage upon her husband's return home as she did on his departure. But if *The Incredibles* simultaneously demarcates the public activity of Bob with the private domesticity of Helen (who never ventures beyond the white picket fence that contains her), then it is the narrative juxtaposition of these scenes that raises several important issues. Indeed, by aligning and then collapsing together these multiple conceptions of housework, *The Incredibles* actually punctures something of its own "feminine mystique" by undercutting the validity of Elastigirl's actions and the purported domestic bliss in which she is partaking.

Domestic life and the performance of housework was certainly idealized in the media as a natural role for women during the postwar period, encouraged to stay within the secure confines and safety of the home space. In 1954, *Home Economics Textbook* published "How to Be a Good Housewife," while a year later in an article credited to a May 1955 issue of *Housekeeping Monthly*, "The Good Wife's Guide," offered women advice that would secure family togetherness and consolidate their own status as domestic caregivers. Although the legitimacy of "The Good Wife Guide" has been brought into disrepute (claimed as either parody or astute hoax), the two-page spread does reflect the tone of many women's magazines circulating across America throughout the 1950s (Rowe-Finkbeiner 25). Publications including *Family Weekly*, *Family Circle*, *Good Housekeeping*, and *McCall's* all sought to enumerate the qualities of a perfect family while painting a picture of the ideal family-oriented woman who would maintain it. Many advertisements for consumer products targeted women by emphasizing their occupational role as housekeepers, stereotyping them in a variety of domestic poses (vacuuming, cooking, serving meals, doing the dishes, and so on) (Courtney and Lockeretz 92–95). Michele Adams and Scott Coltrane have identified that the cultural ideology of separate spheres for men and women "bolstered the conceptual distinction between rational, strong men in control of the public domain and emotional, frail women associated with the private sphere" (408). It was certainly such frailty, entrapment, and festering dissatisfaction felt by women that Friedan's *Feminine Mystique* sought to bring into the public consciousness. It dispelled the myth propagated across magazines and on television of a gratified housewife, and proposed that their *raison d'être* was more than just to confirm and conform to prewar gendered divisions of labor. But by rapidly intercutting between Bob's secret schedule and Helen's domestic routine, *The Incredibles* spotlights the superficiality of the latter's housework activity. Bob's secret charges the domestic front and storybook happy homemaker image with a more insidious, insufficient quality. It therefore comes as little surprise that housework and the monotony of domestic routine features so prominently in the two scenes that hint at Bob's secret life to Helen. In the first, she discovers one of Mirage's hairs when putting his clothes away (leading to an assumption of an extramarital affair and thus weakening the monogamous, lifelong marriage unit prized within a 1950s nuclear family) (Popenoe 528). A subsequent scene focuses on Helen's repetitive gestures with a vacuum cleaner, along the Parr family hallway and then into Bob's office. While continuing to visually place Helen's home life within a domestic-oriented frame, it is telling that the act of housework itself forces her to probe her husband's space in which he maintains a shrine to his superheroic heyday. Yet superheroic history and domestic present collide, as through her housework routine Elastigirl is drawn into direct confrontation with reminders of her past/prewar activism.[5]

The loaded and highly nuanced articulation of housework in *The Incredibles*, one that unfolds within the reality of the 1950s and early 1960s cult of domesticity, relocates Pixar's 2004 film away from prior animated representations of domestic chores. Adams and Coltrane define housework as "household labor or domestic labor" that involves "the physical and emotional work required to maintain homes" (407–8). The creative freedoms of the animated

Figure 11.2.   Animating the drudgery of domestic routine. Source: *The Incredibles* ©Disney Pixar 2004

medium often free repetitive labor from such connotations of laborious *work*, and in some instances even displaces entirely the "gendered pattern of responsibility" for housework that has emerged in a large proportion of Western countries (Adams and Coltrane 407–8). Indeed, household chores and domestic duties have traditionally been gifts for the expressive scope given to animators to explore and elaborate upon the repetitive, routine aspects of laborious effort. Best remembered in this spirit is "Whistle While You Work" from *Snow White and the Seven Dwarfs*, which functions, perhaps, as the archetype for the depiction of housework within an animated context. Douglas Brode has recently reclaimed *Snow White* as moving housework "beyond drudgery" by asserting that the heroine is anything but a servant to her seven male companions (unlike in the Grimms' original fairytale) (178–89). But Booker, in contrast, asserts how the "main talents" of Snow White are straightforward: "singing and housework" (3). It is typical for animation to unify these two skills, crafting a symbiotic sound/image relationship that places domestic duties in the throes of musical accompaniment. In *Snow White*, the playfulness of "whistling while you work" is manifest in the enhanced spectacle of the occasion. The dwarfs' cottage teems with collective and choreographed activity, as each gesture is instantly synchronized to the music. This is crucially a shared activity too. Various woodland animals accompany Snow White as she imprints and asserts her identity through cleanliness (later, she will force each of the seven dwarfs to wash up and thus inaugurates yet another musical number, "The Washing Song"). The re-inscription of housework as a mode of playful performance is further pursued in *Cinderella*. "The Work Song" bears several of the hallmarks of "Whistle While You Work" by privileging the affinity between the domestic task and collective action (a group of mice skillfully craft Cinderella's dress for the ball).⁶ In the film's later "Oh, Sing Sweet Nightingale," an operatic aria sung by Cinderella as she scrubs the palace floor, an altogether conflicting view of the collective is conveyed. Although she sings alone, Cinderella's image is creatively multiplied. Each of her cleaning actions is impossibly reflected and duplicated in the washing bubbles: a repetition that charges this musical soliloquy with a dreamlike excess. Cinderella becomes visually encased within the images of her own domestic routine. But when the bubbles burst, there is little domestic refrain. The music comes to a halt and she is abruptly returned to the harsh reality of her errands.

It is unsurprising that musical accompaniment features so pervasively in the animated business of housework. Judith Weisenfeld has argued that the performance of domestic chores is a particularly acceptable social context "in which people might actually sing" (48). The marriage of sound with industrious action has been traced back to the early 1900s and the importance of music "associated with slave occupations, ranging from field labour to domestic chores such as flailing rice, grinding hominy, spinning, and making baskets" (Nicholls 119). The beneficial elements of song—as a mechanism for survival, for unity, and as welcome distraction—also finds an analogue in the increasing number of psychological studies centering on music's affective attributes. Experiments undertaken by Thomas Edison, Hermann von Helmholtz, Jeff Gundlach, and Kate Hevner since the 1910s have established the relation between musical tempo, tonality, and rhythm upon productivity and work rate (Kellaris 838). A multitude of animated films and cartoons have taken their cue from these sound/image relations to suggest a particular kind of behavioral animated response to musical stimulus, while reconfiguring the domestic space presented in the film as a more theatrical stage. For Betty Boop, singing alleviates the boredom of household maintenance the morning after a "swell party" in the cartoon *House Cleaning Blues*. Despite Betty's claim that she is "getting tired of cleaning things," the sprightly soundtrack and jaunty melody charges her domestic activity with a contradictory energy and vigor. Merged with the film's tableaux-style framing, Betty's comic pratfalls, histrionic behavior, and self-reflexive gestures, the kitchen space is quickly redefined as a stage showcasing this hectic one-woman show. In *The Brave Little Toaster*, the kitchen is likewise coded in theatrical terms, this time becoming a rudimentary dance hall. The "soul injection" of "Tutti Frutti" on the soundtrack (its onscreen source the aptly named Radio) prompts the sentient appliances to reject their disdain for housework, and rouses a more joyful exhibition of domestic cleaning.[7]

In the Disney studio's much-anticipated return to cel-animated technique *The Princess and the Frog* (2009), and again in their subsequent computer-animated feature *Tangled* (2010), a similar musical portrayal of housework provides an outlet for the escapist aspirations of each film's respective working females. *The Princess and the Frog* includes the musical number "Almost There," in which New Orleans waitress Tiana harmonizes about her desire to shun any romantic ambitions and her happily ever after, and instead "work real hard each and every day" to open her own restaurant. Singing to her mother as they dust the floor and set a table for dinner, Tiana maneuvers her broom in grand, sweeping gestures that physicalize the character's playful exuberance and energy. Daily grind is progressively replaced (and displaced) with ardent spectacle, and as Tiana chants her enthusiasm for manual labor, her vocals vie for prominence against an expressionist, art-deco backdrop of vibrant hues married with 1920s jazz age-style score. Written by renowned Disney lyricist Alan Menken, "When Will My Life Begin" from *Tangled* similarly elevates domestic routine to the level of the operatic. The song commences with the enslaved Rapunzel outlining her daily work schedule: "Start on the chores and sweep til the floor's all clean" and "Polish and wax, do laundry, and mop and shine up." The formal arrangement of the sequence immediately spotlights the high-spiritedness and joviality of the occasion. Rapid editing and jump cuts during Rapunzel's solo craft temporal ellipses that accelerate the pace and vibrancy of the musical number. This raises to a higher pitch of emphasis the liveliness and excitement of household duties that combine to structure this "usual morning line-up." But as the song proceeds, Rapunzel's domestic workload itself becomes "tangled" together with creative activities such as reading, painting, drawing, pottery, ballet, candle making, sewing, and even ventriloquism. Such conflation of domestic drudgery with more lighthearted, artistic enterprises in *Tangled* quickly redefines the industry of housework according to the merriment of monotonous routine.

The elaborate spectacle of animated housework arguably reached its creative peak in *Beauty and the Beast*, a film that borrows generously from the theatrical codes and conventions of the Hollywood musical. Though choreographer Busby Berkeley is a figure commonly associated with the geometry-in-motion of experimental, abstract, and avant-garde animated film (Starr 77–83), his unique presentational style provides a prism through which the Disney film can be scrutinized. In the musical number "Be Our Guest," cutlery and crockery parade in florid masses, ornately coordinated into concentric circles that optically delight. Choral presentation accentuates their uniformity, matching the fullness of Broadway-style orchestral sound with a vibrant, chaotic film frame replete with a mass of bodies and objects arranged in geometrical lines and symmetrical shapes. The "over the head" shot—another Berkeley technique and a staple of his Hollywood career since *Whoopee!* (1930)—provides the song's centerpiece, albeit with an army of soup spoons and napkins "freshly pressed" that swirl and loop in unison. If the dinner scene in *The Incredibles* stages a suburban family disconnected from one other, then this hypnotic "culinary cabaret" performed for the benefit of protagonist Belle (the beauty) provides a vivid counterpoint to the familial chaos and disunity of the Parr family's "leftover night." In "Human Again" (a song omitted from *Beauty and the Beast*'s theatrical run, but reinserted for the 2002 home video release), pairs of mops dynamically participate in a similarly rhythmical series of gestures. Reprising the suddenly sentient broom magically awoken from its slumber by Sorcerer Mickey Mouse in *Fantasia* (1940), their precision of movement evokes a dance troupe well versed in its ballroom routine. A high-angled shot frames the multitude, and as each object pulses with energy and in harmonious freedom, their simultaneous movements are matched to the crescendo of the rousing chorus of the accompanying soundtrack.

Animated portrayals of housework uniformly disclose to the spectator instances of the ordinary, albeit on an extraordinary and magnified scale. One type of routinized labor is substituted for the routine of performance: the *domestic* momentarily conjoined with the *theatric*. But *The Incredibles* instead reverses the polarities, so that the extraordinary (and, for that matter, the *incredible*) must play out within the confines of the domestic ordinary or

Figure 11.3. The animated majesty of the marauding mops in *Beauty and the Beast*. Source: *Beauty and the Beast* ©Disney Pixar 2002

everyday. The result of this union is often explicit. The saturated colors of the opening fifties prologue (including the vibrant tint of Elastigirl's super-suit) have been deliberately drained, leaving behind a muted, subdued visual palette of dreary pastel colors. The pixelated space of the computer-animated screen appears to have been irretrievably bleached of its vibrant shades and tones. *The Incredibles* also jettisons animation's enduring associations with both the fairy-tale narrative and the musical format. As Helen stands alone in the Parr family hallway, the soundtrack to this solemn image is provided by the droning vacuum as it follows its routine path. No longer a collective activity (Bob is supposedly at work, the children at school), *The Incredibles* paints a lonely reality of household chores that dramatizes Elastigirl's enforced return to the domestic realm.

One salient point of contact that possibly conjoins *The Incredibles* to earlier animated representations of household labor is the fluctuating levels of effortlessness awarded to the chores themselves. Describing "Whistle While You Work," Margaret Horsfield has argued that the eponymous Snow White "effortlessly flaps away the cobwebs from the dwarfs' home" (14). The majesty of the heroine's movements, gleefully mirrored by the anthropo-morphic creatures that envelop her, inscribes each domestic activity with multiple conceptions of the popular. Not only are these housework songs exploitable across multimedia platforms (soundtracks, stage shows, and interactive "sing-a-long" videos), but the chores they accompany are painted as acts to be relished. The result is an enjoyable ensemble of activity that favors the collective over the individual. As Snow White sings convincingly, "It won't take long when there's a song to help you set the pace." The visibly effort*less* behavior of the kitchen appliances in *The Brave Little Toaster*, and in particular the mops in *Beauty and the Beast*, certainly unfolds along comparable lines. In *Beauty*, cleanliness functions as an emotional catharsis for its human characters, imprisoned by a spell as household objects (Lumière the candlestick was a maître d'hotel, Cogsworth the clock formerly a major-domo). Yet by decentering housework from human agency entirely through effortless automation, both *The Brave Little Toaster* and *Beauty and the Beast* illustrate how animation (to be *animated* or *enlivened*) can decrease the drudgery of household labor and reconfigure housework as a more dynamic and trouble-free enterprise.

The polymorphous vigor of Elastigirl and her faculties for protean, proto-plasmic change similarly enable a greater fluidity and effortlessness to her otherwise laborious routine. She gracefully extends her body when vacuuming, elongating her arm from right to left to exaggerate the simplest of gestures. Through her ease of motion, the enforced relocation of Elastigirl into "secret" domestic exile engages with the introduction of labor-saving devices into modernized suburban residences. Winn suggests that while the 1950s "remains the golden age of the American nuclear family," within these social structures the postwar woman was forced to "exchange her drill for her vacuum cleaner" (177). The science of home economics transferred the role of the woman from "family sustenance to consumption," with the decade permitting domestic appliances to be paid for in installments through "hire-purchase" schemes (Adams and Coltrane 408). Furthermore, through the "must-have" arrival of the automatic washing machine, refrigerator, and electric stove, the white middle-class American housewife was convinced that housework functioned to express her "individual creativity and affirming her femininity" (Coontz 38). *The Incredibles* is certainly acquainted with such lifestyle shifts. The line uttered to Helen by Edna Mode (the film's half-Japanese, half-German fashion designer), that her latest supersuit is "machine washable, darling. That's a new feature," situates the film within the emerging novelty of the household appliance. But Helen's natural abilities and dynamism of movement make her entire body (ironically) conducive to domestic duties: the perfect appliance to efficiently assuage the demands of the household task. Just like those inventive labor-saving devices that impossibly fix Betty Boop's home in *House Cleaning Blues*, Elastigirl remains well equipped for her domestic future, even if Helen herself (and the spectator) knows such functionality to be wasted at home.

CONCLUSION: THE FEMININE ELASTIQUE?

Throughout *The Incredibles*, Helen/Elastigirl can be viewed as a textual mirror retroactively reflecting the wider cult of domesticity that lay dormant in the 1950s, but which progressively came to the fore during the early 1960s. The interpretation offered here is both guided by, and anchored in, the striking connections that the film makes between its overwhelming fifties style and the shifting social role of the era's women, manifest in the figure of Helen Parr. However, Elastigirl's particular agency within *The Incredibles* has, for the main, been relatively underdeveloped across the sparse literature produced around the film itself. This may be a symptom of straightforward scholarly bias, and animation's placement more broadly at the margins of critical inquiry (a position that is still in need of adjustment despite the industrious efforts of contemporary animation studies). The neglect of Elastigirl's visible correspondence with the cult of domesticity from analyses of *The Incredibles* might also stem from the controversy that still envelops Friedan's provocative research on the postwar woman's domestic incarceration. Her labeling of the suburban family home as a "comfortable concentration camp," and the dissatisfaction with material (and marital) comfort that she exposed among many American women of the fifties and sixties, continues to be fervently discussed well beyond the fiftieth anniversary of *The Feminine Mystique*'s original publication (Friedan 271). A film like *The Incredibles* that resuscitates regressive or archaic depictions of women through Elastigirl's compulsory domestic containment is, perhaps, unpalatable in a contemporary era indelibly marked by the subsequent progress of feminist activism (Dennis, "Incredible Propaganda"). The ease with which Elastigirl withdraws from "Super" into civilian life (unlike her disgruntled

Figure 11.4.   Helen is well suited to her flexibility as a mother and homemaker.
Source: *The Incredibles* ©Disney Pixar 2004

husband), and her faculties for (re)shaping her body to fit the demands of the homemaker ideal, betrays a degree of ambivalence toward the historical legacy of second-wave feminism, and the ideological coding of the domestic space as necessarily one of entrapment and restriction.

Indeed, the lack of critical elaboration on Elastigirl is especially remarkable given the particular narrative trajectory of Helen and her subsequent return to superheroism in the second half of the film. With Elastigirl's extreme elasticity comes embodied tension. But rather than recoil and spring back into a state of domestic traditionalism (as with Alice in *Alice in Wonderland* [1951], or Wendy in *Peter Pan*, 1953), Elastigirl ultimately snaps into action to adopt a new social stance. Her innate superpowers and fundamental lack of "normality" (that is, her *incredibleness*) permits her to defy social expectations and return to civic activities, resuming a public role that had previously been annulled. Elastigirl's ability to embody simultaneity, to be both *able* and *flexible*, invites comparison with those values prized within the fifties woman, albeit marked by their unfortunate rarity:

> Contemporary women may resent the pressure to be a superwoman and "do it all," but in that era [the 1950s] the prevailing wisdom was that *only* a superwoman could choose to do *anything* with her life in addition to marriage and motherhood, and that such superwomen were few and far between. (Coontz xxii)

Rupturing the domestic confines of the home, Elastigirl moves from a private interior out into the public sphere, extending beyond her identity as a wife and mother but never discrediting or rendering obsolete either. Friedan herself wrote of a woman's "search for identity" amid the "comfortable concentration camp" of the home that served to collapse a woman's individuality into the housewife image (294). Tensions of identity and social standing likewise represent the inner turmoil of Elastigirl, who finally returns to her prior activism to stave off the threat of the film's antagonist, Syndrome. It is, perhaps, no accident that the primary villain of *The Incredibles* goes by such a provocative and hubristic moniker, one that is revealed to have replaced the character's original childhood name, Buddy Pine. During the late 1950s, several doctors "had begun to refer to women's persistent complaints of fatigue and depression as 'the housewife's syndrome'" (Coontz 22). With all the playful interaction between super/secret identities that recurs throughout *The Incredibles*, the problem "with no name" is reanimated as the Syndrome with a new one. But just as *this* Syndrome threatens the livelihood of Elastigirl and the domestic life she has kept, another condition circulates among her more private existence.

Enforcing the impression of continuity between *The Incredibles* and the fifties cult of domesticity, it is tempting to attach outright Elastigirl's liberated return to active public service to modern women's movements (particularly considering the connotations between second-wave feminism and the sociology of "superwomanhood") (Tong 27–28). But the chronological considerations of *The Incredibles* tap into the era's broader socializing experiences and shifting cultural landscape. Shedding its own identity as merely a passive bridge between the Second World War and radical feminism, the 1950s and 1960s have been reclaimed as a period of reestablishment through the consolidation of identity. From the end of African American segregation and civil rights to the advancement of capitalism and the promotion of the self, America's cultural framework was dented with the widespread quest to assert distinctiveness. Elastigirl's carefully chosen words in *The Incredibles* therefore resonate not just within the context of the era's resurgent feminist movement, but with a wider 1960s America in the throes of sociocultural redefinition. As the superheroic mother prepares her children for an imminent attack (by Syndrome, of course), she proclaims to their young ears, "Your identity is your most valuable possession. Protect it." Within the cultural framework of fifties and sixties America, this statement would become the mantra of anti-Communist women's groups such as the Minute Women of the U.S.A., echoing all the way to the gay rights marches on the steps of Independence Hall in Philadelphia and back again.

NOTES

1. The tendency toward a 1950s aesthetic on television continues across Western moving image culture. In the United Kingdom, series such as *The Hello Girls* (1996–1998), *Born and Bred* (2002–2005), *United* (2011), *The Hour* (2011–), *Call the Midwife* (2012–) and *The Bletchley Circle* (2012) have each drawn inspiration from a range of topics including sports, nursing, and television reports of the Suez crisis.

2. Since the original theatrical release of *The Incredibles* in November 2004, the representational scope of feature-length computer-animated films has been notably broadened to now include Depression-era America (*Everyone's Hero*, 2007) and early twentieth-century France (*A Monster in Paris*, 2011). However, among the growing number of all-digital period pieces, only a small proportion have opted to replicate a 1950s-style Americana. Based on the 1985 children's book by Chris Van Allsburg, Robert Zemeckis's motion-capture animated film *The Polar Express* (2004) takes place primarily on Christmas Eve 1956, in Grand Rapids, Michigan. With more than a hint of comic pastiche, the American, British, and Spanish joint production *Planet 51* (2009) also co-opts an idealized fifties U.S. suburbia as the setting for the planet Glipforg, an intergalactic utopia teeming with white picket fences, jukeboxes, and alien Stepford wives.

3. Not forgetting, of course, Bird's specially animated episode of Steven Spielberg's *Amazing Stories* anthology from 1987 titled "Family Dog." This twenty-minute vignette detailed the events in the dysfunctional Binsford family home, told from the perspective of their bull terrier.

4. The limited style of animation was parodied in a special feature contained on the DVD release of *The Incredibles* in 2005. The segment titled *Mr. Incredible and Pals* was an intentional spoof of the low-budget and low-quality television animation that aired during the 1950s and 1960s. This included the incorporation of the inexpensive and derided "Syncro-Vox" technique in which real human lips are superimposed over static cartoon images to create the illusion that each animated character can talk.

5. Just prior to her unplanned return as Elastigirl, Helen is shown staring intently at a black and white photograph of her with sidekick pilot Snug (while asking her old friend for a fighter jet), thus implying a more direct connection between the Parr family matriarch and World War II activism.

6. The live-action/animated hybrid *Enchanted* (2007) parodies the sustained musicality and excessive theatricality of domestic chores within feature-length Disney animation. The fantasy musical comedy contains a number titled "Happy Working Song," in which a plenitude of (non-animated) urban animals enter into a New York apartment to perform a range of domestic chores. But *Enchanted* opts to displace Disney's collective sentimentality and "gay refrain" with self-reflexive humor, as the animals begin to eat each other, drop crockery, and litter laundry across the floor.

7. An episode of the animated series *The Simpsons* (1989–) titled "Simpsoncalifragilisti-cexpiala(Annoyed Grunt)cious" and originally broadcast in February 1997, includes the irreverent song "Cut Every Corner," which explicitly parodies the alleged economy and efficiency of domestic chores when combined with musical accompaniment. A parody of "A Spoonful of Sugar" from the musical *Mary Poppins* (1964), lyrics to "Cut Every Corner" include "Just do a half-assed job" and "If you cut every corner, you'll have more time for play," to which Bart Simpson responds in rhyme "It's the American way!"

WORKS CITED

Adams, Michele, and Scott Coltrane. "Housework." *Men and Masculinities: A Social, Cultural, and Historical Encyclopedia*. Ed. Michael Kimmel and Amy Aronson. Santa Barbara, CA: ABC-CLIO, 2004. 407–10. Print.

Alice in Wonderland. Dir. Clyde Geronimi, Hamilton Luske, and Wilfred Jackson. Walt Disney, 1951. Walt Disney, 2011. DVD.

Anton, Audrey. "The Nietzschean Influence in *The Incredibles* and the Sidekick Revolt." *The Amazing Transforming Superhero! Essays on the Revision of Characters in Comic Books, Film and Television*. Ed. Terrence R. Wandtke. Jefferson, NC: McFarland, 2007. 209–30. Print.

Banner, Lois. *Marilyn: The Passion and the Paradox*. New York: Bloomsbury, 2012. Print.

Barrier, Michael. "The Juggler." 24 Nov. 2004. Web. 4 Feb. 2013.

Beauty and the Beast. Dir. Gary Trousdale and Kirk Wise. Walt Disney, 1991. Walt Disney, 2010. DVD.

Bell, Jonathan. "The Incredibles." *ICON* 20 Feb. 2005. Web. 4 Feb. 2013.

Booker, M. Keith. *Disney, Pixar, and the Hidden Messages of Children's Films*. Santa Barbara: Praeger, 2009. Print.

Bordwell, David, and Kristin Thompson. *Minding Movies: Observations on the Art, Craft, and Business of Filmmaking*. Chicago: University of Chicago Press, 2011. Print.

Bradshaw, Peter. "The Incredibles." *The Guardian* 19 Nov. 2004. Web. 4 Feb. 2013.

The Brave Little Toaster. Dir. Jerry Rees. Kushner-Locke, 1987. Walt Disney, 1988. DVD.

Brode, Douglas. *Multiculturalism and the Mouse: Race and Sex in Disney Entertainment*. Austin: University of Texas Press, 2005. Print.

Brown, Jeffrey A. *Black Superheroes, Milestone Comics and Their Fans*. Jackson: University Press of Mississippi, 2001. Print.

Bukatman, Scott. "Secret Identity Politics." *Contemporary Comic Book Superheroes*. Ed. Angela Ndalianis. New York: Routledge, 2009. 109–25. Print.

Cars. Dir. John Lasseter. Pixar, 2006. Film.

Cinderella. Dir. Clyde Geronimi, Hamilton Luske, and Wilfred Jackson. Walt Disney, 1950. Walt Disney, 2012. DVD.

Coontz, Stephanie. *A Strange Stirring: The Feminist Mystique and American Women at the Dawn of the 1960s*. New York: Basic, 2011. Print.

Courtney, Alice E., and Sarah Wernick Lockeretz. "An Analysis of the Roles Portrayed by Women in Magazine Advertisements." *Journal of Marketing Research* 8.1 (Feb. 1971): 92–95. *JSTOR*. Web. 4 Feb. 2013.

Croft, Stuart. *Culture, Crisis and America's War on Terror.* New York: Cambridge University Press, 2006. Print.

Dennis, Jon. "Incredible Propaganda." *The Guardian* 7 Dec. 2004. Web. 1 May 2013.

Dunn, David Hastings. "The Incredibles: An Ordinary Day Tale of a Superpower in the Post 9/11 World." *Millennium: Journal of International Studies* 34.2 (Feb. 2006): 559–62. *SAGE Journals.* Web. 4 Feb. 2013.

Elsaesser, Thomas. *Weimar Cinema and After: Germany's Historical Imaginary.* London and New York: Routledge, 2000. Print.

Enchanted. Dir. Kevin Lima. Walt Disney, 2007. Film.

Everyone's Hero. Dir. Colin Brady. IDT Entertainment, 2006. Film.

Fantasia. Dir. James Algar, John Hubley, and Wilfred Jackson. Walt Disney, 1940. Walt Disney, 2011. DVD.

Final Fantasy: The Spirits Within. Dir. Hironobu Sakaguchi. Square Pictures, 2001. Film.

Friedan, Betty. *The Feminine Mystique.* London: Penguin, 1963. Print.

Geraghty, Lincoln. ed. *Directory of World Cinema: American Hollywood.* Bristol: Intellect, 2011. Print.

Haynes, Natalie. "All These TV Series Set in the 1950s Are Really Contemporary Drama." *The Independent* 3 Sept. 2012. Web. 4 Feb. 2013.

Hine, Thomas. *Populuxe.* New York: Knopf, 1986. Print.

hooks, bell. *Feminist Theory: From Margin to Center.* Boston: South End Press, 1984. Print.

Horowitz, Daniel. "Rethinking Betty Friedan and *The Feminine Mystique*: Labor Union Radicalism and Feminism in Cold War America." *American Quarterly* 48.1 (1996): 1–42. *Project MUSE.* Web. 4 Feb. 2013.

———. *Betty Friedan and the Making of* The Feminist Mystique*: The American Left, The Cold War, and Modern Feminism.* Amherst: University of Massachusetts Press, 2000. Print.

Horsfield, Margaret. *Biting the Dust: The Joys of Housework.* New York: Picador, 1998. Print.

House Cleaning Blues. Dir. Dave Fleischer. Paramount, 1937. Web. 4 Feb. 2013.

Howard, Vicki. *Brides, Inc.: American Weddings and the Business of Tradition.* Philadelphia: University of Pennsylvania Press, 2006. Print.

The Incredibles. Dir. Brad Bird. Pixar, 2004. Film.

"*The Incredibles* Production Notes." *Pixar Talk* n.d. Web. 4 Feb. 2013.

The Iron Giant. Dir. Brad Bird. Warner Brothers, 1999. Film.

Kellaris, James J. "Music and Consumers." *Handbook of Consumer Psychology.* Ed. Curtis P. Haugtvedt, Paul M. Herr, and Frank R. Kardes. New York: Psychology Press, 2008. 837–56. Print.

Lopes, Paul. *Demanding Respect: The Evolution of the American Comic Book.* Philadelphia: Temple University Press, 2009. Print.

A Monster in Paris. Dir. Bibo Bergeron. Bibo Films. 2011. Film.

Nicholls, David, ed. *The Cambridge History of American Music.* New York: Cambridge University Press, 1998. Print.

Papamichael, Stella. "The Incredibles (2004)." *BBC Films* 25 Nov. 2004. Web. 4 Feb. 2013.

Peter Pan. Dir. Clyde Geronimi, Hamilton Luske, and Wilfred Jackson. Walt Disney, 1953. Walt Disney, 2012. DVD.

Planet 51. Dir. Jorge Blanco. Ilion Animation Studios, 2009. Film.

The Polar Express. Dir. Robert Zemeckis. ImageMovers, 2004. Film.

Popenoe, David. "American Family Decline, 1960–1990: A Review and Appraisal." *Journal of Marriage and Family* 55.3 (Aug. 1993): 527–42. *JSTOR.* Web. 4 Feb. 2013.

The Princess and the Frog. Dir. Ron Clements and John Musker. Walt Disney, 2009. Film.

Rowe-Finkbeiner, Kristen. *The F-Word: Feminism In Jeopardy: Women, Politics, and the Future.* Emeryville, CA: Seal Press, 2004. Print.

Scott, A. O. "Being Super in Suburbia Is No Picnic." *The New York Times* 5 Nov. 2004. Web. 4 Feb. 2013.

"Simpsoncalifragilisticexpiala(Annoyed Grunt)cious." *The Simpsons.* Dir. Chuck Sheetz. Fox, Gracie Films. 7 Feb. 1997. Television.

Skoble, Aeon J. "Superhero Revisionism in *Watchmen* and *The Dark Knight Returns.*" *Super-heroes and Philosophy: Truth, Justice and the Socratic Way.* Ed. Tom Morris and Matt Morris. Peru, IL: Open Court, 2005. 43–63. Print.

Snow White and the Seven Dwarfs. Dir. David Hand. Walt Disney, 1937. Walt Disney, 2009. DVD.

Starr, Cecille. "Busby Berkeley and America's Pioneer Abstract Film-makers." *Unseen Cine-ma: Early American Avant-garde Film 1893–1941; a Retrospective of Restored and Pre-served Films Detailing the Unknown Accomplishments of American Pioneer Filmmakers.* Ed. Bruce Posner. New York: Black Thistle Press, 2003. 77–83. Print.

Tangled. Dir. Nathan Greno and Byron Howard. Walt Disney, 2010. Film.

Telotte, J. P. *Animating Space: From Mickey to Wall-E.* Lexington: University Press of Ken-tucky, 2010. Print.

Tong, Rosemarie. *Feminist Thought: A More Comprehensive Introduction.* Boulder, CO: Westview Press, 1998. Print.

Toy Story 2. Dir. John Lasseter. Pixar, 1999. Film.

Up. Dir. Pete Docter. Pixar, 2009. Film.

Weisenfeld, Judith. *Hollywood Be Thy Name: African American Religion in American Film, 1929–1949.* Berkeley: University of California Press, 2007. Print.

Wertham, Fredric. *Seduction of the Innocent: The Influence of Comic Books on Today's Youth.* New York: Rinehart, 1954. Print.

Winn, Peter. "Back to the Future: A GI Bill for the Twenty-First Century." *Taking Parenting Public: The Case for a New Social Movement.* Ed. Sylvia Ann Hewlett, Nancy Rankin, and Cornel West. Lanham, MD: Rowman & Littlefield, 2002. 175–207. Print.

Young, William H. *American Popular Culture through History: The 1950s.* Westport, CT: Greenwood Press, 2004. Print.

Chapter Twelve

I Couldn't Do It Without Her

Big Love, Sister Wives, *and Housework*

Rita M. Jones

When the sister wives in HBO's *Big Love* (2006–2011) and TLC's *Sister Wives* (2011–present) do housework, it stands out. The women transport laundry and children from house to house, discuss the best strategies for stockpiling dry goods, and negotiate a night with a husband shared by at least three wives. Simultaneously, these characters show viewers something more unusual: the actual completing of the housework, the daily tasks required to keep a household and a family functioning smoothly. Representations of American households have all but covered up these tasks, such as cleaning dishes, paying bills, and coordinating children's after-school schedules. It takes the tripling or quadrupling of the work via plural marriage to make the work visible. We often see characters in popular shows standing over sinks or stirring pots of food on the stove, but they participate in these tasks to signal a domestic scene rather than to *do* domestic work. In *Big Love* and *Sister Wives*, the women fold laundry, clean countertops, and pay bills be-cause this work has to get done. The two shows focus on how the sister wives make housework a prominent and normal part of everyday discussions. These women depict their work in the home as vital, usual, and in a constant state of change.

Sister Wives and *Big Love* highlight the vast amount of housework the women complete each day, but these women do their work within the con-fines of a strictly patriarchal space. The families in the two shows share similar elements: multiple wives, many children, decisions to go public as polygamists, and white families located in the intermountain western United States. The women's interactions with one another regarding housework and the daily operations of the home create distinctions between the families. The wives in *Sister Wives*, Meri, Janelle, Christine, and Robyn, treat domestic labor as normal, vital, and pleasurable, and they engage one another and their husband, Kody Brown, in conversations about their work. Consistent with reality television formats, *Sister Wives* intersperses segments of "watching" the family via documentary-like footage with segments of the wives and husband on a couch recounting to the camera topics addressed in the documentary scenes. Conversely, the women in *Big Love*, Barb, Nicki, and Margie, display housework as onerous, unrewarding, and something someone else should do.[1] Bill Henrickson, their husband, refuses to be bothered by "women's work," and the sister wives fail to have honest and thorough conversations with one another about delegating work. The wives approach their roles in the house using a small business management model, which falls apart because home life exists in constant states of change and growth. Children are born or get sick, someone wants to move into the paid labor force, or a car breaks down. Each occurrence requires wives to rewrite a schedule, and they may need to make changes hourly. Ultimately, the sister wives in both shows demonstrate how housework, when performed by women family members, without pay and as part of family obligations, is incompatible with American understandings of "work" and not worthy of public recognition.

Treatments of housework have a long and well-established history, and for the purposes of this paper, I will be using the terms "housework" and "work in the home" to cover three types of work in the home: home infrastructure (physical structure of the home and revenue), home care (cleaning, laundry, and cooking), and child care (organizing schedules, driving, and rearing). For some time, scholars such as Ann Crittenden and Kathleen Gerson have separated home maintenance and home care from child care. Separating these categories certainly helps us fine-tune our understandings of the impact women make in each area, but the approach does not work well when we discuss *Big Love* and *Sister Wives*. A wife, for example, makes dinner while watching kids and asking a sister wife for help in repairing a garbage disposal. The representation of the lived experience in a home comes across as fluid rather than compartmentalized. In her important contribution to research regarding women's work in the home, Ruth Schwartz Cowan reminds us how the compartmentalizing works well for roles in the paid labor force. She identifies three elements of labor in the home that distinguish it from market labor and, thus, its devaluing. She notes that housework is "unpaid labor, performed in isolated workplaces, by unspecialized workers" (7). Untrained, unpaid, and previously unrepresented, the sister wives' housework exemplifies these elements. Early researchers like Cowan and Susan Strasser also emphasize the ways women's housework, which grew greatly during the nineteenth century in America, complemented notions of women's "natural" proclivity to remain within the home (Cowan 68; Strasser 181). The sister wives in *Big Love* and *Sister Wives* create an opportunity to complicate and extend our understanding of contemporary housework because even though they do not have specialized training and do not receive wages for their work, they labor alongside one another and discuss their contributions to the family in economic terms.

In each series the sister wives exist in a seemingly endless cycle of cleaning dishes, folding laundry, and managing budgets, and their work is, of course, exaggerated by the fact that they are completing these tasks for three or more houses at once. Most representations of housework fall within Louis Althusser's explanation of how ideology functions. He explains that ideology represents "not the system of the real relations which govern the existence of individuals, but the imaginary relation of those individuals to the real relations in which they live" (165). Most television shows set in the domestic sphere show us the home and, occasionally, some indications of work in the home, using imaginary relations and actions rather than actual ones. Closing the door on a minivan or turning off a vacuum stands in for what we imagine to be representations of work in the home. The wives in *Sister Wives* and *Big Love* engage in housework regularly and typically complete the work on-screen. They address through their actions and words the actual and real connections they have to the work. We see women completing the work, and since we rarely see this work accomplished, it initially looks odd to us. Unfamiliar representations catch our attention, even when we see something, such as housework, that occurs every day.

Plural marriage and its multiplication of wives and children allows viewers to see housework, but its uncommon structure encourages a dismissal of housework as antiquated and oppressive. Television critics have noted that the housework and daily routines of the women are significant aspects of these two shows, but because the family structure is non-normative, even critics cannot focus their comments on the very housework they initially say is most important. Reviewing *Sister Wives*, for example, Frank Stuever of the *Washington Post* argues the "domestic minutiae" of "the food supply, the house floor plan, the division of labor, the minor spats" ("TLC's 'Sister Wives'") make the show worth watching, but he devotes only these small comments to housework and moves on to the oddities of one man with many wives. Similarly, Schuyler Velasco notes on Salon.com that "the show offers a peek into an unfamiliar world: the sprawling dormlike home where the whole brood lives in attached houses, the rigorous scheduling of Brown's date nights and sleeping arrangements" ("Secrets of the Polygamists"). Velasco demonstrates that the show is indeed successful in representing housework as both familiar and new, but it falls beneath the more unfamiliar spectacle of a man trying to remember which wife he is to sleep with on any given night. The oddities of plural marriage and the strong patriarchal structure reassert the nineteenth-century separation of public and private spheres, making housework look outdated rather than respected.

Although the shows expand popular understandings of plural marriage, they also reassert the strong patriarch of each family. The Henricksons and the Browns exemplify particular variations on plural marriage, resembling the Apostolic United Brethren (AUB), who often live in suburbs and outwardly appear no different from their monogamous counterparts (Bennion, "Many Faces" 169). Most popular representations of polygamous families in America claim a lineage with the Church of Jesus Christ of Latter Day Saints, even though the LDS church denies most of these affiliations. Some practitioners of plural marriage are members of the Fundamentalist Church of Latter-Day Saints (FLDS), others are part of clans stemming from one or two patriarchs, and some are loosely connected with several churches, usually founded by a patriarch, or a family leader (Bennion, *Evaluating* 17; Zeitzen 94–95). These groups create unity by dictating where members live and enforcing dress codes, choosing typically rural and isolated areas and, specifically for women, prairie-style dresses and long hair (Bennion, "History" 113). Both series include representations of FLDS-based families, but the Henricksons and Browns overtly reject the restrictions. They do share beliefs in the primacy of a patriarch, eternal families that are formed on earth and continue into the afterlife, and modesty (Bennion, "History" 108). The sister wives defer to their husbands and perform household labor, connecting them more to representations of antiquated nineteenth-century angels in the home than liberated twenty-first century women.

The wives' positive representations of housework cannot overcome popular notions of women trapped within the confines of the domestic sphere. Women have struggled to represent housework in a positive light since the nineteenth century. Catharine E. Beecher and Harriet Beecher Stowe's *The American Woman's Home* (1869) is one manual from the nineteenth century that included information ranging from home decoration to raising children and caring for the aged. Beecher and Stowe designed the book to be used as a reference guide, but the compendium nature of the guide also served to enforce an appropriate form of housework. As Nicole Tonkovich explains, Beecher and Stowe wanted "to establish [domesticity's] respectability by placing it in a coherent scientific and philosophical system" (xxvii). Moving domestic labor into these realms also moved it into a public conversation. Stowe and Beecher argued that running a home and raising a family required planning; they argued that women needed training and resources to maintain an efficient home from which family members could launch successfully into the public sphere. We see similar representations in the pilot episode of *Sister Wives*, when we learn that Janelle and Christine openly negotiate, discuss, and support the different roles they take on in order to make the family function smoothly. Janelle, who works full time outside the home, feels fortunate that she does not resemble her workplace colleagues who, before leaving work, bemoan the fact that they still have to go home and make dinner. "Not me!" quips Janelle, knowing Christine is at home preparing an evening meal for all the family members because, as Christine points out, her "role is making the family run smoothly" ("Meet Kody"). Janelle and Christine expose the often unseen work of women in the home. These two women complicate viewers' ability to label Christine's work. Is she liberated and doing what she wants? Is she unable to see how she participates in her own oppression? These binary choices tend to limit viewers' options. Consequently, popular rhetoric that categorizes women who work only in the home as drudges wins out.

Rather than liberating one another, the wives of *Big Love* and *Sister Wives* may be seen as holding one another back. Plural marriage, rarely represented in popular culture as anything but vacant-eyed women in prairie dresses, furthers negative assessments of the wives. Viewers can only place Janelle's actions in a dominant position and Christine's in a submissive one. The overriding rhetoric of housework categorizes wife as "a full-time job encompassing homemaker, hostess, cheerleader, mother, chauffeur, Jill-of-all-trades" (Kingston 9). Certainly Janelle needs Christine to fulfill all of these roles if Janelle wants to earn wages, but Christine ends up looking like "the domestic backup and emotional support required so her husband could go out and make a living" (Kingston 9) to both Kody and Janelle rather than a sister wife, who supports and shares duties. Just as the women on *Sister Wives* struggle to complicate the notion of housework as oppressive, Bennion critiques *Big Love* for failing to "take in the many advantages of being a polygamist wife, such as sharing and friendship" (*Evaluating* 138). She explains that "women have to work together to survive, realizing very early in the marriage that if they intentionally wound their co-wife, family life will be disrupted, because there will come a time when a woman's survival rests in her co-wife's hands" (128). Whereas Christine and Janelle engage in dialogue, Barb, Nicki, and Margie in *Big Love* cannot place individual desires aside long enough to contemplate the greater needs of the family. Bill fuels their individualism, as Bennion argues, by "pit[ting] one wife against another" (139) and exerting strong patriarchal control over the wives and children. The wives' work in *Big Love* slips easily into conventional representations of housewives under the thumb of patriarchy.

Both sets of wives create structures for completing all elements of housework, including caring for children, cooking, budgeting, and working out of the home for pay, and they do so in the chaos of family life. Barb, Nicki, and Margie hold weekly meetings, calling to mind Charlotte Perkins Gilman's professionalization of housework in *Women and Economics* (1898). Gilman emphasized a model where families would live in groups, with a common kitchen overseen by properly trained cooks, and individual living spaces with bedrooms and family rooms, cleaned by trained professionals. Gilman's approach rejected the Beecher and Stowe model that relied upon a woman in every home, unconnected with more public spaces. Gilman's model would enable women who did not enjoy or were not good at housekeeping to work outside the home for pay. Similarly, women who enjoyed these labors and caring for children could specialize in these roles *and* be paid for the work. Regardless of where they work, all of the women and the knowledge of their work would become topics of public conversation. As Cowan argues, without public recognition, housework continues to stay within the isolated, unpaid, and untrained space. Regular meetings provide Barb, Nicki, and Margie opportunities to communicate with one another about housework, but problems arise from using a static model—a meeting—to fit a dynamic unit—a family. They try to negotiate schedules to accommodate special occasions such as birthdays ("Pilot"), but attempting to create a single schedule for one husband, three wives, and seven kids that will survive even a few days is doomed to fail. Even without multiple wives and sets of children, families function fluidly. Lacking alternative representations in everyday life, the Henrickson wives only know a management structure that they have seen represented by mainstream business culture. Viewers know and can see the small-business "departmental meeting" on commercials for just about every product, but they cannot recognize organizational representations that shift constantly, like the Henrickson household structure does.

Big Love and *Sister Wives* foreground the infrastructural elements of a household, which must include discussions about the physical layout of a house and the family budget. Infrastructure is a topic rarely included overtly in representations of housework. The physical layout of a house significantly affects the flow of labor. Homes without washers and dryers, for example, require additional time and resource expenditures (money, travel) than homes with these appliances. Houses with multiple carpeted rooms near one another decrease time required for vacuuming and physical strain to move the vacuum. Drawing attention to these details, *Big Love* and *Sister Wives* expose an important and often invisible element of housework. Of course housing stands out in these shows, since both represent either custom-built single homes or multiple homes inhabited by one husband and multiple wives and children. We recognize the significance of stairs in the home, as we see wives run up and down them with laundry or alternate between making a bed upstairs to checking on dinner and kids downstairs. Rather than focus on how living space has an effect on the efficiency of housework, viewers repurpose the depiction into the spectacle of plural marriage. The shows' representations of housework, then, come off merely as odd because few people live in two, let alone four, houses with multiple wives and sets of children. Within plural marriage, family housing structure often reflects the dynamics of the family itself. Zeitzen points out that some families opt for separate homes located near one another in order to lessen the constant negotiation of each wife's personality or to make each wife feel special (97). Further, Bennion indicates that other families seek to celebrate the communal elements of plural marriage and choose super-sized, custom-built homes with dozens of bedrooms (*Evaluating* 53–57). We see both kinds of housing structures in the shows, and regardless of what philosophy underpins the family— separate houses for separate personalities or thriving in a kind of commune— the wives' ideas about housing must play a central role in decisions or the foundation falls apart.

 Big Love portrays household layout as a critical element to women's housework and family harmony. We learn quickly in *Big Love* that Margie disagrees with both the housing infrastructure and also the dynamics of how housework is done. At the start of the show, the Henricksons hide their plural marriage from the public. To maintain the appearance of normalcy in the neighborhood, they have recently moved into three separate homes that are side-by-side but connected in the back through one large yard space. To their neighbors, Bill and Barb are married and renting homes to Nicki and Margie. Bill consistently enters and exits through Barb's house and accesses Nicki's and Margie's houses through the backdoors. The wives and children access one another's homes through the backdoors because they consistently need to pick up laundry from another house or borrow food from someone's kitchen. They further demarcate the separation of each wife and her biological children by referring to each house by the respective wife's name. They deemphasize the holistic nature of each wife's work by suggesting she is responsible for only one house, one set of children. Naming each house masks the constant interactions among the wives and their work in the home. This living arrangement is a relatively new one for the Henricksons, and all three wives and their children formerly lived in a single home with an annex in the back for Margie. In the second episode of the series, Bill scolds Margie for spending too much time in Barb's house and not enough time in her own house. When he comes home and discovers her asleep on Barb's couch with her boys crying in the playpen, he tells Margie to go to her own home. She wants to be at Barb's because "I like it here. Everyone's always here" ("Viagra Blue"). Margie desires the communal nature of a plural marriage and resists the isolation typical of housework. Her actions indicate a need for her family to recognize her contributions, and separate houses thwart that acknowledgment.

 Margie's actions also demonstrate how housing layouts impact housework. Barb's house functions as a common meeting area for the entire family, hosting at least one full-family dinner a week and commonly serving as an everyday breakfast location, where the other wives and children are always welcome. In terms of efficiency, Margie's actions make sense. Since the larger family convenes at Barb's so often, Margie decreases the number of times she needs to pack up her three kids and tote them through the backyard to Barb's. Misunderstanding the function of Barb's house, Margie spends her days with her kids in Barb's house, rather than upacking boxes in her own home. In two different episodes in season one, Barb asks Margie to return to her own home and give Barb some space ("Home Invasion" and "The Affair"). Margie indicates, through words and actions, that she prefers the more communal structure of their previous home, but her opinion is not validated by the other members of the family, who all enjoy the separate homes.

In order to keep up with the cost of three homes, Bill occasionally needs a wife to work outside the home. Deciding to work outside the home for pay is another fundamental component of a family's infrastructure, and when wives decide to move into the paid labor force, they must address the topic with their sister wives. As the series begins, Barb works outside the home as a substitute teacher, and early in season two, she receives an early-morning call from the school. As she dashes from the house, she leaves Nicki with additional duties for Barb's biological children: finish Teeny's costume for a school play; pick up tights for her at the store; pick her up from school at 3:20; pick up Sarah after work; and mend Ben's jeans. Nicki suddenly also leaves and transfers all of Barb's and Nicki's tasks and kids to Margie. Never do the sister wives ask one another if they can leave; each operates individually, assuming one of the others will remain at home as wife. While at work, Barb receives an offer to fill in for the year for a teacher out on maternity leave, and she agrees without talking to Nicki and Margie first. Bill reminds her that her actions directly affect her sister wives, and we recognize that Barb simply assumed her sister wives would not only step in to take care of her kids but also any residual housework and food preparation ("Eclipse"). Barb, like Bill, operates under the ideology that working outside for pay supersedes working in the home. Even though she does work at home, she cannot necessarily see it as comparable to the work she does at the school.

Running a household using a small business model causes strife among the sister wives, and they implement the once-and-done model when deciding who will work where. Nicki protests that one wife cannot make unilateral decisions such as working outside the home and expecting her sister wives to pick up the slack. She informs Barb, "I'm not your personal assistant . . . and neither is Margie" ("Eclipse"). This episode highlights the role of "wife": someone at home to take care of children, clean, ensure groceries are purchased and meals cooked, make medical appointments, and attend parent-teacher conferences. Without her sister wives, Barb would not be able to accept the teaching offer. She would need to research, at the very least, after-school care options and car pools or simply reject the offer and remain at home. Even in the midst of housework itself, Barb exemplifies how ideology masks our actual experiences. She cannot see who completes the housework, even when she participates in it. Barb retreats to the imaginary representations she does see. Those common depictions suggest that a position in the paid labor force transfers her from the status of first wife to second husband, relying upon the invisible support of her wives to keep the household functioning in her absence. Because paid labor is valued more than housework, she bypasses talking with her sister wives regarding her decision to take the job. From the physical home to who will work outside it, the wives of *Big Love* struggle to recognize their actual experiences with housework.

Openly discussing all facets of life, the Brown family stands in stark contrast to the Henricksons, and the wives foreground housework, beginning with the infrastructure of the home. They start the series in a custom-built home that has three kitchens, a communal living space, and separate bedroom quarters for each mother and her children. When Kody and Robyn prepare for marriage, early in season one, Robyn and her three children move to a rental home about a block away from the main Brown residence ("Wives on the Move"). The customized home obviously benefits Kody, who can easily kiss all children and wives goodnight before retiring to one wife's bedroom, but more importantly, we see it benefitting the wives by easing housework. Because Christine manages the house and children during the day, she needs to be able to move efficiently through the home to complete tasks including cleaning and cooking. In fact, shots cut from Janelle's son leaving a sink overflowing with dirty dishes from breakfast, to Christine talking about keeping things running "smoothly," and finally to an immaculate and empty sink. In *Sister Wives* the dirty-to-clean, full-to-empty sink represents the work required to feed a household rather than a mere representation of domestic space. We recognize that Christine washed these dishes. She moves from kitchen to kitchen, floor to floor doing housework. These cuts also represent the physical layout of the house. Stairs that separate floors, for example, increase labor for women performing household duties, as they must move up and down several times to complete tasks. Precisely because Christine may be cleaning three sets of kitchen sinks in a single day, every day, can the public actually *see* the physical layout and work in a home. Christine has to be shown doing three times the work in order to break through the lack of representation of housework.

Significantly, *Sister Wives* and *Big Love* make clear who completes much of the work of running a home. Arlie Hochschild famously outlined the notion of the second shift. After working outside the home for pay, people still need to return home to complete household tasks, known as the second shift. Hochschild describes this shift as including a wide variety of work from child care, to laundry, to repairing home appliances. Her research found that women completed "jobs that fix them into a rigid routine," multitask jobs, and often forgo leisurely activities to complete maintenance (9). Men, on the other hand, may or may not help out with the second shift, and often when they do, they have "more control over *when* they make their contributions than women do" (9). While Barb Henrickson dashes home after teaching with a bag of groceries in hand and informs Bill "ten more minutes on the meatloaf," Bill moves through the houses greeting his wives and chatting with his children ("Pilot"). Barb must ensure dinner is ready every night at or about the same time, while Bill can decide how and when to spend quality time with his kids. Seeing Barb and Bill perform work inside and outside the home creates space to represent the second shift as an important contribution to American life. *Sister Wives* similarly depicts the second shift, exemplified in the opening episode, "Meet Kody and the Wives." Meri, Janelle, Christine, and their thirteen children spend time outside cleaning up the fall yard, raking leaves, and clearing dead or felled trees, and Janelle participates after returning from a day at work outside the home. During the bulk of the shots, Kody is absent and appears briefly with a chainsaw, ultimately creating more work for his wives and children. Although *Sister Wives* reasserts the second shift as women's domain and never-ending, it also elevates the work through the women's open conversations about the shift as important work, without which the family would fail. Janelle and Christine refuse to ignore the demands of housework, and Janelle admits without hesitation that she has someone at home to either assist her with or absolve her from the second shift.

The shows emphasize the amount of work required to run a household efficiently by consistently showing the women with arms full of laundry or children, yet the families employ different strategies for understanding the importance of that work. The Henricksons represent housework as dominant American culture does, as something degrading, unrewarding, and focusing on women. The Browns engage in housework as rewarding and significant. The sister wives ensure topics about housework are at the forefront of the couch conversations, and we see them performing these tasks in the documentary shots. Because they perform their labors often in an isolated home, the sister wives know they need recognition from one another in order to complete their housework effectively. They also require a communal space in which to complete their work. While living in Utah, Janelle leaves the house before seven in the morning. She forthrightly explains that the large family needs her paycheck and that she needs Christine. Janelle prefers to work outside the home, admitting, "I get to do the things I like to do, too, not just the household stuff" like "cooking or chauffeuring. I just like being the mom" ("Meet Kody"). For Janelle, "being the mom" does not require her to be present in her children's lives at all times, though she misses them and calls them regularly from work when they get home from school to see how their day went. Her "mom" role requires her to earn money to support her children, her sister wives, and her sister wives' children. Janelle admits succeeding outside the home requires Christine's labor in the home, not just because "she likes to do that" but because it is vital to the success of all the family members. When we see Christine helping kids with projects and cooking food in the kitchen, she is smiling. As she talks on the couch about her work in the home, she is smiling. Her "mom" role requires her to be ever-present at home, contributing hourly to the house and its occupants. Kody underscores the delegation of duties, acknowledging that Christine "is actually mothering the twelve kids" ("Meet Kody"). Everyone in the Brown household recognizes each wife's actual relationships with housework. Janelle dislikes cleaning and constantly caring for children, but Christine pours her sense of self into those roles. Representing both simultaneously helps to break down narrow standards that value one over another.

Acknowledging housework requires constant work, mimicking the endless cycle of caring for children, making food, and vacuuming. Christine needs her sister wives to validate her contributions in the midst of ideological representations that devalue and fail to show work performed within the home. While in Utah, she proclaims proudly that she is "the domestic one," and she is often shown in her kitchen making a special treat for a family member, ironing, and discussing why toasters are fire hazards. Whether she is in the midst of a task or recounting it during the couch talk, Christine expresses joy for her work. She likes what she does and emphasizes that her work matters. She talks about how she saves the family money by buying in bulk and canning or preserving food ("The Price"). She, Meri, and Robyn find great pleasure in their relationship as sister wives, and they spread that happiness into the work they perform for the home. In "Polygamist Party," the three go grocery shopping for dinner. We see them pushing a cart and laughing so hard that, at times, they use the cart for support. They take items off the shelves and read the packaging together. In this segment they complete a mundane but necessary part of housework: buying food. Shopping for groceries in *Sister Wives* exposes the labor required to feed families. Cabinets and refrigerators at home contain products only if someone puts them there. They define their lives as "a girl party" that happens anytime, anywhere, and they recognize that Janelle does not want to participate in either the 365, 24/7 girl party, or the work required to run a household efficiently. They value, however, that she spends hours outside the home participating in the paid labor force to ensure that grocery store trips continue. All four women appreciate each other's contributions and refuse to see the separation of the duties as negative. When three of them live in one home with the other residing only a block away, they consistently validate one another's work.

Relocating to Nevada impedes the sister wives' abilities to assert their actual relationships with housework and acknowledge one another's contributions. They cannot find a home that will accommodate its many members. Instead, the family spreads out to four, single-family homes across the city, and the wives' support network falters. Christine, the major housework contributor, feels the sting of invisibility most. In Utah, everyone knew Christine wanted quality time with her newborn, Truely. In Nevada, Christine openly exhibits intense frustration with Truely for occupying too much time. We see Christine slovenly dressed, her carpet filled with stains, and clothes piled up around her on washing machines and ironing boards. She cannot complete her work, even though the move reduces her housework by one-third. The move also, however, requires her to take on jobs that Janelle typically completed, including taking care of monthly bills for her house ("Confronting Failure"). Christine's loss of joy in raising her daughter and working in her home cannot be explained away by, for example, the additional task of balancing a checkbook. Her relegation to the isolated space of a single-family home impedes her work, since her sister wives are not physically present each day to reap the rewards of Christine's labors and acknowledge her important contributions to the home and family. She no longer has a dozen children around her, and her husband's extended visits come only every fourth day. Christine cannot overcome on her own the more typical and negative characteristics of housework. She needs the support of her sister wives to affirm the daily work she contributes to the family.

Christine communicates and commiserates with her sister wives to create spaces for publicizing housework, but the sister wives of *Big Love* only speak openly about housework to complain or to tell another sister wife to do more work. They recreate the larger public perception of housework as something someone else needs to do in the isolated space of a single-family home. In *Big Love*, Barb and Nicki consistently place additional duties and higher expectations on Margie. Because they operate their family using a small business model, they unsurprisingly assert a hierarchy of first, second, and third wives. As the third, Margie has little ability to contradict her sister wives unless she forms a temporary alliance with one of them or cajoles Bill into chastising Barb or Nicki on Margie's behalf. Neither of these methods creates a community that will support women's housework as valuable and necessary, and neither method disrupts dominant representations of households where no one ever seems to perform work. Part of the hierarchy in the show, specifically in terms of Margie, stems from her introduction to the family. She worked at one of Bill's Home Plus stores, he asked her to become a babysitter, and then he married her ("Certain Poor Shepherds"). Margie never fully moves out of the role of family babysitter, someone who cares for children in the confines of an isolated home without witnesses. Bill, Barb, and Nicki all expect Margie to take care of her own house and children and the other sister wives' children whenever they need her to. Indeed, in "Eclipse," when left with everyone's children, Margie turns to one of the kids and exasperatedly sighs, "Hi. I'm the babysitter." Margie unwillingly becomes her sisters' wife because of a lack of honest communication among the women. Unlike Christine, Margie cannot create an alternative and positive representation of housework.

Through Margie, *Big Love* reasserts dominant constructions of house-work as negative. The sister wives re-create these depictions in the show's pilot, as Barb, Nicki, and Bill rush off to take care of family business a few hours away from the suburbs. Because they view Margie as the family's wife, they do not consult with her and simply inform her she will be at home with everyone's children to look after. At first, Margie thinks she will have all the kids only for a few hours, but Barb calls to tell her she will actually have them overnight. When we see Margie, she is in the midst of domestic chaos with Wayne, one of Nicki's sons, peeing on Margie's floor, Margie's youngest crying in her arms, and the other young sons running and screaming throughout the house. Boxes and laundry and food clutter the house, as Margie struggles to comprehend the news of the family's delayed return. Barb provides instructions for Margie, and these instructions, of course, also include information about Barb's kids. After the family returns, Margie talks to Barb about the situation. She tells Barb, "I try to contribute. I try to do my part," but "I can't take care of my own boys, let alone Nicki's" ("Pilot"). Margie recognizes her limitations, where she is failing, and where she needs support from her sister wives. As Nicki walks in, Barb reminds Margie that they are all in this family by choice, emphasizing common rhetoric given to and about women who demand more recognition and support for their work in the home. All Margie can respond with is "I'm a crappy mother," indicat-ing she has given in to both the popular rhetoric and Barb's response that it's all Margie's responsibility. Nicki steps in briefly to quip, "Margie's right, Barb. None of it's easy," but she neither thanks Margie for her work nor develops plans to lessen the burdens. Margie's frustration and failures as a housekeeper and mother certainly counter the typically absent work per-formed daily in the home. They ultimately, however, validate arguments that women who stay at home are oppressed and deluded.

Big Love and *Sister Wives* demonstrate how difficult it is to provide a space to reassess housework, particularly to reassess it as something positive and worthwhile. The sister wives of the shows assert their work against the tide that casts housework as menial and the incorrect course for twenty-first century, liberated American women. In her response to the end of *Big Love*'s third season, Virginia Heffernan argues that Bill Henrickson's patriarchal approach, an element of his polygamous beliefs, contributes to his wives' unhappiness. She sees the rise of patriarchal control in the show shift because up to that point the "series has taken pains to suggest that polygamy can be a successful, if unconventional, way to run a household" ("Together Forever"). The wives work together to relieve one another once in a while, and use their specific skills, such as Nicki's appliance repair work, to keep the homes running. Similarly, Courtney Hazlett, in reviewing the first season of *Sister Wives*, sees that the Browns' "lifestyle affords a certain degree of freedom— each wife, for example, is doing exactly what they want thanks to their built-in support system" ("Sister Wives"). Plural marriage allows critics and viewers to see the work and negotiation the women complete to run a home. Plural marriage also causes a depreciation of women's work in the home, as depictions of a strong patriarch make the women appear tied to the home, rather than happy in the home. Three or four wives working in the home allows viewers to see the actual relationships women have with housework, but the imagined relationships remain impossible to resist. The women's work, however, remains a central feature of both television shows, and the two series make important contributions to popular understandings of women doing actual housework on a daily basis.

NOTE

1. Although Bill Henrickson courts and marries Ana Marcovic in the third season, Ana only stays on as fourth wife for two days, and because of her brief role as wife, I will not treat her in this discussion. She connects to the family in a peripheral way until the end of the series, but she does not function as a domestic laborer in the Henrickson household.

WORKS CITED

"The Affair." *Big Love: The Complete First Season*. Home Box Office, 2006. DVD.

Althusser, Louis. "Ideology and Ideological State Apparatuses (Notes Toward an Investigation)." *Lenin and Philosophy and Other Essays*. Trans. Ben Brewster. New York: Monthly Review Press, 1971. 127–86. Print.

Beecher, Catharine E., and Harriet Beecher Stowe. *The American Woman's Home*. 1869. Ed. Nicole Tonkovich. New Brunswick, NJ: Rutgers University Press, 2004. Print.

Bennion, Janet. *Evaluating the Effects of Polygamy on Women and Children in Four North American Mormon Fundamentalist Groups: An Anthropological Study*. Lewiston, NY: Edwin Mellen Press, 2004. Print.

———. "History, Culture, and Variability of Mormon Schismatic Groups." *Modern Polygamy in the United States: Historical, Cultural, and Legal Issues*. Ed. Cardell K. Jacobson with Lara Burton. New York: Oxford University Press, 2011. 101–24. Print.

———. "The Many Faces of Polygamy: An Analysis of the Variability in Modern Mormon Fundamentalism in the Intermountain West." *Modern Polygamy in the United States: Historical, Cultural, and Legal Issues*. Ed. Cardell K. Jacobson with Lara Burton. New York: Oxford University Press, 2011. 163–84. Print.

"Certain Poor Shepherds." *Big Love: The Complete Fifth Season*. Home Box Office, 2001. DVD.

"Confronting Failure." *Big Love*. TLC. 16 Dec. 2012. Television.

Cowan, Ruth S. *More Work for Mother: The Ironies of Household Technology from the Open Hearth to the Microwave*. 1984. New York: Basic, 1993. Print.

"Eclipse." *Big Love: The Complete First Season*. Home Box Office, 2006. DVD.

Gilman, Charlotte Perkins. *Women and Economics: A Study of the Economic Relation Between Men and Women as a Factor in Social Evolution*. 1898. University of Pennsylvania. Web. 15 Dec. 2010.

Hazlett, Courtney. "'Sister Wives' Defy Criticism to Open Up on TV." TODAY.com. 28 Sept. 2010. Web. 18 Jan 2013.

Heffernan, Virginia. "Together Forever." *New York Times*. 22 Mar. 2009. Web. 19 Oct. 2011.

Hochschild, Arlie, with Anne Machung. *The Second Shift: Working Families and the Revolution at Home*. Rev. ed. New York, NY: Penguin, 2012. Print.

"Home Invasion." *Big Love: The Complete First Season*. Home Box Office, 2006. DVD.

Kingston, Anne. *The Meaning of Wife: A Provocative Look at Women and Marriage in the Twenty-First Century*. New York: Picador, 2004. Print.

"Meet Kody and the Wives." *Sister Wives: Season 1*. TLC, 2010. DVD.

"Pilot." *Big Love: The Complete First Season*. Home Box Office, 2006. DVD.

"Polygamist Party." *Sister Wives: Season 2*. Vol. 1. TLC, 2011. DVD.

"The Price of Failure." *Sister Wives: Season 2*. Vol. 1. TLC, 2011. DVD.

Strasser, Susan. *Never Done: A History of American Housework*. New York: Henry Holt, 2000. Print.

Stuever, Hank. "TLC's 'Sister Wives': Frank, Entertaining TV about Polygamist Browns in Utah." *Washington Post*. 25 Sept. 2010. Web. 17 Jan. 2013.

Velasco, Schuyler. "Secrets of the Polygamists." Salon.com. 16 Oct. 2010. Web. 17 Jan. 2013.

"Viagra Blue." *Big Love: The Complete First Season*. Home Box Office, 2006. DVD.

Tonkovich, Nicole. "Introduction." *The American Woman's Home*. By Catharine E. Beecher and Harriet Beecher Stowe. New Brunswick, NJ: Rutgers University Press, 2004. ix–xxxi. Print.

"Wives on the Move." *Sister Wives: Season 1*. TLC, 2010. DVD.

Zeitzen, Miriam Koktvedgaard. *Polygamy: A Cross-Cultural Analysis*. Oxford: Berg, 2008. Web. 11 Dec. 2012.

Suggested Reading

BOOKS

Armstrong, Pat, and Hugh Armstrong. *The Double Ghetto: Canadian Women and Their Segregated Work.* Cambridge, ON: Oxford University Press, 1994. Print.

Babcock, Linda, and Sara Laschever. *Women Don't Ask: Negotiation and the Gender Divide.* Princeton, NJ: Princeton University Press, 2003. Print.

Beer, William R. *Househusbands: Men and Housework in American Families.* New York: Praeger, 1983. Print.

Benoit, Cecilia. *Women, Work and Social Rights: Canada in Historical and Comparative Perspective.* Toronto: Prentice-Hall Canada, 2000. Print.

Bonner, Kieran. *Power and Parenting: A Hermeneutic of the Human Condition.* London and New York: Macmillan/St. Martin's Press, 1998. Print.

Booth, Alan, and Ann Crouter. *Men in Families: When Do They Get Involved? What Difference Does It Make?* Mahwah, NJ: Lawrence Erlbaum Associates, 1998. Print.

Boydston, Jeanne. *Home and Work: Housework, Wages, and the Ideology of Labor in the Early Republic.* New York: Oxford University Press, 1990. Print.

Bradley, Patricia. *Mass Media and the Shaping of American Feminism, 1963–1975.* Jackson: University Press of Mississippi, 2003. Print.

Chabon, Michael. *Manhood for Amateurs: The Pleasures and Regrets of a Husband, Father, and Son.* New York: Harper Perennial, 2009. Print.

Cohen, Lizabeth. *A Consumers' Republic: The Politics of Mass Consumption in Postwar America.* New York: Knopf, 2003. Print.

Coltrane, Scott, and Michele Adams. "Men, Women and Housework." *Gender Mosaics: Social Perspectives.* Ed. Dana Vannoy. Los Angeles: Roxbury Publishing, 2001. 145–54. Print.

Connell, Robert William. *The Men and the Boys.* Berkeley: University of California Press, 2000. Print.

Coontz, Stephanie. *A Strange Stirring: The Feminine Mystique and American Women at the Dawn of the 1960s.* Philadelphia: Perseus, 2011. Print.

———. *The Way We Never Were: American Families and the Nostalgia Trap.* New York: Basic, 1992. Print.

Cowan, Ruth S. *More Work for Mother: The Ironies of Household Technology from the Open Hearth to the Microwave.* 1983. New York: Basic, 1993. Print.

Dunne, Gillian. "Lesbians at Home: Why Can't a Man Be More Like a Woman?" *Family Patterns: Gender Relations.* 3rd ed. Ed. Bonnie Fox. New York: Oxford University Press, 2009. Print.

Ehrenreich, Barbara. *Nickel and Dimed: On (Not) Getting by in America.* New York: Picador, 2001. Print.

———. *The Hearts of Men: American Dreams and the Flight from Commitment.* 1983. Anchor, 1987. Print.

Foot, David, and Daniel Stoffman. *Boom, Bust and Echo: How to Profit from the Coming Demographic Shift.* Toronto: Stoddart, 1996. Print.

Fox, Bonnie, ed. *Family Patterns, Gender Relations.* 1994. New York: Oxford University Press, 2009. Print.

Friedan, Betty. *The Feminine Mystique.* 1963. Rpt. New York and London: Norton, 1997. Print.

Graesch, Anthony P., Jeanne E. Arnold, Enzo Ragazzini, and Elinor Ochs. *Life at Home in the 21st Century.* Los Angeles: Cotsen Institute of Archaeology, 2012. Print.

Hayden, Dolores. *Redesigning the American Dream.* 1984. New York: Norton, 2002. Print.

Hays, Sharon. *The Cultural Contradictions of Motherhood.* New Haven, CT: Yale University Press, 1995. Print.

Hesse-Bibber, Sharlene Nagy, and Gregg Lee Carter. *Working Women in America: Split Dreams.* 2000. New York: Oxford University Press, 2005. Print.

Heymann, Jody. *The Widening Gap: Why America's Working Families Are in Jeopardy and What Can Be Done About It.* New York: Perseus, 2000. Print.

Hite, Shere. *The Hite Report: Women and Love: A Cultural Revolution in Progress.* New York: Knopf, 1987. Print.

Hochschild, Arlie. *The Second Shift: Working Families and the Revolution at Home.* Rev. ed. New York: Penguin, 2012. Print.

———. *The Time Bind: When Work Becomes Home and Home Becomes Work.* New York: Metropolitan Books, 1997. Print.

Horowitz, Daniel. *The Anxieties of Affluence: Critiques of American Consumer Culture, 1939–1979.* Amherst: University of Massachusetts Press, 2004. Print.

———. *Betty Friedan and the Making of* The Feminine Mystique. Amherst: University of Massachusetts Press, 1998. Print.

Horsfield, Margaret. *Biting the Dust: The Joys of Housework.* New York: Picador, 1998. Print.

Johnson, Lesley, and Justine Lloyd. *Sentenced to Everyday Life: Feminism and the Housewife.* Oxford: Berg, 2004. Print.

Kamen, Paula. *Her Way: Young Women Remake the Sexual Revolution.* New York: NYU Press, 2000. Print.

Kirk, Gwyn, and Margo Okazawa-Rey. *Women's Lives: Multicultural Perspectives.* 1998. Boston: McGraw-Hill, 2007. Print.

Kleinberg, S. Jay, Eileen Boris, and Vicki Ruiz, eds. *The Practice of U.S. Women's History.* New Brunswick, NJ: Rutgers University Press, 2007. Print.

Komarovsky, Mirra. *Women in the Modern World: Their Education and Their Dilemmas.* Boston: Little, Brown, 1953. Print.

Kossek, Ellen Ernst, and Susan Lambert. *Work and Life Integration: Organizational, Cultural and Individual Perspectives.* Mahwah, NJ: Lawrence Erlbaum Associates. 2005. Print.

Krull, Catherine. "Families and the State: Family Policy in Canada." *Canadian Families Today.* Ed. David Cheal. New York: Oxford University Press, 2007. 257–72. Print.

Leavitt, Sarah. *From Catharine Beecher to Martha Stewart: A Cultural History of Domestic Advice.* Chapel Hill: University of North Carolina Press, 2002. Print.

Lerman, Nina, Ruth Oldenziel, and Arwen P. Mohun, eds. *Gender and Technology: A Reader.* Baltimore: Johns Hopkins University Press, 2003. Print.

Levitt, Steven, and Stephen J. Dubner. *Freakonomics: A Rogue Economist Explores the Hidden Side of Everything.* New York: Morrow, 2005. Print.

Lewis, Stephen. *Race Against Time.* Toronto: House of Anansi Press, 2005. Print.

Lorber, Judith. *Paradoxes of Gender.* New Haven, CT: Yale University Press, 1994. Print.

Mainardi, Pat. "The Politics of Housework." *Feminist Frameworks: Alternative Theoretical Accounts of the Relations between Women and Men.* 1978. Ed. Alison Jagger and Paula S. Rothenberg. New York: McGraw-Hill, 1984. 51–56. Print.

Matthews, Glenna. *Just a Housewife: The Rise and Fall of Domesticity in America*. New York: Oxford University Press, 1989. Print.

McHugh, Kathleen Anne. *American Domesticity: From How-To Manual to Hollywood Melodrama*. Oxford: Oxford University Press, 1999. Print.

Mendelson, Cheryl. *Home Comforts: The Art and Science of Keeping House*. New York: Scribner, 1999. Print.

Merriam, Eve. *After Nora Slammed the Door*. World Pub. Co., 1964. Google Books.

Meyerowitz, Joanne, ed. *Not June Cleaver: Women and Gender in Postwar America*. Philadelphia: Temple University Press, 1994. Print.

Moen, Phyllis, ed. *It's About Time: Couples and Careers*. Ithaca, NY: Cornell University Press, 2003. Print.

Myrdal, Alva, and Viola Klein. *Women's Two Roles: Home and Work*. London: Routledge & Kegan Paul, 1956.

National Trust. *The National Trust Manual of Housekeeping: The Care of Collections in Historic Houses Open to the Public*. Amsterdam and London: Butterworth-Heinemann, 2005. Print.

Orenstein, Peggy. *Flux: Women on Sex, Work, Kids, Love and Life in a Half-Changed World*. New York: Doubleday, 2000. Print.

Padavic, Irene, and Barbara Reskin. *Women and Men at Work*. 2nd ed. Thousand Oaks: Pine Forge Press, 2002. Print.

Parasuraman, J. H. Saroj, ed. *Integrating Work and Family*. Westport, CT: Quorum, 1997. Print.

Pitt-Catsouphes, Marcie, Ellen Ernst Kossek, and Stephen Sweet, eds. *The Work and Family Handbook: Multidisciplinary Perspectives, Methods and Approaches*. Mahwah, NJ: Lawrence Erlbaum Associates, 2006. Print.

Plant, Rebecca Jo. *Mom: The Transformation of Motherhood in Modern America*. Chicago: University of Chicago Press, 2010. Print.

Pollack, Neal. *Alternadad*. New York: Pantheon, 2007. Print.

Press, Andrea. *Women Watching Television: Gender, Class and Generation in the American Television Experience*. Philadelphia: University of Pennsylvania Press, 1991. Print.

Reskin, Barbara, and Patricia Roos, eds. *Job Queues, Gender Queues: Explaining Women's Inroads into Male Occupations*. Philadelphia: Temple University Press, 1990. Print.

Risman, Barbara. *Families as They Really Are*. New York: Norton, 2010. Print.

Romero, Mary. *Maid in the U.S.A.* New York: Routledge, 1992. Print.

Shaevitz, Marjorie Hansen. *The Superwoman Syndrome*. New York: Warner Books, 1985. Print.

Steele, Betty. *The Feminist Takeover: Patriarchy to Matriarchy in Two Decades*. Gaithersburg, MD: Human Life International, 1987. Print.

Stewart, Martha. *Homekeeping Handbook*. New York: Clarkson Potter, 2006. Print.

Strasser, Susan. *Never Done: A History of American Housework*. New York: Henry Holt, 2000. Print.

Tone, Andrea. *The Age of Anxiety*. New York: Basic, 2009. Print.

Tong, Rosemarie. *Feminist Thought: A More Comprehensive Introduction*. 3rd ed. Boulder, CO: Westview Press, 2009. Print.

Valian, Virginia. *Why So Slow? The Advancement of Women*. Cambridge, MA: MIT Press, 1998. Print.

Waldman, Ayelet. *Bad Mother: A Chronicle of Maternal Crimes, Minor Calamities, and Occasional Moments of Grace*. New York: Doubleday, 2009. Print.

Warner, Judith. *Perfect Madness: Motherhood in the Age of Anxiety*. New York: Penguin, 2005. Print.

Williams, Christine. *Still a Man's World: Men Who Do "Women's Work."* Berkeley: University of California Press, 1995. Print.

Williams, Joan. *Reshaping the Work-Family Debate: Why Men and Class Matter*. Cambridge, MA: Harvard University Press, 2010.

Woloch, Nancy. *Women and the American Experience*. New York: McGraw-Hill, 1984. Print.

ARTICLES AND BLOGS

Acker, Joan. "Hierarchies, Jobs, Bodies: A Theory of Gendered Organizations." *Gender and Society* 4.2 (1990): 139–58. Print.

Aumann, Kerstin, Ellen Galinsky, and Kenneth Matos. "The New Male Mystique." *Families and Work Institute* (2011). Families and Work Institute. Web.

Belkin, Lisa. "The Opt-Out Revolution." *New York Times Magazine*, 26 Oct. 2003. Web.

Berkowitz, Dana, and William Marsiglio. "Gay Men: Negotiating Procreative, Father and Family Identities." *Journal of Marriage and the Family* 69 (2007): 366–81. Print.

Cady, Kathryn. "Labor and Women's Liberation: Popular Readings of *The Feminine Mystique*." *Women's Studies in Communication* 32 (2009): 348–79. Print.

Cruz, Michael. "Why Doesn't He Just Leave? Gay Male Domestic Violence and the Reasons Victims Stay." *Journal of Men's Studies* 11.3 (2003): 309–23. Print.

Dewan, Shailene, and Robert Gebeloff. "More Men Enter Fields Dominated by Women." *New York Times,* 20 May 2012: A1. Web.

Dijkstra, Sandra. "Simone de Beauvoir and Betty Friedan: The Politics of Omission." *Feminist Studies* 6 (Summer 1980): 290–303. Print.

Folbre, Nancy. "Feminism's Uneven Success." Economix, 19 Dec. 2011. *New York Times*. Web.

Galinsky, Ellen, Kerstin Aumann, and James T. Bond. "Times Are Changing: Gender and Generation at Work and at Home." Families and Work Institute, 2008 National Study of the Changing Workforce, August 2011. Web.

Green, Penelope. "A Country's Attic, on Display." *New York Times*, 2 May 2012: D7. Web.

Hall, Elaine. "Smiling, Deferring, and Flirting: Doing Gender by Giving 'Good Service.'" *Work and Occupations* 20.4 (1993): 452–71. Print.

Heymann, Jody, Aloson Earle, and Amresh Hanchate. "Bringing a Global Perspective to Community, Work, and Family." *Community, Work & Family* 7.2 (2004): 47–271. Web.

Hirschman, Linda. "Homeward Bound." *American Prospect*, 20 Dec. 2005. Web.

Hoffnung, Michele. 2004. "Wanting It All: Career, Marriage, and Motherhood During College-Educated Women's 20s." *Sex Roles* 50 (2004): 711–23. Web.

Lambert, Susan. "Added Benefits: The Link between Work-Life Benefits and Organizational Citizenship Behavior." *Academy of Management Journal* 43 (2003): 801–15. Print.

Le Bourdais, Celine, and Evelyne Lapierre-Adamcyk. "Changes in Conjugal Life in Canada: Is Cohabitation Progressively Replacing Marriage?" *Journal of Marriage and Family* 66 (2004): 929–42. Print.

Lerum, Kari. "Sexuality, Power, and Camaraderie in Service Work." *Gender and Society* 18(6) (2004): 756–76. Print.

Mainiero, Lisa, and Sherry Sullivan. "Kaleidoscope Careers: An Alternate Explanation for the 'Opt-Out' Revolution." *The Academy of Management Executive* 19.1 (2005): 106–23. Print.

McGaw, Judith A. "Women and the History of American Technology." *Signs* 7.4 (Summer, 1982): 798–828. Print.

McKinley, Jesse. "Scrub the Halls." *New York Times*, 7 Dec. 2011. D1. Web.

Merriam, Eve. "Are Housewives Necessary?" *The Nation*, 31 Jan. 1959: 96–99. Print.

Nickles, Shelley. "More Is Better: Mass Consumption, Gender, and Class Identity in Postwar America." *American Quarterly* 54 (2002): 582–622. Print.

Orenstein, Peggy. "The Other Mother." *New York Times Magazine*, 24 July 2004. Web.

Press, Andrea. "Gender and Family in Television's Golden Age and Beyond." *ANNALS of the American Academy of Political and Social Science* 625 (Sept. 2009): 139–51. Web.

Schiebinger, Londa, and Shannon K. Gilmartin. "Housework Is an Academic Issue: How to Keep Talented Women Scientists in the Lab, Where They Belong." *Academe* 96.1 (2010). Web.

Senior, Jennifer. "All Joy and No Fun." *New York*, 4 July 2010. Web.

Singleton, Andrew, and JaneMaree Maher. "The 'New Man' Is in the House: Young Men, Social Change, and Housework." *Journal of Men's Studies* 12.3 (2004): 227–40. Print.

Smith, Calvin D. "Men Don't Do This Sort of Thing: A Case Study of the Social Isolation of House Husbands." *Men and Masculinities* 1.2 (1998): 138–72. Print.

Stone, Pamela. "The Rhetoric and Reality of 'Opting Out.'" *Contexts* 6.4 (2007): 14–19. Print.

Sullivan, Maureen. "Rozzie and Harriet? Gender Family Patterns of Lesbian Coparents." *Gender and Society* 10.6 (1996): 747–67. Print.

Swisher, Raymond, Stephen A. Sweet, and Phyllis Moen. "The Family-Friendly Community and Its Life Course Fit for Dual-Earner Couples." *Journal of Marriage and Family* 66 (2004): 281–92. Print.

Voydanoff, Patricia. "The Effects of Work and Community Resources and Demands on Family Integration." *Journal of Family and Economic Issues* 25 (2004): 7–23. Print.

Wurtzel, Elizabeth. "1% Wives Are Helping Kill Feminism and Make the War on Women Possible." *The Atlantic*, 15 Jun 2012. Web.

Zeitz, J. "Rejecting the Center: Radical Grassroots Politics in the 1970s—Second-Wave Feminism as a Case Study." *Journal of Contemporary History* 43.4 (2008): 673–88. Print.

Index

About the Editors and Contributors

Elizabeth Patton is Program Coordinator and full-time faculty in the Johns Hopkins University MA in Communication program in Washington, D.C. She received her PhD in 2013 from the Department of Media, Culture, and Communication at New York University. Her research includes media history; representations of gender, class, and race within mass media; and the impact of communication technology on space, family, and work-life balance. Her dissertation, "(Home)work and the Bedroom-Study: Work, Leisure and Communication Technology," investigates the socioeconomic significance of market-based work in the bedroom and the introduction of communication technology in the home. Elizabeth has also contributed to the *Encyclopedia of Identity* (2010) and written reviews for the *Journal of Popular Culture*.

Mimi Choi received her MA from Ryerson University's Literatures of Modernity program in Toronto, Canada, after more than two decades of professional writing and editing experience in the financial, book, and magazine publishing industries. Her academic research interests include British and American novels, feminist theory and gender studies, and reception theory. Mimi served as research assistant on *The Collected Poems of Miriam Waddington: A Critical Edition* by Dr. Ruth Panofsky, and plans to undertake her doctoral studies in 2014.

* * *

Nicole Williams Barnes is a doctoral candidate in Communication at Georgia State University. She is interested in the ways gender roles manifest as a constraint upon women's self-identification with a focus on the Cold War period. She is currently working on a dissertation examining the ways American mass media through the 1950s functioned to persuade women to accept their place within the home as both traditional and natural.

Kristi Branham is assistant professor of Gender and Women's Studies in the Department of Community and Diversity Studies at Western Kentucky University in Bowling Green. She earned her PhD in literature with concentrations in social theory and women's studies from the University of Kentucky. Her research focuses on American women's popular culture from 1850 to 1950.

Nancy Bressler is currently earning her PhD in Media and Communication, as well as a graduate certificate in Women's Studies, at Bowling Green State University. Her research interests include media studies, with an emphasis on the intersections of critical/cultural studies, feminist theory, and popular culture. Her previous research has concentrated on the role of media in American culture and how television images influence and contribute to American identity. Specifically, she focuses on the intersections of gender and economic class on television and the role humor plays in the concealment and identification of common ideologies.

Nicola Goc is a senior lecturer in Journalism, Media and Communications at the University of Tasmania. She has written widely on female representation and the media. Her most recent book is *Women, Infanticide and the Press 1822–1922: News Narratives in England and Australia* (2013). A collector of snapshot photographs since her teens, her current research focus is on female subjectivity and vernacular (snapshot) photography. She is currently working on a funded research project focusing on snapshot photography, female subjectivity, and the migrant experience.

Christopher Holliday completed a Film Studies PhD at King's College, London. His research is aimed at developing an approach to the computer-animated film that elaborates upon its unique visual currencies and formal attributes, organized as a generic framework that supports the study of computer-animated films as a new genre of contemporary cinema. Primary research interests include the nuances of film style, fictional world creation, and conceptions of animated performance within the context of the digital media and traditional animation.

Kristi Rowan Humphreys is assistant professor of Critical Studies and Artistic Practice at Texas Tech University in Lubbock, where she teaches within the Fine Arts doctoral program. She earned her PhD in the Humanities, Aesthetic Studies at the University of Texas at Dallas, and she specializes in popular culture, musical theater, and novelist William Faulkner. She also is a working stage and commercial actress, having performed in over forty stage productions. Her most recent publication, coauthored by William Harrison Taylor and titled "Satan's Most Popular Pawn? Harry Potter and Modern Christian Cosmology," is forthcoming in the anthology *A History of Evil in Popular Culture: What Hannibal Lecter, Stephen King, and Vampires Reveal about America.*

Since 2008, **Rita M. Jones** has been director of the Women's Center and Affiliate Faculty in Women, Gender, and Sexuality Studies at Lehigh University in Bethlehem, Pennsylvania. After completing her PhD in English at Washington State University, Rita was assistant professor and director of the Women's Studies Program at the University of Northern Colorado before moving to Lehigh. Her research interests include mothers, pregnancy and childbirth, and women and housework.

Andrea Krafft is a PhD candidate in the Department of English at the University of Florida in Gainesville, where she is writing her dissertation about the intersections of the fantastic and the domestic in postwar American literature. She has presented on this research at both the 2013 Popular Culture Association national conference and the 34th International Conference on the Fantastic in the Arts. Her research interests include twentieth-century American literature, speculative fiction, domesticity, humor writing, and advertising studies.

Ryan Lescure (MA, San Francisco State University) is a lecturer of Communication Studies at San Francisco State University. He teaches courses such as Gender and Communication and Fundamentals of Oral Communication. His courses are taught with a special emphasis on social justice. Additionally, he has worked as a member of a teaching team in courses such as Communication and Masculinities, Sexual Identity and Communication, Field Research Strategies, and Communication and Culture. His research primarily focuses on the intersections between communication, gender, sexuality, media, culture, and power.

Hannah Swamidoss, an independent researcher, completed her PhD in Literary Studies from the University of Texas at Dallas with an emphasis on British fiction, children's literature, and postcolonial studies. Her dissertation explores the concept of "third culture" in British literature and examines a range of authors from Jane Austen to Frances Hodgson Burnett. Her recent publications include "'When I Cannot Still the Longing of My Heart': Third-Culture Displacement and the Image of the Child in Allen Say's *Tree of Cranes* and *Grandfather's Journey*" in *Red Feather Journal* (Spring 2013) and "The Interstitial Body and Moral Formation: Third-Culture Displacement and Subject Formation in Charles Kingsley's *The Water-Babies*" in *Otherness: Essays and Studies* (Spring 2013).

Gust A. Yep (PhD, University of Southern California) is professor of Communication Studies, core graduate faculty of Sexuality Studies, and faculty of the EdD Program in Educational Leadership at San Francisco State University. He has three active research programs: (1) communication at the intersections of culture, race, class, gender, sexuality, and nation; (2) communication in HIV/AIDS programs in communities of color; and, (3) queer theory and communication. He is author and editor of three books, including *Queer Theory and Communication: From Disciplining Queers to Queering the Discipline(s)* and *Privacy and Disclosure of HIV in Interpersonal Relationships: A Sourcebook for Researchers and Practitioners*. Yep's awards include the National Communication Association (NCA) Randy Majors Memorial Award for Outstanding Lesbian, Gay, Bisexual, and Transgender Scholarship in Communication (2006) and Distinguished Faculty Award for Professional Achievement in Research at San Francisco State University (2011). He has served on editorial boards including *Canadian Online Journal of Queer Studies in Education, Communication Studies, Communication Yearbook, International and Intercultural Communication Annual, Journal of Homosexuality, Journal of International and Intercultural Communication,* and *Women's Studies in Communication*. In 2006–2008, he served as the editor of the National Communication Association Non-Serial Publications Program. He is currently on the Executive Board of *QED: A Journal in GLBTQ World Making*, a new interdisciplinary academic journal.